SURREY
County Cricket Club
First-Class Records
1846-1994

compiled by
Michael Ayers

Foreword by
Rt. Hon. John Major, M.P.

First published in Great Britain by
Limlow Books Limited
St Peter's Hill, Litlington, Royston SG8 0QF
1995

British Library Cataloguing-in-Publication Data.
A catalogue record for this book is available from the British Library.

ISBN 1 874524 15 7

Printed by Peartree Printers, Derby

CONTENTS

FOREWORD
INTRODUCTION

SECTION 1 - TEAM RECORDS

Results of First-Class Matches 1846-1994	9
Abandoned Matches	10
Highest and Lowest Scores by Surrey against each County	10
Highest and Lowest Scores against Surrey by each County	11
Highest Innings Totals	11
Highest Fourth Innings Totals	14
Highest Fourth Innings Total Without Loss by Surrey	15
Highest Match Aggregates	15
Lowest Match Aggregates for a Completed Match	16
Lowest Innings Totals	17
Matches Completed in One Day	17
Decisive Results	17
Tied Matches	23
Close Results	23
Victory After Following-On	24
Defeat After Opponents Followed On	24
Most Runs in a Day	24
Four Hundreds in an Innings for Surrey	25
Three Hundreds in an Innings	25
Seven Fifties in an Innings for Surrey	26
Six Fifties in an Innings for Surrey	26
Five Fifties in an Innings	26
Eight Fifties in a Match against Surrey	28
Seven Fifties in a Match	28
Record Innings Totals for Surrey Involving Hundreds and Fifties	29
Eleven Bowlers Used in an Innings	29
Most Bowlers Used in a Match (Both Sides)	29
Most Extras Conceded in an Innings	30
Unusual Dismissals	31

SECTION 2 - INDIVIDUAL BATTING RECORDS

Highest Individual Innings	32
First-Class Centurions for Surrey	34
Hundred in Each Innings	36
Hundred on Debut	37
Three or More Centuries in Successive Innings	37
Most Fifties in Successive Innings	38
Carrying Bat Through Both Innings of a Match for Surrey	39
Carrying Bat Through a Completed Innings and Last Out in the Other	40
Carrying Bat Through a Completed Innings	40
Most Runs in a Day	41

Batsmen Scoring Over 50% of Total in Each Innings 42
Monopolising the Scoring While at the Wicket 42
Hundred With A Runner 42
Most Runs Added During a Batsman's Innings 42
Fastest Hundreds 42
Fifty with Fewest Scoring Strokes 42
Hundred Before Lunch 42
Hundreds by Two Batsmen in a Pre-Lunch Session 45
2000 Runs in a Season 45
1000 Runs in a Season 45
Earliest Dates for Reaching Milestones 49
1000 Runs in a Month 49
10000 Runs for Surrey 49
Leading Surrey Batsmen 50

SECTION 3 - PARTNERSHIP RECORDS

Highest Wicket Partnerships for Surrey 54
Highest Wicket Partnerships against Surrey 56
Two Hundred and Fifty Run Partnerships 58

SECTION 4 - INDIVIDUAL BOWLING RECORDS

Nine or More Wickets in an Innings 61
Fifteen or More Wickets in a Match 62
Hat-Tricks 62
Wicket with First Ball 64
Five Wickets in an Innings on Debut for Surrey 64
Bowling Unchanged Through Both Innings of a Completed Match 64
125 Wickets in a Season 65
Most Wickets in a Season 65
Best Average for a Hundred Wickets in a Season 66
Most Balls Bowled in an Innings for Surrey 67
Most Runs Conceded in an Innings against Surrey 67
Some Expensive Analyses for Surrey 68
Most Expensive Analysis against Surrey 68
Outstanding Spells of Wicket-Taking 68
Bowlers Taking Five Wickets in an Innings Most Times 68
500 Wickets in a Career for Surrey 69
Leading Surrey Bowlers 69

SECTION 5 - ALL-ROUND RECORDS

100 Runs and 10 Wickets in a Match 72
Season Double 72
10000 Runs and 1000 Wickets in a Career 72

SECTION 6 - WICKET-KEEPING RECORDS

Most Dismissals in an Innings 73
Most Dismissals in a Match 73
Most Dismissals in a Season 74
Highest Totals without Byes 74
Most Dismissals in a Career 74

SECTION 7 - FIELDING RECORDS

Most Catches in an Innings 75
Most Catches in a Match 75
Most Catches in a Season 76
Most Catches in a Career 76

SECTION 8 - GROUND RECORDS

Summary of Results of all First-Class Matches by Ground 77
The Oval 81
Guildford 82

SECTION 9 - RECORDS AGAINST EACH OPPONENT

Summary of Results of First-Class Matches 1846-1994 83
County Matches 84
University Matches 101
Test-playing Countries 102
Other Matches 106

SECTION 10 - PLAYERS' RECORDS

Surrey Captains 1846-1994 108
Surrey Caps 1884-1994 108
Most Appearances for Surrey 110
Youngest Players on Debut for Surrey 110
Oldest Players on Debut for Surrey 111
Oldest Players for Surrey 111
Longest Career for Surrey 111
Longest Lived Surrey Players 111
Family Relationships of Surrey Players 112
University Blues 113
Surrey Players' Test Career Records 115
Surrey Career Records 116

Surrey in 1905
back row: **H.Strudwick A.Baker M.T.Jackson F.C.Holland E.H.L.Nice J.B.Hobbs W.E.Davis**
front row: **E.G.Hayes N.A.Knox Lord Dalmeny** *(captain)* **T.W.Hayward W.S.Lees**

FOREWORD

As a life long supporter of Surrey County Cricket Club I am delighted that at last we have a complete set of Club Records to study.

It is entirely appropriate that they should be published this year which is, of course, Surrey's 150th Anniversary.

For the dedicated Surrey fan this book will provide great entertainment and probably settle once and for all many of the talking points and disputes that have been around for years. At last we can be sure which was the highest total scored by Surrey without a century (535 v Nottinghamshire at The Oval in 1891) and at which match Extras were the highest score (I shall spare the blushes of the county concerned!).

Among the other wonderful details the reader can also discover that Surrey's youngest player on debut was G.A.R.Lock at 17 years and eight days against Kent in 1946.

Conversely, the oldest player on debut for Surrey was W.Clarke at 53 years and 162 days against England at The Oval in 1852. Now that gives me pause for thought - hope is rekindled for someone born in 1943, although there might be clashes with my other job!

Michael Ayers has done a great service in assembling this book - I am sure it will be widely appreciated by Surrey followers and, indeed, all cricket fans. It is the ideal tonic to keep us occupied between seasons and when the rain falls.

John Major
Downing Street
December 1994

INTRODUCTION

I should like to dedicate this publication to all the scorers and statisticians who have produced scorecards and records for Surrey and the other seventeen counties over the years. I should especially like to remember Tom Billson and George Russ.
This book contains the records of Surrey County Cricket Club since it was formally inaugurated after a dinner at The Horns Tavern on 18th October 1845. The first occasion on which Surrey took the field as a county side was in a match played against M.C.C. on 25th and 26th May 1846, which they lost narrowly by 48 runs. Surrey's first victory was achieved in their next match - against Kent a month later. Surrey won by 10 wickets.
Since then, some 3241 first-class matches have been played over nearly 150 years. It has been a pleasure to study the achievements of so many great cricketers and I am grateful to have played a tiny part, as Surrey First Team Scorer and Club Statistician, in the history of this fine club.

Acknowledgements

I should like to thank John Major, the Prime Minister, for writing the Foreword: I hope that he is able to take time off from his 'other job' to enjoy some good cricket at The Oval.
I should particularly like to thank those who have spent many hours recording Surrey's performance over the years. It has made my job so much easier to have available the meticulous records of George Russ and Stu Emsley, Philip Bailey, Bill Frindall, the Surrey Statistics Group and others. Special thanks also to Richard Allnatt, Norman Bates, Brian Cowley and Michael Pearce for their contributions, to Derek Lodge for his painstaking research and to Peter Griffiths for his guidance.
I must thank my wife Libby for her untiring work, typing and checking the enormous amount of information that was required for this publication.
My personal thanks also to David Baggett, Brian Hunt, Mike Smith, Andrew Hignell, Bert Avery, Victor Isaacs, Howard Milton, Malcolm Lorimer, Dennis Lambert, Eddie Solomon, Laurie Newell, Peter Wynne-Thomas, Michael Hill and Nigel Johns, Norman Epps, Robert Brooke, Les Hatton, Roy Wilkinson for confirming the data, and to David Baggett for his additional assistance in proof-reading.

In addition to the various editions of *Wisden Cricketers' Almanack, Surrey County Cricket Club Yearbooks* and the Association of Cricket Statisticans and Historians publications, the following have been invaluable:

Philip Bailey, Philip Thorn, Peter Wynne-Thomas, *Who's Who of Cricketers*, Hamlyn, 1993
Bill Frindall, *The Wisden Book of Cricket Records*, Headline, 1993
Bill Frindall, *The Wisden Book of Test Cricket*, MacDonald and Jane's, 1979
David Lemmon, *The History of Surrey C.C.C.*, Christopher Helm, 1989
Louis Palgrave, *The Story of The Oval*, Cornish, 1949
William Powell, *The Wisden Guide to Cricket Grounds*, Stanley Paul, 1989
Gordon Ross, *A History of County Cricket - Surrey*, Arthur Baker, 1971
Peter Wynne-Thomas, *Surrey Cricketers 1839-1980*, A.C.S., 1980

Michael Ayers
Berkshire

January 1995

SECTION 1 - TEAM RECORDS

RESULTS OF FIRST-CLASS MATCHES 1846-1994

	All First-Class Matches						County Championship						
Season	P	W	D	L	T	A	P	W	D	L	T	A	Pos
1846	2	1	1	0	-	-	2	1	1	0	-	-	-
1847	4	0	0	3	1	-	2	0	0	1	1	-	-
1848	1	1	0	0	-	-	-	-	-	-	-	-	-
1849	4	2	0	2	-	-	2	1	0	1	-	-	-
1850	5	4	1	0	-	-	4	4	0	0	-	-	-
1851	6	4	2	0	-	-	5	4	1	0	-	-	-
1852	7	2	1	4	-	-	5	0	1	4	-	-	-
1853	2	1	0	1	-	-	2	1	0	1	-	-	-
1854	4	3	1	0	-	-	4	3	1	0	-	-	-
1855	3	0	0	3	-	-	2	0	0	2	-	-	-
1856	3	3	0	0	-	-	3	3	0	0	-	-	-
1857	8	7	0	1	-	-	5	5	0	0	-	-	-
1858	6	5	1	0	-	-	2	2	0	0	-	-	-
1859	6	4	0	2	-	-	1	0	0	1	-	-	-
1860	7	2	3	2	-	-	4	2	1	1	-	-	-
1861	11	5	2	4	-	-	8	3	1	4	-	-	-
1862	11	4	2	5	-	-	8	4	1	3	-	-	-
1863	10	4	4	2	-	-	7	3	3	1	-	-	-
1864	11	8	3	0	-	-	8	6	2	0	-	-	-
1865	16	8	4	4	-	-	12	7	2	3	-	-	-
1866	13	5	1	7	-	-	10	4	1	5	-	-	-
1867	14	4	4	6	-	-	10	3	4	3	-	-	-
1868	16	6	0	8	2	-	12	5	0	6	1	-	-
1869	15	3	2	10	-	-	12	3	2	7	-	-	-
1870	18	5	0	13	-	-	14	5	0	9	-	-	-
1871	16	1	4	11	-	-	13	0	4	9	-	-	-
1872	15	8	2	5	-	-	12	7	2	3	-	-	-
1873	15	3	2	10	-	-	14	2	2	10	-	-	-
1874	12	4	2	6	-	-	10	3	1	6	-	-	-
1875	12	3	2	7	-	-	10	3	2	5	-	-	-
1876	15	3	2	9	1	-	12	2	1	8	1	-	-
1877	14	6	3	5	-	-	12	6	3	3	-	-	-
1878	14	3	3	8	-	-	12	3	3	6	-	-	-
1879	11	3	3	5	-	-	10	3	3	4	-	-	-
1880	15	2	5	8	-	-	14	2	5	7	-	-	-
1881	15	4	1	10	-	-	14	4	1	9	-	-	-
1882	17	6	3	8	-	-	14	4	3	7	-	-	-
1883	21	10	5	6	-	-	20	10	5	5	-	-	-
1884	21	10	5	6	-	-	18	9	5	4	-	-	-
1885	23	14	5	4	-	-	20	12	4	4	-	-	-
1886	20	15	1	4	-	-	16	12	1	3	-	-	-
1887	19	14	2	3	-	-	16	12	2	2	-	-	-
1888	19	13	3	3	-	-	14	12	1	1	-	-	-
1889	17	13	1	3	-	-	14	10	1	3	-	-	-
1890	**17**	**9**	**4**	**4**	**-**	**-**	**14**	**9**	**2**	**3**	**-**	**-**	**1st**
1891	**17**	**12**	**2**	**3**	**-**	**-**	**16**	**12**	**2**	**2**	**-**	**-**	**1st**
1892	**19**	**14**	**2**	**3**	**-**	**-**	**16**	**13**	**1**	**2**	**-**	**-**	**1st**
1893	19	10	1	8	-	-	16	7	1	8	-	-	5th
1894	**26**	**19**	**2**	**4**	**1**	**-**	**16**	**13**	**0**	**2**	**1**	**-**	**1st**
1895	**28**	**18**	**5**	**5**	**-**	**-**	**26**	**17**	**5**	**4**	**-**	**-**	**1st**
1896	30	17	3	10	-	-	26	17	2	7	-	-	4th
1897	28	19	5	4	-	-	26	17	5	4	-	-	2nd
1898	26	13	9	4	-	2	24	11	9	4	-	2	4th
1899	**31**	**13**	**15**	**3**	**-**	**-**	**26**	**10**	**14**	**2**	**-**	**-**	**1st**
1900	33	10	16	7	-	-	28	9	12	7	-	-	7th
1901	35	12	17	6	-	1	27	7	14	6	-	1	6th
1902	36	9	17	10	-	-	28	8	15	5	-	-	4th
1903	34	11	11	12	-	1	27	7	9	11	-	1	11th
1904	34	9	12	13	-	-	28	6	10	12	-	-	11th
1905	33	15	10	7	1	1	27	14	6	6	1	1	4th
1906	33	21	7	5	-	-	28	18	6	4	-	-	3rd
1907	33	15	14	4	-	-	28	12	12	4	-	-	4th
1908	33	17	12	4	-	1	29	13	12	4	-	1	3rd
1909	34	17	8	9	-	-	30	16	7	7	-	-	5th
1910	33	18	7	8	-	-	30	16	7	7	-	-	2nd
1911	34	19	8	7	-	-	30	15	8	7	-	-	5th
1912	28	8	13	7	-	2	24	7	12	5	-	2	7th
1913	27	14	8	5	-	-	26	13	8	5	-	-	3rd
1914	**26**	**15**	**9**	**2**	**-**	**2**	**26**	**15**	**9**	**2**	**-**	**2**	**1st**
1919	25	8	14	3	-	-	20	7	10	3	-	-	4th
1920	25	15	4	6	-	-	24	15	3	6	-	-	3rd
1921	28	15	8	5	-	-	24	15	7	2	-	-	2nd
1922	27	13	13	1	-	-	24	13	10	1	-	-	3rd
1923	30	12	14	4	-	-	26	11	13	2	-	-	4th
1924	28	9	16	3	-	2	24	9	14	1	-	2	3rd
1925	27	14	10	3	-	-	26	14	10	2	-	-	2nd
1926	30	7	19	4	-	-	26	7	15	4	-	-	5th
1927	30	8	18	4	-	-	26	8	15	3	-	-	6th
1928	32	5	24	3	-	-	28	5	20	3	-	-	6th
1929	33	10	15	8	-	-	28	8	13	7	-	-	10th
1930	34	5	25	4	-	1	27	3	20	4	-	1	8th
1931	32	7	21	4	-	1	27	6	17	4	-	1	8th
1932	33	9	21	3	-	1	27	9	16	2	-	1	5th
1933	30	7	18	5	-	-	26	6	15	5	-	-	9th
1934	31	8	14	9	-	-	26	6	12	8	-	-	11th
1935	30	8	15	7	-	1	26	7	14	5	-	-	11th
1936	34	9	17	8	-	-	30	9	14	7	-	-	6th
1937	31	10	14	7	-	-	26	8	13	5	-	-	8th
1938	31	13	11	7	-	-	26	12	8	6	-	-	3rd
1939	33	13	12	8	-	-	28	11	10	7	-	-	8th
1946	32	8	12	12	-	-	26	6	9	11	-	-	11th
1947	29	11	10	8	-	1	25	10	8	7	-	1	6th
1948	30	13	5	12	-	-	26	13	4	9	-	-	2nd
1949	31	12	9	10	-	-	26	11	7	8	-	-	5th
1950	**33**	**18**	**9**	**6**	**-**	**-**	**28**	**17**	**7**	**4**	**-**	**-**	**1st**
1951	32	9	17	6	-	-	28	7	15	6	-	-	6th
1952	**33**	**23**	**6**	**4**	**-**	**-**	**28**	**20**	**5**	**3**	**-**	**-**	**1st**
1953	**34**	**16**	**12**	**6**	**-**	**-**	**28**	**13**	**11**	**4**	**-**	**-**	**1st**
1954	**33**	**17**	**13**	**3**	**-**	**-**	**28**	**15**	**10**	**3**	**-**	**-**	**1st**
1955	**34**	**27**	**0**	**7**	**-**	**-**	**28**	**23**	**0**	**5**	**-**	**-**	**1st**
1956	**35**	**18**	**10**	**7**	**-**	**1**	**27**	**15**	**7**	**5**	**-**	**1**	**1st**
1957	**35**	**25**	**6**	**4**	**-**	**-**	**28**	**21**	**4**	**3**	**-**	**-**	**1st**
1958	**34**	**16**	**12**	**6**	**-**	**-**	**28**	**14**	**9**	**5**	**-**	**-**	**1st**
1959	36	14	15	7	-	-	28	12	11	5	-	-	2nd
1960	32	12	14	6	-	1	27	9	12	6	-	1	7th
1961	34	5	14	15	-	-	28	4	11	13	-	-	15th
1962	33	13	16	4	-	-	28	10	15	3	-	-	5th
1963	34	5	23	6	-	-	28	5	17	6	-	-	11th
1964	30	12	15	3	-	1	27	11	13	3	-	1	4th
1965	33	8	21	4	-	-	28	7	17	4	-	-	8th
1966	30	9	18	3	-	1	28	8	17	3	-	-	7th
1967	32	9	19	4	-	-	28	8	16	4	-	-	4th
1968	32	5	20	7	-	-	28	4	17	7	-	-	15th
1969	29	8	19	2	-	-	24	7	16	1	-	-	3rd
1970	26	7	15	4	-	-	24	6	14	4	-	-	5th
1971	**27**	**12**	**11**	**4**	**-**	**-**	**24**	**11**	**10**	**3**	**-**	**-**	**1st**
1972	23	4	14	5	-	-	20	3	12	5	-	-	12th
1973	23	10	10	3	-	-	20	9	8	3	-	-	2nd

	All First-Class Matches						County Championship						
Season	P	W	D	L	T	A	P	W	D	L	T	A	Pos
1974	21	6	10	5	-	-	20	6	10	4	-	-	7th
1975	21	9	9	3	-	-	20	8	9	3	-	-	6th
1976	22	7	11	4	-	-	20	6	10	4	-	-	9th
1977	23	3	14	6	-	1	21	3	12	6	-	1	12th
1978	24	3	13	8	-	-	22	3	12	7	-	-	16th
1979	23	7	13	3	-	1	21	6	12	3	-	1	3rd
1980	24	12	8	4	-	-	22	10	8	4	-	-	2nd
1981	22	7	10	5	-	1	21	7	9	5	-	1	6th
1982	24	6	12	6	-	-	22	6	10	6	-	-	5th
1983	25	8	13	4	-	-	24	7	13	4	-	-	8th
1984	26	7	13	6	-	-	24	6	12	6	-	-	8th
1985	26	5	16	5	-	-	24	5	14	5	-	-	6th
1986	25	8	11	6	-	-	24	8	10	6	-	-	3rd
1987	26	7	15	4	-	-	24	7	13	4	-	-	4th
1988	25	9	11	5	-	-	22	7	10	5	-	-	4th
1989	23	4	12	7	-	-	22	4	11	7	-	-	12th
1990	24	4	17	3	-	-	22	4	15	3	-	-	9th
1991	23	9	8	6	-	-	22	8	8	6	-	-	5th
1992	23	6	10	7	-	-	22	5	10	7	-	-	13th
1993	19	6	6	7	-	-	17	6	5	6	-	-	6th
1994	18	7	4	7	-	-	17	7	3	7	-	-	7th
Total	3241	1271	1227	737	6	24	2773	1104	1045	619	5	22	

ABANDONED MATCHES (24)

1898 (2)	v Derbyshire	The Oval	1930	v Northamptonshire	The Oval
	v Warwickshire	Birmingham	1931	v Warwickshire	Birmingham
1901	v Yorkshire	The Oval	1932	v Lancashire	Manchester
1903	v Hampshire	The Oval	1935	v Cambridge Univ	The Oval
1905	v Lancashire	The Oval	1947	v Derbyshire	Chesterfield
1908	v Lancashire	The Oval	1956	v Warwickshire	The Oval
1912 (2)	v Gloucestershire	Cheltenham	1960	v Essex	The Oval
	v Yorkshire	Sheffield	1964	v Leicestershire	Ashby-de-la-Zouch
1914 (2)	v Leicestershire	The Oval	1966	v West Indians	The Oval
	v Sussex	Hove	1977	v Lancashire	Manchester
1924 (2)	v Essex	The Oval	1979	v Essex	The Oval
	v Leicestershire	Leicester (AR)	1981	v Hampshire	The Oval

HIGHEST AND LOWEST SCORES BY SURREY AGAINST EACH COUNTY

	High			*Low*		
Derbyshire	611-9d	The Oval	1904	60	The Oval	1935
Durham	538-6d	Darlington	1994	236	Darlington	1994
Essex	613-6d	The Oval	1990	14	Chelmsford	1983
Glamorgan	560-8d	The Oval	1947	50	Cardiff (AP)	1948
Gloucestershire	579	Bristol	1901	27	Cheltenham	1874
Hampshire	742	The Oval	1909	64	Basingstoke	1986
Kent	648	Canterbury	1990	44	Maidstone	1884
Lancashire	707-9d	The Oval	1990	33	The Oval	1873
Leicestershire	576	The Oval	1947	35	Leicester (GR)	1894
Middlesex	582-9d	The Oval	1919	35	Islington	1868
Northamptonshire	619-5d	Northampton	1920	58	The Oval	1913
Nottinghamshire	706-4d	Nottingham	1947	16	The Oval	1880
Somerset	811	The Oval	1899	35	The Oval	1937
Sussex	698	The Oval	1888	51	Petworth	1849
Warwickshire	634	The Oval	1906	61	The Oval	1962
Worcestershire	544	Worcester	1904	57	The Oval	1958
Yorkshire	560-6d	The Oval	1933	31	Holbeck	1883

HIGHEST AND LOWEST SCORES AGAINST SURREY BY EACH COUNTY

	High			Low		
Derbyshire	438-9d	Ilkeston	1993	42	The Oval	1887
Durham	357	Durham Univ	1992	120	The Oval	1993
Essex	616-5d	The Oval	1904	37	Leyton	1899
Glamorgan	550-6d	The Oval	1936	31	The Oval	1957
Gloucestershire	544	The Oval	1928	39	Clifton	1888
Hampshire	603-7d	Southampton	1994	32	The Oval	1885
Kent	579-8d	The Oval	1935	20	The Oval	1870
Lancashire	863	The Oval	1990	27	Manchester	1958
Leicestershire	516-8d	The Oval	1929	35	Leicester (GR)	1897
(Leicestershire scored 35 in each innings of the match)						
Middlesex	568-9d	The Oval	1919	25	The Oval	1885
Northamptonshire	529-9	The Oval	1958	32	The Oval	1905
Nottinghamshire	548-9	The Oval	1898	40	The Oval	1955
Somerset	507-6d	Weston-s-Mare	1946	36	Weston-s-Mare	1955
Sussex	705-8d	Hastings	1902	31	The Oval	1857
Warwickshire	585-7	The Oval	1905	45	The Oval	1953
Worcestershire	446-7	Guildford	1979	25	The Oval	1954
Yorkshire	704	The Oval	1899	26	The Oval	1909

HIGHEST INNINGS TOTALS

For Surrey

811	v Somerset	The Oval	1899
742	v Hampshire	The Oval	1909
707-9d	v Lancashire	The Oval	1990
706-4d	v Nottinghamshire	Nottingham	1947
698	v Sussex	The Oval	1888
650	v Hampshire	The Oval	1883
650	v Oxford University	The Oval	1888
648	v Kent	Canterbury	1990
645-9d	v New Zealanders	The Oval	1949
635	v Somerset	The Oval	1885
634	v Lancashire	The Oval	1898
634	v Warwickshire	The Oval	1906
631	v Sussex	The Oval	1885
619-5d	v Northamptonshire	Northampton	1920
617-6d	v Oxford University	The Oval	1928
617	v Kent	The Oval	1897
616-5d	v Northamptonshire	The Oval	1921
614	v Oxford University	The Oval	1889
613-6d	v Essex	The Oval	1990
611-9d	v Derbyshire	Derby	1904
609	v Warwickshire	The Oval	1898
604-4d	v Nottinghamshire	Nottingham	1994
602	v Warwickshire	The Oval	1897
594-8d	v Cambridge University	The Oval	1923
592-9d	v Hampshire	The Oval	1936
582-9d	v Middlesex	The Oval	1919
579	v Hampshire	The Oval	1897
579	v Gloucestershire	Bristol	1901
579-4d	v Hampshire	Southampton	1919
579-5d	v Middlesex	Lord's	1926
579-4d	v Somerset	The Oval	1931

576	v Derbyshire	The Oval	1911
576	v Leicestershire	The Oval	1947
570-6d	v Derbyshire	The Oval	1994
570-8d	v Essex	Brentwood	1934
568	v Warwickshire	Birmingham	1897
567	v Lancashire	Manchester	1928
565	v Cambridge University	The Oval	1930
562	v Warwickshire	Birmingham	1906
560	v Leicestershire	The Oval	1897
560-6d	v Yorkshire	The Oval	1933
560-8d	v Glamorgan	The Oval	1947
559-8d	v Middlesex	The Oval	1901
558-7d	v MCC	Lord's	1934
557-7d	v Gloucestershire	The Oval	1927
557	v Somerset	The Oval	1992
556	v Lancashire	The Oval	1899
556	v Cambridge University	The Oval	1927
555-4d	v Somerset	The Oval	1929
553	v Sussex	Hove	1988
552	v Sussex	Hastings	1902
552-8d	v Sussex	Hastings	1923
551-7	v Yorkshire	The Oval	1899
550	v Derbyshire	Derby	1905
550	v Hampshire	The Oval	1935
550-6d	v Glamorgan	The Oval	1936
549-6d	v Leicestershire	The Oval	1905
549-6d	v Yorkshire	Lord's	1914
548-7d	v Glamorgan	The Oval	1937
547	v Sussex	The Oval	1938
547-5d	v Kent	Blackheath	1925
544	v Worcestershire	Worcester	1904
544	v Middlesex	The Oval	1914
543	v Cambridge University	The Oval	1887
543	v Cambridge University	The Oval	1895
542	v Nottinghamshire	The Oval	1914
541	v Warwickshire	The Oval	1914
541-5d	v Leicestershire	The Oval	1926
540	v Sussex	The Oval	1908
540	v Yorkshire	The Oval	1911
539	v Sussex	Hove	1900
538-6d	v Durham	Darlington	1994
536	v Yorkshire	The Oval	1898
536-7d	v Worcestershire	Worcester	1982
535	v Nottinghamshire	The Oval	1913
534	v Kent	The Oval	1898
533-7d	v Glamorgan	Cardiff (AP)	1928
532-7d	v Kent	The Oval	1908
532-6d	v Sussex	The Oval	1919
532-6d	v Sussex	The Oval	1922
531	v Hampshire	The Oval	1913
530-9	v Northamptonshire	Northampton	1928
529	v Lancashire	The Oval	1921
528-8d	v Leicestershire	The Oval	1900
528-6	v Essex	The Oval	1947
525-5d	v Nottinghamshire	The Oval	1946
524-9d	v Essex	Leyton	1926
523-7d	v Somerset	Taunton	1911
523-5	v Derbyshire	The Oval	1900
523	v Oxford University	The Oval	1919
522-7d	v Nottinghamshire	The Oval	1927

521-9d	v Somerset	The Oval	1938
520	v Warwickshire	The Oval	1895
518-5d	v Yorkshire	The Oval	1984
517	v Leicestershire	Leicester (AR)	1901
517	v Kent	The Oval	1922
517	v Hampshire	Southampton	1990
516-8d	v Leicestershire	The Oval	1929
512	v Derbyshire	Derby	1896
512	v Somerset	The Oval	1936
512-8d	v Cambridge University	The Oval	1938
509	v Kent	Blackheath	1914
509	v Middlesex	Lord's	1937
509-7d	v Nottinghamshire	Nottingham	1934
507	v Middlesex	The Oval	1889
507	v Somerset	The Oval	1908
506	v Leicestershire	Leicester (GR)	1899
506	v Leicestershire	The Oval	1909
506-4d	v Essex	Leyton	1928
506	v Hampshire	Southampton	1933
505-3d	v Oxford University	The Oval	1926
505	v Northamptonshire	The Oval	1928
503-5d	v Worcestershire	Worcester	1913
503-4d	v Warwickshire	The Oval	1931
501	v Sussex	Hove	1885
501	v Australians	The Oval	1886
501	v Leicestershire	The Oval	1994
501-9d	v Sussex	The Oval	1913
501-8d	v Leicestershire	Leicester (AR)	1922
501	v Nottinghamshire	Nottingham	1930
501	v Kent	The Oval	1934
501-3d	v Somerset	The Oval	1949
500-4d	v Gloucestershire	The Oval	1898
500	v Leicestershire	Leicester (GR)	1900
500	v Essex	The Oval	1936
500	v Glamorgan	Cardiff (AP)	1936

Against Surrey

863	- Lancashire	The Oval	1990
705-8d	- Sussex	Hastings	1902
704	- Yorkshire	The Oval	1899
632	- Australians	The Oval	1948
629	- Australians	The Oval	1934
616-5d	- Essex	The Oval	1904
603-7d	- Hampshire	Southampton	1994
600-7d	- Sussex	The Oval	1903
597	- Essex	The Oval	1946
588-4	- Lancashire	Manchester	1928
585-7	- Warwickshire	The Oval	1905
582-7d	- Yorkshire	Sheffield	1935
579-8d	- Sussex	Hove	1904
579-8d	- Kent	The Oval	1935
577	- Oxford University	Reigate	1909
572	- Cambridge University	The Oval	1930
572	- South Africans	The Oval	1935
568-9d	- Middlesex	The Oval	1919
561	- Sussex	The Oval	1899
559	- Hampshire	The Oval	1993
558	- Lancashire	The Oval	1913

557-7	- Kent	The Oval	1922
556-7d	- Lancashire	Manchester	1902
552	- Oxford University	The Oval	1930
552-9d	- Hampshire	Southampton	1992
550-6d	- Glamorgan	The Oval	1936
548-9	- Nottinghamshire	The Oval	1898
544	- Gloucestershire	The Oval	1928
542-9d	- Sussex	Hove	1903
539-5d	- Yorkshire	The Oval	1922
539	- Essex	The Oval	1990
537-2d	- Middlesex	The Oval	1947
537-5d	- West Indians	The Oval	1950
536	- Sussex	Hove	1932
534-9	- Lancashire	Manchester	1933
530	- Oxford University	The Oval	1933
529-9	- Northamptonshire	The Oval	1958
528	- Australians	The Oval	1938
526-7d	- Lancashire	The Oval	1929
522-9d	- Lancashire	Manchester	1927
521	- England	The Oval	1866
519-6d	- Yorkshire	Leeds	1936
516-8d	- Leicestershire	The Oval	1929
515-6d	- Sussex	The Oval	1908
514-5d	- Middlesex	The Oval	1929
510	- Warwickshire	Birmingham	1906
510	- Kent	Blackheath	1928
507-6d	- Somerset	Weston-super-Mare	1946
503	- England	The Oval	1862
501	- Nottinghamshire	The Oval	1882
501	- Warwickshire	Birmingham	1911

HIGHEST FOURTH INNINGS TOTALS

For Surrey

460	(lost by 5 runs)	v MCC	Lord's	1938
370	(lost by 43 runs)	v Sussex	The Oval	1896
354-9	(won by 1 wkt)	v Gloucestershire	Gloucester (KS)	1994
350	(lost by 94 runs)	v Hampshire	Portsmouth	1947
344	(lost by 9 runs)	v Worcestershire	The Oval	1911
341-7	(won by 3 wkts)	v Hampshire	Portsmouth	1937
340-5	(drawn)	v Essex	The Oval	1911
340-8	(won by 2 wkts)	v Essex	Chelmsford	1947
334-8	(won by 2 wkts)	v Middlesex	The Oval	1987
327-8	(drawn)	v Somerset	Weston-super-Mare	1990
325-8	(drawn)	v Gloucestershire	The Oval	1976
325-9	(drawn)	v Middlesex	The Oval	1992
322-8	(won by 2 wkts)	v Glamorgan	Guildford	1982
314	(lost by 32 runs)	v Essex	Westcliff-on-Sea	1938
310-3	(drawn)	v Worcestershire	The Oval	1907
306-9	(won by 1 wkt)	v Yorkshire	Bradford	1992
305-5	(drawn)	v Oxford University	Oxford	1990
302-9	(drawn)	v Gloucestershire	Cheltenham	1990
302	(lost by 96 runs)	v Lancashire	The Oval	1993
301-3	(won by 7 wkts)	v Gloucestershire	The Oval	1939

Against Surrey

427-4 (lost by 6 wkts)	- Cambridge University	The Oval	1925
416-6 (lost by 4 wkts)	- Kent	Blackheath	1934
392-8 (lost by 2 wkts)	- Middlesex	The Oval	1994
376-7 (lost by 3 wkts)	- Worcestershire	Worcester	1961
375 (won by 37 runs)	- Glamorgan	The Oval	1927
352-7 (lost by 3 wkts)	- Nottinghamshire	The Oval	1992
350 (won by 19 runs)	- Middlesex	The Oval	1921
337-5 (lost by 5 wkts)	- Sussex	Hove	1990
336 (won by 75 runs)	- Kent	The Oval	1921
333 (won by 119 runs)	- Leicestershire	The Oval	1926
330 (won by 60 runs)	- Somerset	Taunton	1962
328-4 (drawn)	- Middlesex	Lord's	1939
325 (won by 12 runs)	- Sussex	Horsham	1931
324 (won by 77 runs)	- Somerset	The Oval	1926
323-8 (drawn)	- Middlesex	The Oval	1923
322-4 (lost by 6 wkts)	- Middlesex	Lord's	1921
319-6 (lost by 4 wkts)	- Middlesex	The Oval	1946
316-6 (lost by 4 wkts)	- Oxford University	The Oval	1924
316-7 (lost by 3 wkts)	- Northamptonshire	The Oval	1994
307 (won by 21 runs)	- Australians	The Oval	1912
305 (won by 14 runs)	- Lancashire	Manchester	1939
302-4 (drawn)	- Sussex	The Oval	1933
301-8 (lost by 2 wkts)	- Worcestershire	Bournville	1911

HIGHEST FOURTH INNINGS TOTAL WITHOUT LOSS BY SURREY

270-0 (set 346 to win)	v Kent	The Oval	1900

HIGHEST MATCH AGGREGATES

1650-20	v Lancashire	The Oval	1990
Surrey 707-9d & 80-1 Lancashire 863		Match drawn	
1480-26	v Middlesex	The Oval	1994
Surrey 425 & 313-3d Middlesex 350-5d & 392-8		Middlesex won by 2 wickets	
1475-27	v Northamptonshire	Northampton	1920
Northamptonshire 306 & 430 Surrey 619-5d & 120-2		Surrey won by 8 wickets	
1469-31	v Cambridge University	The Oval	1921
Cambridge University 346 & 460-6d Surrey 399 & 264-5		Match drawn	
1451-29	v Kent	Canterbury	1990
Kent 425 & 378-9 Surrey 648		Match drawn	
1427-22	v Sussex	Hastings	1902
Sussex 705-8d & 170-4 Surrey 552		Match drawn	
1409-25	v Middlesex	The Oval	1919
Middlesex 568-9d & 193-5d Surrey 403 & 245-1		Match drawn	

LOWEST MATCH AGGREGATES FOR A COMPLETED MATCH

Aggregate	Opponent	Venue	Year
157-22	v Worcestershire	The Oval	1954
	Worcestershire 25 & 40, Surrey 92-3d	Surrey won by an innings & 27 runs	
175-35	v MCC	Lord's	1872
	MCC 16 & 71, Surrey 49 & 39-5	Surrey won by 5 wkts	
204-30	v Kent	The Oval	1889
	Kent 48 & 53, Surrey 92 & 11-0	Surrey won by 10 wkts	
221-30	v Lancashire	Manchester	1888
	Lancashire 35 & 63, Surrey 123	Surrey won by an innings & 25 runs	
224-30	v Gloucestershire	Cheltenham	1874
	Surrey 27 & 73, Gloucestershire 124	Glos won by an innings & 24 runs	
226-30	v Yorkshire	Hull	1879
	Surrey 50 & 58, Yorkshire 118	Yorkshire won by an innings & 10 runs	
229-30	v Yorkshire	Holbeck	1883
	Yorkshire 116, Surrey 31 & 82	Yorkshire won by an innings & 3 runs	
232-29	v Sussex	The Oval	1857
	Surrey 166, Sussex 35 & 31	Surrey won by an innings & 100 runs	
234-30	v Leicestershire	Leicester (GR)	1897
	Leicester 35 & 35, Surrey 164	Surrey won by an innings & 94 runs	
241-34	v Yorkshire	Sheffield	1869
	Surrey 52 & 67, Yorkshire 82 & 40-4	Yorkshire won by 6 wkts	
243-30	v Warwickshire	The Oval	1953
	Warwickshire 45 & 52, Surrey 146	Surrey won by an innings & 49 runs	
246-30	v MCC	Lord's	1867
	MCC 129, Surrey 38 & 79	MCC won by an innings & 12 runs	
254-30	v Middlesex	The Oval	1851
	Middlesex 87 & 36, Surrey 131	Surrey won by an innings & 8 runs	
259-30	v Kent	Tunbridge Wells	1856
	Kent 54 & 58, Surrey 147	Surrey won by an innings & 35 runs	
259-32	v Kent	Canterbury	1862
	Kent 83 & 46, Surrey 114 & 16-2	Surrey won by 8 wkts	
259-30	v Nottinghamshire	Nottingham	1878
	Surrey 45 & 84, Notts 88 & 42-0	Nottinghamshire won by 10 wkts	
264-30	v Derbyshire	Derby	1907
	Derbyshire 79 & 45, Surrey 140	Surrey won by an innings & 16 runs	
268-30	v Middlesex	The Oval	1885
	Surrey 166, Middlesex 25 & 77	Surrey won by an innings & 64 runs	
272-30	v MCC	Lord's	1951
	MCC 62 & 70, Surrey 140	Surrey won by an innings & 8 runs	
274-35	v North	Sheffield	1857
	North 73 & 63, Surrey 93 & 45-5	Surrey won by 5 wkts	
275-30	v MCC	Lord's	1869
	MCC 134 & 4-0, Surrey 51 & 86	MCC won by 10 wickets	
276-30	v Nottinghamshire	Nottingham	1876
	Surrey 26 & 100, Notts 150	Notts won by an innings & 24 runs	
277-30	v Kent	The Oval	1870
	Kent 20 & 97, Surrey 160	Surrey won by innings & 43 runs	
279-30	v Nottinghamshire	Nottingham	1871
	Notts 168, Surrey 48 & 63	Notts won by an innings & 57 runs	
280-30	v Kent	The Oval	1846
	Kent 83 & 56, Surrey 137 & 4-0	Surrey won by 10 wkts	
280-21	v Middlesex	Lord's	1977
	Surrey 49 & 89, Middlesex 0-0* & 142-1	Middlesex won by 9 wkts	
281-30	v Leicestershire	The Oval	1899
	Leicestershire 74 & 40, Surrey 167	Surrey won by an innings & 53 runs	
287-30	v Sussex	Petworth	1849
	Surrey 68 & 51, Sussex 168	Sussex won by an innings & 49 runs	

288-30	v Yorkshire	Sheffield	1876
	Surrey 74 & 41, Yorkshire 173	Yorkshire won by an innings & 58 runs	
293-30	v Derbyshire	Derby	1895
	Derbyshire 63 & 57, Surrey 173	Surrey won by an innings & 53 runs	

LOWEST INNINGS TOTALS

For Surrey

14	v Essex	Chelmsford	1983
16	v Nottinghamshire	The Oval	1880
26	v Nottinghamshire	Nottingham	1876
27	v Gloucestershire	Cheltenham	1874

Against Surrey

16	- MCC	Lord's	1872
20	- Kent	The Oval	1870
25	- Middlesex	The Oval	1885
25	- Worcestershire	The Oval	1954
26	- Yorkshire	The Oval	1909
27	- Lancashire	Manchester	1958

MATCHES COMPLETED IN ONE DAY

Surrey (166)	Sussex (35 & 31)	The Oval	1857
MCC (16 & 71)	Surrey (49 & 39-5)	Lord's	1872
Lancashire (35 & 63)	Surrey (123)	Manchester	1888
Leicestershire (35 & 35)	Surrey (164)	Leicester (GR)	1897
Warwickshire (45 & 52)	Surrey (146)	The Oval	1953

DECISIVE RESULTS

Surrey Victories

By an Innings and			
485	v Sussex	The Oval	1888
468	v Hampshire	The Oval	1909
379	v Somerset	The Oval	1899
375	v Somerset	The Oval	1891
367	v Oxford University	The Oval	1889
357	v Warwickshire	The Oval	1898
345	v Kent	The Oval	1898
341	v Northamptonshire	The Oval	1921
331	v Glamorgan	Cardiff (AP)	1936
318	v Kent	The Oval	1908
303	v Hampshire	The Oval	1897
301	v Somerset	The Oval	1885
285	v Leicestershire	The Oval	1897
280	v Hampshire	The Oval	1885
272	v Yorkshire	The Oval	1898
270	v Leicestershire	The Oval	1906
261	v Essex	The Oval	1894
259	v Leicestershire	The Oval	1896
252	v Hampshire	Southampton	1885
239	v Warwickshire	The Oval	1920
237	v Derbyshire	Derby	1887

235	v Cambridge University	The Oval	1923
231	v Nottinghamshire	Nottingham	1994
230	v Hampshire	The Oval	1899
228	v Yorkshire	Bradford	1888
224	v Worcestershire	The Oval	1930
223	v Warwickshire	The Oval	1895
222	v Warwickshire	The Oval	1897
221	v Hampshire	The Oval	1865
221	v Sussex	The Oval	1885
214	v Derbyshire	The Oval	1911
214	v Northamptonshire	The Oval	1906
213	v Somerset	The Oval	1883
209	v Australians	The Oval	1886
206	v Leicestershire	The Oval	1904
206	v Sussex	The Oval	1922
205	v Durham	The Oval	1993
204	v Somerset	The Oval	1908
203	v Warwickshire	The Oval	1985
201	v Leicestershire	The Oval	1947
200	v Gloucestershire	The Oval	1894
200	v Sussex	The Oval	1922

By Runs

388	v Sussex	The Oval	1939
380	v Hampshire	Southampton	1896
352	v Essex	Southend-on-Sea	1907
343	v Worcestershire	The Oval	1905
342	v Hampshire	The Oval	1908
337	v Hampshire	The Oval	1906
323	v Gloucestershire	The Oval	1924
316	v Nottinghamshire	The Oval	1911
303	v Gloucestershire	Bristol	1913
299	v Derbyshire	The Oval	1887
299	v Northamptonshire	The Oval	1920
298	v Glamorgan	Swansea	1924
291	v Lancashire	The Oval	1902
290	v Durham	Darlington	1994
289	v Sussex	The Oval	1906
287	v Essex	Leyton	1912
283	v Derbyshire	The Oval	1909
279	v Sussex	The Oval	1897
274	v Gloucestershire	The Oval	1936
268	v Essex	Leyton	1906
265	v Leicestershire	The Oval	1930
262	v Yorkshire	The Oval	1938
261	v Essex	Leyton	1900
260	v Gloucestershire	The Oval	1913
256	v Northamptonshire	Northampton	1961
253	v Hampshire	The Oval	1904
251	v Leicestershire	Leicester (AR)	1913
250	v Gloucestershire	The Oval	1889
249	v Worcestershire	The Oval	1939
247	v Hampshire	Bournemouth	1900
246	v Somerset	The Oval	1903
241	v Somerset	The Oval	1914
240	v Sussex	The Oval	1856
238	v MCC	Lord's	1957
238	v Worcestershire	The Oval	1908
235	v Derbyshire	The Oval	1905

234	v Kent	The Oval	1986
233	v Lancashire	The Oval	1985
230	v Kent	Maidstone	1872
230	v Oxford University	The Oval	1905
229	v Middlesex	Lord's	1932
229	v Somerset	Taunton	1921
227	v Worcestershire	Guildford	1983
222	v Kent	Blackheath	1923
222	v Leicestershire	Leicester (GR)	1957
221	v Lancashire	Manchester	1920
221	v Somerset	Bath	1922
215	v Oxford University	The Oval	1953
213	v Gloucestershire	The Oval	1969
212	v Derbyshire	The Oval	1952
212	v Middlesex	The Oval	1949
212	v Kent	Blackheath	1951
210	v Nottinghamshire	Nottingham	1952
207	v Lancashire	Manchester	1891
207	v Somerset	The Oval	1947
205	v Durham	The Oval	1993
204	v Somerset	The Oval	1963
204	v Yorkshire	Sheffield	1920
203	v Kent	Maidstone	1881
202	v Essex	The Oval	1921
202	v Leicestershire	Leicester (GR)	1946
201	v Essex	Leyton	1895
200	v Middlesex	The Oval	1938

By 10 Wickets

v Kent	The Oval	1846
v Yorkshire	The Oval	1851
v Sussex	Brighton	1854
v Nottinghamshire	The Oval	1864
v Yorkshire	Sheffield	1865
v Sussex	The Oval	1866
v Middlesex	Prince's	1872
v Middlesex	The Oval	1875
v Kent	The Oval	1876
v Middlesex	The Oval	1883
v Sussex	Hove	1884
v Hampshire	Southampton	1884
v Kent	Beckenham	1886
v Sussex	Hove	1888
v Kent	The Oval	1889
v Yorkshire	The Oval	1891
v Kent	Canterbury	1891
v Gloucestershire	Bristol	1891
v Gloucestershire	Cheltenham	1892
v Kent	The Oval	1892
v Yorkshire	The Oval	1893
v Nottinghamshire	The Oval	1893
v Cambridge University XII *(won by 11 wickets)*	Cambridge	1894
v Yorkshire	The Oval	1894
v Middlesex	Lord's	1895
v Kent	Catford	1895
v Sussex	The Oval	1895
v Warwickshire	Birmingham	1896
v Gloucestershire	The Oval	1896
v Somerset	The Oval	1896

v Kent	The Oval	1896
v Sussex	Hove	1896
v Derbyshire	Derby	1897
v Essex	Leyton	1897
v Sussex	Hove	1898
v Derbyshire	Derby	1899
v Derbyshire	Derby	1900
v Worcestershire	Worcester	1900
v Leicestershire	Leicester (AR)	1901
v Gloucestershire	The Oval	1901
v Middlesex	Lord's	1902
v Warwickshire	The Oval	1902
v Cambridge University	Cambridge	1903
v Lancashire	Liverpool	1905
v Middlesex	The Oval	1905
v Hampshire	Aldershot	1906
v Gloucestershire	The Oval	1906
v West Indians	The Oval	1906
v Derbyshire	Chesterfield	1906
v Derbyshire	The Oval	1906
v Gloucestershire	The Oval	1907
v Derbyshire	The Oval	1908
v Hampshire	Bournemouth	1909
v Derbyshire	Derby	1910
v Leicestershire	The Oval	1911
v Worcestershire	The Oval	1912
v Nottinghamshire	The Oval	1913
v Kent	The Oval	1919
v Essex	Leyton	1919
v Nottinghamshire	Nottingham	1920
v Leicestershire	The Oval	1920
v Somerset	The Oval	1921
v Somerset	The Oval	1922
v Gloucestershire	The Oval	1922
v Warwickshire	Birmingham	1922
v Glamorgan	Cardiff (AP)	1923
v Somerset	Taunton	1925
v Leicestershire	Leicester (AR)	1927
v Northamptonshire	Northampton	1928
v Middlesex	Lord's	1930
v Warwickshire	The Oval	1935
v Worcestershire	Worcester	1935
v Oxford University	The Oval	1937
v Kent	The Oval	1937
v Sussex	Horsham	1938
v Somerset	Weston-s-Mare	1939
v Somerset	The Oval	1946
v Worcestershire	The Oval	1949
v Worcestershire	Worcester	1950
v Middlesex	The Oval	1950
v Leicestershire	The Oval	1950
v Nottinghamshire	Nottingham	1951
v Sussex	The Oval	1952
v Worcestershire	Kidderminster	1952
v Yorkshire	The Oval	1953
v Derbyshire	Derby	1954
v Essex	The Oval	1954
v Nottinghamshire	The Oval	1954
v Worcestershire	Worcester	1954
v Worcestershire	The Oval	1955

v Australians	The Oval	1956
v Cambridge University	Cambridge	1957
v Northamptonshire	Northampton	1957
v Kent	The Oval	1957
v Leicestershire	The Oval	1957
v Warwickshire	Birmingham	1957
v Kent	The Oval	1958
v Cambridge University	Guildford	1959
v Glamorgan	Cardiff (AP)	1959
v Kent	Blackheath	1959
v Somerset	Bath	1959
v Nottinghamshire	The Oval	1960
v Lancashire	The Oval	1962
v Cambridge University	The Oval	1962
v Gloucestershire	Gloucester	1964
v Sussex	Hove	1964
v Lancashire	The Oval	1966
v Leicestershire	Guildford	1967
v Oxford University	Oxford	1968
v Sussex	Hove	1973
v Nottinghamshire	Guildford	1974
v Kent	Folkestone	1979
v Hampshire	Portsmouth	1979
v Essex	The Oval	1980
v Middlesex	The Oval	1981
v Nottinghamshire	The Oval	1982
v Worcestershire	Worcester	1983
v Nottinghamshire	Nottingham	1983
v Northamptonshire	The Oval	1987
v Sussex	Hove	1993
v Lancashire	Manchester	1994

Surrey Defeats

By an Innings and

296	- England	The Oval	1866
296	- Australians	The Oval	1948
217	- Yorkshire	Huddersfield	1881
205	- South Africans	The Oval	1935
203	- Yorkshire	Sheffield	1938

By Runs

392	- England	The Oval	1859
353	- Middlesex	Lord's	1911
345	- Essex	Southend-on-Sea	1933
323	- Essex	The Oval	1914
317	- Somerset	Bath	1994
316	- Worcestershire	Stourbridge	1910
304	- Northamptonshire	Northampton	1993
297	- Yorkshire	Bradford	1904
295	- Lancashire	Manchester	1949
292	- Kent	The Oval	1903
283	- Essex	Chelmsford	1990
281	- Somerset	The Oval	1993
279	- Gloucestershire	Cheltenham	1934
260	- Essex	The Oval	1903
256	- Middlesex	Lord's	1936
256	- Warwickshire	Guildford	1994
255	- Australians	The Oval	1961

248	- Yorkshire	Sheffield	1958
244	- Sussex	Hastings	1929
233	- Warwickshire	Coventry	1952
228	- Nottinghamshire	Nottingham	1905
225	- Nottinghamshire	Nottingham	1984
224	- Somerset	The Oval	1897
223	- Sussex	Hastings	1920
221	- Middlesex	Lord's	1903
221	- Leicestershire	The Oval	1910
216	- Lancashire	The Oval	1881
215	- Kent	Blackheath	1933
209	- Essex	Chelmsford	1982
206	- Kent	Blackheath	1908
205	- MCC	The Oval	1867
205	- Middlesex	The Oval	1896
204	- Oxford University	Oxford	1909
202	- Nottinghamshire	Nottingham	1907
200	- Cambridge University	The Oval	1883

By 10 Wickets

- Nottinghamshire	Nottingham	1852
- Sussex	The Oval	1852
- The North	The Oval	1862
- Oxford University	The Oval	1865
- Hampshire	Southampton	1866
- Sussex	Hove	1867
- MCC	Lord's	1869
- Kent	The Oval	1871
- Yorkshire	The Oval	1871
- Nottinghamshire	The Oval	1871
- Yorkshire	The Oval	1872
- Gloucestershire	The Oval	1876
- Nottinghamshire	The Oval	1876
- Gloucestershire	Clifton	1877
- Nottinghamshire	Nottingham	1878
- Kent	Maidstone	1878
- Gloucestershire	The Oval	1879
- Cambridge University	The Oval	1879
- Gloucestershire	Cheltenham	1880
- Middlesex	Lord's	1881
- Middlesex	The Oval	1881
- Middlesex	Lord's	1883
- Nottinghamshire	The Oval	1901
- Hampshire	Southampton	1902
- London County	The Oval	1902
- Kent	Beckenham	1905
- Kent	Blackheath	1907
- Gloucestershire	Bristol	1908
- Lancashire	Manchester	1912
- Yorkshire	Bradford	1919
- Oxford University	The Oval	1921
- Kent	Blackheath	1922
- West Indians	The Oval	1923
- Cambridge University	The Oval	1924
- Yorkshire	Bradford	1925
- Yorkshire	Leeds	1927
- Worcestershire	Worcester	1930
- Kent	The Oval	1935
- Worcestershire	The Oval	1938
- Essex	Colchester	1939

	- Middlesex	Lord's	1946
	- Australians	The Oval	1948
	- Lancashire	Manchester	1959
	- Lancashire	The Oval	1959
	- Australians	The Oval	1961
	- Northamptonshire	The Oval	1963
	- Warwickshire	Coventry	1963
	- Glamorgan	Neath	1968
	- Indians	The Oval	1974
	- Middlesex	Lord's	1974
	- Middlesex	The Oval	1978
	- Essex	Chelmsford	1980
	- Middlesex	The Oval	1983
	- Hampshire	Southampton	1992

TIED MATCHES

Surrey (112 & 160)	Kent (127 & 145)	The Oval	1847
MCC (175 & 122)	Surrey (204 & 93)	The Oval	1868
Middlesex (112 & 167)	Surrey (93 & 186)	The Oval	1868
Middlesex (138 & 322)	Surrey (215 & 245)	The Oval	1876
Surrey (97 & 124)	Lancashire (147 & 74)	The Oval	1894
Kent (202 & 84)	Surrey (125 & 161)	The Oval	1905

CLOSE RESULTS

Surrey Victories

By One Run			
	v Lancashire	The Oval	1948
By Two Runs			
	v Gloucestershire	The Oval	1948
	v Leicestershire	Guildford	1969
By Four Runs			
	v Warwickshire	Birmingham	1989
By Five Runs			
	v Australians	The Oval	1909
	v Hampshire	Southampton	1913
By One Wicket			
	v Nottinghamshire	Nottingham	1864
	v Nottinghamshire	The Oval	1865
	v MCC	The Oval	1871
	v Gloucestershire	The Oval	1872
	v Kent	Gravesend	1885
	v Lancashire	The Oval	1885
	v Sussex	Hove	1887
	v Northamptonshire	Northampton	1911
	v Sussex	The Oval	1914
	v Northamptonshire	Northampton	1932
	v Middlesex	The Oval	1934
	v Northamptonshire	Kettering	1954
	v Sussex	Hove	1954
	v Leicestershire	The Oval	1975
	v Gloucestershire	Cheltenham	1979
	v Hampshire	Bournemouth	1991
	v Yorkshire	Guildford	1991
	v Yorkshire	Bradford	1992
	v Gloucestershire	Gloucester	1994

Surrey Defeats

By One Run			
	- Leicestershire	The Oval	1961
By Two Runs			
	- Sussex	Hove	1855
	- Kent	Maidstone	1870
	- Rhodesia	Salisbury	1959
By Three Runs			
	- Manchester	Eccles	1857
	- Hampshire	The Oval	1982
By Five Runs			
	- Essex	The Oval	1900
	- MCC	Lord's	1938
	- Yorkshire	Sheffield	1950
By One Wicket			
	- England	The Oval	1855
	- The North	Manchester	1862
	- Nottinghamshire	The Oval	1874
	- Middlesex	The Oval	1900
	- Kent	The Oval	1906
	- Sussex	Horsham	1910
	- Hampshire	Southampton	1924
	- Middlesex	The Oval	1948
	- Lancashire	Manchester	1991

VICTORY AFTER FOLLOWING-ON

Surrey (175 and 253) beat North (257 and 118)	The Oval	1858
Surrey (110 and 297) beat Hampshire (208 and 140)	The Oval	1866
Surrey (179 and 334) beat Cambridge University (339 and 160)	The Oval	1868

DEFEAT AFTER OPPONENTS FOLLOWED ON

MCC (91 and 216) beat Surrey (197 and 101)	The Oval	1847
Lancashire (113 and 314) beat Surrey (226 and 141)	The Oval	1880
Yorkshire (137 and 247) beat Surrey (293 and 76)	The Oval	1890
Middlesex (108 and 377) beat Surrey (287 and 119)	Lord's	1893
Kent (117 and 332) beat Surrey (301-8 dec. and 76)	Guildford	1992

MOST RUNS IN A DAY

By Surrey

645	v Hampshire	The Oval	1909
616	v Northamptonshire	The Oval	1921
607	v Northamptonshire	Northampton	1920

By Both Sides

666	Northamptonshire (59-2) v Surrey (607-4)	Northampton	1920
647	Sussex (115) v Surrey (532-6)	The Oval	1919
626	Surrey (337-2) v Hampshire (289)	Southampton	1919
601	Surrey (361-5) v Middlesex (240)	The Oval	1919

FOUR HUNDREDS IN AN INNINGS FOR SURREY

706-4 dec v Nottinghamshire Nottingham 1947
D.G.W.Fletcher 194, H.S.Squires 154, E.R.T. Holmes 122, J.F.Parker 108**

THREE HUNDREDS IN AN INNINGS

For Surrey

500-4d v Gloucestershire The Oval 1898
D.L.A.Jephson 166, W.Brockwell 105, R.Abel 104**
556 v Lancashire The Oval 1899
R.Abel 178, W.H.Lockwood 131, D.L.A.Jephson 100
811 v Somerset The Oval 1899
R.Abel 357, T.W.Hayward 158, V.F.S.Crawford 129*
495-5 dec v Worcestershire The Oval 1900
*R.Abel 221, E.G.Hayes 150, W.H.Lockwood 104**
552 v Sussex Hastings 1902
R.Abel 179, T.W.Hayward 144, H.S.Bush 122
549-6 dec v Leicestershire The Oval 1905
J.N.Crawford 142, Lord Dalmeny 138, T.W.Hayward 122*
576 v Derbyshire The Oval 1911
T.W.Hayward 202, H.S.Bush 135, E.G.Goatly 105
523-7 dec v Somerset Taunton 1911
E.G.Hayes 101, A.Ducat 101, J.W.Hitch 100*
509 v Kent Blackheath 1914
T.W.Hayward 122, J.B.Hobbs 122, D.J.Knight 105
549-6 dec v Yorkshire Lord's 1914
J.B.Hobbs 202, E.G.Hayes 134, T.W.Hayward 116
619-5 dec v Northamptonshire Northampton 1920
H.A.Peach 200, A.Ducat 149, P.G.H.Fender 113**
616-5 dec v Northamptonshire The Oval 1921
A.Sandham 292, A.Jeacocke 138, A.Ducat 134*
594-8 dec v Cambridge University The Oval 1923
A.Jeacocke 156, W.J.Abel 117, A.Ducat 115
477 v Somerset The Oval 1925
T.F.Shepherd 133, A.Ducat 128, J.B.Hobbs 111
617-6 dec v Oxford University The Oval 1928
A.Sandham 198, T.F.Shepherd 142, R.J.Gregory 107
579-4 dec v Somerset The Oval 1931
P.G.H.Fender 139, A.Sandham 131, J.B.Hobbs 128*
503-4 dec v Warwickshire The Oval 1931
J.B.Hobbs 147, T.F.Shepherd 140, A.Ducat 125
478 v Lancashire Manchester 1933
R.J.Gregory 142, F.R.Brown 108, H.S.Squires 101*
550 v Hampshire The Oval 1935
T.H.Barling 168, A.Sandham 107, H.S.Squires 101
495 v Sussex Hove 1937
R.J.Gregory 124, E.R.T Holmes 115, A.Sandham 102

Against Surrey

577 - Oxford University Reigate 1909
M.G.Salter 152, J.A.Seitz 120, C.V.L.Hooman 117
568-9 dec - Middlesex The Oval 1919
H.W.Lee 163, J.W.Hearne 113, E.L.Kidd 100
557-7 - Kent The Oval 1922
J.Seymour 129, H.T.W.Hardinge 119, F.E.Woolley 100

516-8 dec - Leicestershire The Oval 1929
*G.L.Berry 156, E.W.Dawson 140, J.C.Bradshaw 105**
536 - Sussex Hove 1932
E.H.Bowley 146, K.S.Duleepsinhji 126, H.W.Parks 120
489 - Sussex Eastbourne 1935
*John G.Langridge 111, A.Melville 110, H.W.Parks 100**
519-6 dec - Yorkshire Leeds 1936
M.Leyland 163, L.Hutton 163, H.Sutcliffe 129*
597 - Essex The Oval 1946
A.V.Avery 210, T.N.Pearce 116, T.C.Dodds 103*
537-2 dec - Middlesex The Oval 1947
W.J.Edrich 157, D.C.S.Compton 137*, J.D.B.Robertson 127*
632 - Australians The Oval 1948
S.G.Barnes 176, D.G.Bradman 146, A.L.Hassett 110
863 - Lancashire The Oval 1990
N.H.Fairbrother 366, M.A.Atherton 191, G.D.Mendis 102
441 - Middlesex The Oval 1992
M.A.Roseberry 120. J.D.Carr 114, M.R.Ramprakash 117

SEVEN FIFTIES IN AN INNINGS FOR SURREY

493 v Hampshire Portsmouth 1908
J.N.Crawford 124, F.C.Holland 65, J.B.Hobbs 56, A.Marshal 54, T.W.Hayward 53, W.A.Spring 53, E.G.Hayes 52*

SIX FIFTIES IN AN INNINGS FOR SURREY

539 v Sussex Hove 1900
R.Abel 110, W.H.Lockwood 85, N.Miller 81, V.F.S.Crawford 79, W.Brockwell 64, T.W.Hayward 52
535 v Nottinghamshire The Oval 1913
D.J.Knight 90, E.G.Goatly 82, J.B.Hobbs 77, H.S.Harrison 66, T.W.Hayward 63, E.G.Hayes 60
524-9 dec v Essex Leyton 1926
P.G.H.Fender 104, T.F.Shepherd 93, J.B.Hobbs 69, A.Sandham 67, D.R.Jardine 60, A.Jeacocke 51
505 v Northamptonshire The Oval 1928
A.Sandham 119, H.M.Garland-Wells 88, R.J.Gregory 70, J.B.Hobbs 65, E.W.J.Brooks 57, A.Ducat 50

FIVE FIFTIES IN AN INNINGS

For Surrey

650 v Hampshire The Oval 1883
*W.W.Read 168, J.M.Read 91, R.Abel 83, J.Shuter 67, A.Chester 54**
635 v Somerset The Oval 1885
J.M.Read 186, W.W.Read 98, R.Abel 81, M.P.Bowden 51, H.Wood 50*
698 v Sussex The Oval 1888
M.P.Bowden 189, W.W.Read 171, J.Shuter 95, K.J.Key 84, R.Abel 59*
614 v Oxford University The Oval 1889
*R.Abel 138, J.M.Read 136, W.W.Read 91, F.Fielding 75, W.H.Lockwood 53**
464 v Gloucestershire The Oval 1890
J.M.Read 135, W.H.Lockwood 65, H.Wood 63, G.A.Lohmann 57, W.W.Read 51
356 v Australians The Oval 1893
W.Brockwell 67, R.Henderson 60, C.Baldwin 54, T.W.Hayward 53, A.E.Street 51*

560 v Leicestershire The Oval 1897
R.Abel 144, T.W.Hayward 130, K.J.Key 66, W.W.Read 62, H.D.G.Leveson-Gower 53
434 v Lancashire Manchester 1899
W.H.Lockwood 76, T.W.Hayward 67, D.L.A.Jephson 64, H.Wood 61, R.Abel 54*
506 v Leicestershire Leicester (GR) 1899
W.Brockwell 147, T.W.Hayward 80, R.Abel 63, H.B.Richardson 61, E.G.Hayes 54
517 v Leicestershire Leicester (AR) 1901
W.Brockwell 101, R.Abel 75, T.W.Hayward 72, D.L.A.Jephson 68, W.H.Lockwood 57
440 v Derbyshire The Oval 1902
V.F.S.Crawford 101, D.L.A.Jephson 94, W.Brockwell 70, H.S.Bush 56, T.W.Hayward 54*
544 v Worcestershire Worcester 1904
J.E.Raphael 111, E.G.Hayes 94, R.Abel 87, H.D.G.Leveson-Gower 60, A.Stedman 51*
390 v Gents of England The Oval 1908
W.S.Lees 97, A.Marshal 62, E.G.Hayes 56, F.C.Holland 56, S.E.Busher 52
415 v Worcestershire Worcester 1909
T.W.Hayward 74, A.Marshal 60, J.B.Hobbs 58, T.Rushby 58, E.G.Hayes 57*
499 v Hampshire The Oval 1911
E.G.Hayes 91, J.B.Hobbs 87, W.C.Smith 69, A.Ducat 65, T.W.Hayward 52*
442 v Derbyshire Derby 1911
E.G.Hayes 109, W.E.Davis 65, M.C.Bird 62, I.P.F.Campbell 54, H.S.Bush 50
523-7 dec v Somerset Taunton 1911
E.G.Hayes 101, A.Ducat 101, J.W.Hitch 100, E.G.Goatly 64, H.S.Harrison 53*
544 v Middlesex The Oval 1914
C.T.A.Wilkinson 135, A.Ducat 102, H.S.Harrison 68, E.G.Hayes 67, P.G.H.Fender 51
532-6 dec v Sussex The Oval 1919
A.Ducat 190, A.Sandham 90, C.T.A.Wilkinson 80, H.S.Harrison 52, T.Abel 50**
582-9 dec v Middlesex The Oval 1919
A.Sandham 175, J.B.Hobbs 84, A.Ducat 75, W.J.Abel 73*, H.Strudwick 53*
552-8 dec v Sussex Hastings 1923
A.Ducat 120, T.F.Shepherd 106, D.J.Knight 90, J.B.Hobbs 79, P.G.H.Fender 64
439 v Hampshire The Oval 1927
T.F.Shepherd 120, J.B.Hobbs 112, H.A.Peach 77, A.Jeacocke 55, P.G.H.Fender 53
522-7 dec v Nottinghamshire The Oval 1927
A.Sandham 140, J.B.Hobbs 131, P.G.H.Fender 66, T.H.Barling 59, A.Ducat 58*
617-6 dec v Oxford University The Oval 1928
A.Sandham 198, T.F.Shepherd 142, R.J.Gregory 107, A.Jeacocke 62, H.A.Peach 55**
530-9 dec v Northamptonshire Northampton 1928
J.B.Hobbs 117, E.F.Wilson 99, R.J.Gregory 96, A.Ducat 54, C.E.Daily 51
453-5 dec v Leicestershire The Oval 1930
J.B.Hobbs 100, A.Sandham 100, P.G.H.Fender 76, A.Ducat 67, T.F.Shepherd 64
579-4 dec v Somerset The Oval 1931
P.G.H.Fender 139, A.Sandham 131, J.B.Hobbs 128, A.Ducat 83, D.R.Jardine 80**
453 v Cambridge University The Oval 1932
H.S.Squires 103, G.S.Mobey 73, E.F.Wilson 72, T.F.Shepherd 65, R.de W.K.Winlaw 52
457 v Warwickshire The Oval 1933
J.B.Hobbs 100, R.J.Gregory 92, H.T.Barling 67, A.Sandham 57, D.R.Jardine 50
560-6 dec v Yorkshire The Oval 1933
H.S.Squires 178, H.T.Barling 112, A.Sandham 96, R.de W.K.Winlaw 75, P.G.H.Fender 55*
482-7 dec v Gloucestershire The Oval 1934
R.J.Gregory 141, H.T.Barling 104, A.Sandham 81, P.G.H.Fender 54*, H.S.Squires 52*
501 v Kent The Oval 1934
E.R.T.Holmes 100, H.M.Garland-Wells 85, H.S.Squires 85, E.A.Watts 71, R.J.Gregory 60
558-7 dec v MCC Lord's 1934
H.T.Barling 176, H.S.Squires 110, R.J.Gregory 99, H.M.Garland-Wells 79, J.B.Hobbs 50
419-9 dec v Hampshire Bournemouth 1934
H.T.Barling 70, R.J.Gregory 70, E.R.T.Holmes 67, L.B.Fishlock 65, H.S.Squires 51
576 v Leicestershire The Oval 1947
J.F.Parker 134, G.J.Whittaker 105, E.A.Bedser 92, H.S.Squires 78, T.H.Clark 51*

706-4 dec v Nottinghamshire Nottingham 1947
D.G.W.Fletcher 194, H.S.Squires 154, E.R.T.Holmes 122, J.F.Parker 108*, R.J.Gregory 84*
319-5 dec v Sussex The Oval 1967
W.A.Smith 64, M.J.Stewart 62, M.D.Willett 62, M.J.Edwards 53, S.J.Storey 50*
613-6 dec v Essex The Oval 1990
D.M.Ward 208, R.I.Alikhan 138, I.A.Greig 57, A.J.Stewart 51, D.J.Bicknell 50*
411 v Nottinghamshire Nottingham 1992
*G.P.Thorpe 100, A.J.Stewart 85, D.J.Bicknell 77, M.A.Lynch 70, A.D.Brown 50**

Against Surrey

705-8 dec - Sussex Hastings 1902
K.S.Ranjitsinhji 234, C.B.Fry 159, J.Vine 92, F.W.Tate 61*, G.R.Cox 51*
600-7 dec - Sussex The Oval 1903
K.S.Ranjitsinhji 204, J.Vine 101, C.B.Fry 81, G.Brann 54, W.Newham 50
526-7 dec - Lancashire The Oval 1929
F.B.Watson 169, G.E.Tyldesley 74, L.Warburton 74, C.Hallows 58, T.M.Halliday 55*
632 - Australians The Oval 1948
*S.G.Barnes 176, D.G.Bradman 146, A.L.Hassett 110, A.R.Morris 65, D.Tallon 50**
559 - Hampshire The Oval 1993
R.A.Smith 127, M.C.J.Nicholas 95, V.P.Terry 91, R.M.F.Cox 63, C.A.Connor 59
603-7 dec - Hampshire Southampton 1994
M.C.J.Nicholas 145, V.P.Terry 135, A.N.Aymes 76, R.A.Smith 75, G.W.White 57

EIGHT FIFTIES IN A MATCH AGAINST SURREY

470 & 363-3 - Yorkshire The Oval 1902
F.S.Jackson 77 & 81, T.L.Taylor 64 & 88*, Lord Hawke 126, S.Haigh 62, W.A.I.Washington 84, J.T.Brown 55*

SEVEN FIFTIES IN A MATCH

For Surrey

439 & 281-6 dec v Hampshire The Oval 1927
J.B.Hobbs 112 & 104, T.F.Shepherd 120, H.A.Peach 77, A.Sandham 58, A.Jeacocke 55, P.G.H.Fender 53
297 & 369 v Glamorgan The Oval 1927
A.Ducat 54 & 64, A.Jeacocke 75, A.Sandham 57, P.G.H.Fender 56, T.F.Shepherd 56, H.A.Peach 56
405 & 311-4 v Oxford University The Oval 1930
A.Ducat 56 & 87, A.Jeacocke 52 & 66, T.F.Shepherd 122, H.T.Barling 103, E.W.Whitfield 59**
501 & 207-5 dec v Kent The Oval 1934
H.S.Squires 85 & 61, E.R.T.Holmes 100, H.M.Garland-Wells 85, A.Sandham 85, E.A.Watts 71, R.J.Gregory 60
469 & 155-6 v Essex Ilford 1948
J.F.Parker 67 & 53, H.S.Squires 74, D.G.W.Fletcher 70, A.J.W.McIntyre 68, J.C.Laker 56, L.B.Fishlock 51*

Against Surrey

382 & 280-5 dec - London County Crystal Palace 1901
W.G.Grace 71 & 80, C.J.B.Wood 66 & 70, L.C.Braund 115 & 58, G.W.Beldam 52**
426 & 221-2 dec - Cambridge UniversityGuildford 1949
G.H.G.Doggart 124 & 54, J.G.Dewes 81 & 82, D.J.Insole 87, A.G.J.Rimell 62, R.J. Morris 58*

329-7 dec & 245-4 dec - Hampshire Bournemouth 1964
A.C.D.Ingleby-Mackenzie 81, R.E.Marshall 61, J.R.Gray 61, P.J.Sainsbury 59, D.A.Livingstone 51*, H.Horton 51, H.M.Barnard 51*

327-7 dec & 259-3 - Warwickshire The Oval 1975
D.L.Amiss 78 & 76, R.B.Kanhai 78 & 51*, A.I.Kallicharran 54, W.A.Bourne 51*, J.A.Jameson 50*

300-4 dec & 274-4 dec - Warwickshire Birmingham 1980
G.W.Humpage 74 & 54, K.D.Smith 62 & 60, J.Whitehouse 79, T.A.Lloyd 75, D.L. Amiss 50*

RECORD INNINGS TOTALS FOR SURREY INVOLVING HUNDREDS AND FIFTIES

Highest Innings Total Without a Hundred

535		v Nottinghamshire	The Oval	1913

Lowest Completed Innings Total With a Fifty

81	W.S.Surridge (51)	v Derbyshire	Derby	1953

Lowest Completed Innings Total With a Hundred

184	T.Humphrey (103)	v Nottinghamshire	The Oval	1868

K.F.Barrington scored 103 out of 157-9d in the first innings v Northamptonshire at The Oval in 1966.*

Lowest Completed Innings Total With a Double Hundred

344	J.B.Hobbs (205*)	v A.I.F.	The Oval	1919

J.H.Edrich scored 205 out of 321-8d v Gloucestershire at Bristol in 1965.*

ELEVEN BOWLERS USED IN AN INNINGS

By Surrey

455	v Middlesex	The Oval	1866
585-7	v Warwickshire	The Oval	1905

By Opponents

698	- Sussex	The Oval	1888
579	- Hampshire	The Oval	1897

MOST BOWLERS USED IN A MATCH (Both Sides)

20	v Middlesex	The Oval	1990

MOST EXTRAS CONCEDED IN AN INNINGS

(10% or more of innings total)

By Surrey

			b	*lb*	*w*	*nb*	*Extras*	*Inns total*
1847	v MCC	Lord's	13	-	4	1	18	148
1847	v Kent	Aylesford	10	-	7	2	19	99
1867	v Yorkshire	The Oval	20	9	10		39	265
1883	v Kent	The Oval	29	11	2	1	43	299
1885	v Kent	The Oval	21	17	1	1	40	288
1890	v Gloucestershire	The Oval	31	2	-	-	33	238
1907	v Derbyshire	The Oval	3	22	-	2	27	216
1923	v Middlesex	The Oval	32	5	8	-	45	294
1928	v Sussex	Horsham	18	24	-	1	43	387
1928	v Lancashire	The Oval	24	11	4	10	49	486
1937	v Middlesex	Lord's	9	3	20	2	34	202
	(E.R.T. Holmes bowled an over yielding 24 from byes and wides to get a new ball)							
1987	v Glamorgan	The Oval	6	6	4	21	37	152
	(extras were the top score in the innings)							
1989	v Oxford University	Oxford	1	11	-	23	35	201
No-balls now count as an additional 2 runs, whether scored off or not								
1993	v Leicestershire	Leicester (GR)	1	10	1	29	41	255
1993	v Worcestershire	Worcester	9	12	1	28	50	406
1993	v Worcestershire	Worcester	5	14	-	34	53	313
1994	v Hampshire	Southampton	5	14	4	58	81	603
1994	v Derbyshire	The Oval	-	10	-	20	30	208
1994	v Northamptonshire	The Oval	8	12	2	12	34	316
1994	v Somerset	Bath	4	5	6	38	53	428
1994	v Warwickshire	Guildford	1	10	5	32	48	246
1994	v Essex	Colchester	-	12	1	32	45	378
1994	v Middlesex	The Oval	-	13	8	38	59	350
Note also:								
1927	v Lancashire	Manchester	33	11	1	1	46	522
	(most extras in an innings before the change to the no-ball law)							
1928	v Hampshire	The Oval	34	9	-	1	44	454
	(most byes in an innings)							
1991	v Kent	The Oval	2	27	1	5	35	420
	(most leg byes in an innings)							
1992	v Yorkshire	The Oval	3	11	-	25	39	495
	(most no-balls in an innings before the change to the no-ball law)							

By Opponents

			b	*lb*	*w*	*nb*	*Extras*	*Inns total*
1846	- Kent	The Oval	13	-	6	-	19	137
1850	- Kent	The Oval	16	7	5	4	32	246
1863	- Kent	The Oval	17	2	1	-	20	192
1876	- Middlesex	Prince's	19	9	-	-	28	276
1876	- Kent	The Oval	30	1	6	1	38	268
1882	- Sussex	The Oval	7	15	-	-	22	202
1989	- Kent	The Oval	1	9	2	28	40	477
1990	- Leicestershire	The Oval	6	26	1	9	42	420

			b	*lb*	*w*	*nb*	*Extras*	*Inns total*
No-balls now count as an additional 2 runs, whether scored off or not								
1993	- Middlesex	Lord's	-	9	-	34	43	322
1993	- Durham	The Oval	5	21	1	32	59	473
1994	- Worcestershire	The Oval	1	14	10	25	50	470
1994	- Gloucestershire	Gloucester	2	9	3	42	56	354
1994	- Durham	Darlington	3	11	1	28	43	236
1994	- Nottinghamshire	Nottingham	14	35	-	24	73	604
1994	- Middlesex	The Oval	-	11	7	32	50	425
Note also:								
1883	- Hampshire	The Oval	38	7	5	2	52	650
	(most extras in an innings before the change to the no-ball law)							
1887	- Cambridge University	The Oval	40	3	3	-	46	543
	(most byes in an innings)							
1989	- Kent	The Oval	1	9	2	28	40	477
	(most no-balls in an innings before the change to the no-ball law)							
1989	- Warwickshire	Birmingham	-	4	13	7	24	293
	(most wides in an innings)							

UNUSUAL DISMISSALS

Hit the Ball Twice

H.R.J.Charlwood	v Sussex	Hove	1872
J.H.King	v Leicestershire	The Oval	1906

Obstructing the Field

C.A.Absolom	v Cambridge Univ	The Oval	1868

Run Out by the Bowler While Backing Up

R.Swetman (Gloucestershire)	by R.D.Jackman	Bristol	1972

SECTION 2 - INDIVIDUAL BATTING RECORDS

HIGHEST INDIVIDUAL INNINGS

For Surrey

357*	R.Abel	v Somerset	The Oval	1899
338	W.W.Read	v Oxford University	The Oval	1888
316*	J.B.Hobbs	v Middlesex	Lord's	1926
315*	T.W.Hayward	v Lancashire	The Oval	1898
306*	A.Ducat	v Oxford University	The Oval	1919
294*	D.M.Ward	v Derbyshire	The Oval	1994
292*	A.Sandham	v Northamptonshire	The Oval	1921
291	I.A.Greig	v Lancashire	The Oval	1990
290*	A.Ducat	v Essex	Leyton	1921
282*	A.Sandham	v Lancashire	Manchester	1928
277*	T.F.Shepherd	v Gloucestershire	The Oval	1927
276	E.G.Hayes	v Hampshire	The Oval	1909
273*	E.G.Hayes	v Derbyshire	Derby	1904
273	T.W.Hayward	v Yorkshire	The Oval	1899
271	A.Ducat	v Hampshire	Southampton	1919
269	H.T.Barling	v Hampshire	Southampton	1933
263	D.M.Ward	v Kent	Canterbury	1990
261	J.B.Hobbs	v Oxford University	The Oval	1926
255	J.F.Parker	v New Zealanders	The Oval	1949
253	L.B.Fishlock	v Leicestershire	Leicester (GR)	1948
250	R.Abel	v Warwickshire	The Oval	1897
248*	A.Sandham	v Glamorgan	Cardiff (AP)	1928
247	W.W.Read	v Lancashire	Manchester	1887
244*	W.W.Read	v Cambridge University	The Oval	1887
243	R.J.Gregory	v Somerset	The Oval	1938
239	A.Sandham	v Glamorgan	The Oval	1937
236	H.S.Squires	v Lancashire	The Oval	1933
235*	D.J.Bicknell	v Nottinghamshire	Nottingham	1994
235	A.Ducat	v Leicestershire	The Oval	1926
234	C.Baldwin	v Kent	The Oval	1897
234	T.F.Shepherd	v Cambridge University	The Oval	1930
233*	H.T.Barling	v Nottinghamshire	The Oval	1946
232	J.N.Crawford	v Somerset	The Oval	1908
231	R.Abel	v Essex	The Oval	1896
230	A.Sandham	v Essex	The Oval	1927
229*	T.W.Hayward	v Derbyshire	Derby	1896
227*	M.J.Stewart	v Middlesex	The Oval	1964
226*	J.H.Edrich	v Middlesex	The Oval	1967
226	J.B.Hobbs	v Nottinghamshire	The Oval	1914
225	W.Brockwell	v Hampshire	The Oval	1897
221	R.Abel	v Worcestershire	The Oval	1900
221	J.B.Hobbs	v West Indians	The Oval	1933
221	T.E.Jesty	v Essex	The Oval	1986
219	R.Abel	v Kent	The Oval	1898
219	T.W.Hayward	v Northamptonshire	The Oval	1906
219	A.Sandham	v Australians	The Oval	1934
218	E.G.Hayes	v Oxford University	The Oval	1906
218	A.Ducat	v Nottinghamshire	Nottingham	1930
217	R.Abel	v Essex	The Oval	1895
216*	A.R.Butcher	v Cambridge University	Cambridge	1980
216	J.H.Edrich	v Nottinghamshire	Nottingham	1962
216	G.P.Thorpe	v Somerset	The Oval	1992
215	R.Abel	v Nottinghamshire	The Oval	1897

215*	J.B.Hobbs	v Essex	Leyton	1914
215	J.B.Hobbs	v Warwickshire	Birmingham	1925
215	A.Sandham	v Somerset	Taunton	1932
213	D.L.A.Jephson	v Derbyshire	The Oval	1900
212	T.F.Shepherd	v Lancashire	The Oval	1921
212	F.R.Brown	v Middlesex	The Oval	1932
211	P.B.H.May	v Nottinghamshire	Nottingham	1954
210*	T.F.Shepherd	v Kent	Blackheath	1921
210	H.S.Squires	v Derbyshire	The Oval	1949
210	L.B.Fishlock	v Somerset	The Oval	1949
209*	A.Sandham	v Somerset	The Oval	1921
208	T.W.Hayward	v Warwickshire	The Oval	1906
208	A.Ducat	v Essex	Leyton	1928
208	D.M.Ward	v Essex	The Oval	1990
207*	T.F.Shepherd	v Kent	Blackheath	1925
207	P.B.H.May	v Cambridge University	The Oval	1954
207	K.F.Barrington	v Nottinghamshire	The Oval	1964
206*	A.J.Stewart	v Essex	The Oval	1989
206	E.R.T.Holmes	v Derbyshire	Chesterfield	1935
205*	R.Abel	v Middlesex	The Oval	1901
205*	J.B.Hobbs	v A.I.F.	The Oval	1919
205*	B.Constable	v Somerset	The Oval	1952
205*	J.H.Edrich	v Gloucestershire	Bristol	1965
205	J.B.Hobbs	v Hampshire	The Oval	1909
204*	T.W.Hayward	v Warwickshire	The Oval	1909
204*	A.Ducat	v Northamptonshire	Northampton	1921
204*	J.F.Parker	v Derbyshire	The Oval	1947
204	W.E.Roller	v Sussex	The Oval	1885
204	J.B.Hobbs	v Somerset	The Oval	1929
204	A.Sandham	v Warwickshire	Birmingham	1930
203*	J.B.Hobbs	v Nottinghamshire	Nottingham	1924
203	A.Ducat	v Sussex	The Oval	1920
202*	A.W.Smith	v Oxford University	The Oval	1994
202	E.G.Hayes	v Middlesex	The Oval	1907
202	T.W.Hayward	v Derbyshire	The Oval	1911
202	J.B.Hobbs	v Yorkshire	Lord's	1914
201*	A.Jeacocke	v Sussex	The Oval	1922
200*	H.A.Peach	v Northamptonshire	Northampton	1920
200*	J.B.Hobbs	v Warwickshire	Birmingham	1928
200*	M.J.Stewart	v Essex	The Oval	1962
200	A.Sandham	v Essex	Leyton	1923
200	J.B.Hobbs	v Hampshire	Southampton	1926
200	H.S.Squires	v Cambridge University	The Oval	1931

Against Surrey

366	N.H.Fairbrother	- Lancashire	The Oval	1990
300*	F.B.Watson	- Lancashire	Manchester	1928
300	R.Subba Row	- Northamptonshire	The Oval	1958
280*	R.G.Duckfield	- Glamorgan	The Oval	1936
255*	W.G.Quaife	- Warwickshire	The Oval	1905
255	W.Barber	- Yorkshire	Sheffield	1935
252*	D.G.Bradman	- Australians	The Oval	1930
251*	C.Washbrook	- Lancashire	Manchester	1947
248	J.O'Connor	- Essex	Brentwood	1934
240	S.J.McCabe	- Australians	The Oval	1934
236*	W.Gunn	- Nottinghamshire	The Oval	1898
236	G.E.Tyldesley	- Lancashire	The Oval	1923
235	D.C.S.Compton	- Middlesex	Lord's	1946

234*	K.S.Ranjitsinhji	- Sussex	Hastings	1902
233	M.R.Ramprakash	- Middlesex	Lord's	1992
232*	G.H.Hirst	- Yorkshire	The Oval	1905
232	E.de C.Weekes	- West Indians	The Oval	1950
232	H.Sutcliffe	- Yorkshire	The Oval	1922
231	J.L.Bryan	- Cambridge University	The Oval	1921
229	C.B.Fry	- Sussex	Hove	1900
229	F.E.Woolley	- Kent	The Oval	1935
228	E.Wainwright	- Yorkshire	The Oval	1899
225	H.W.Lee	- Middlesex	The Oval	1929
224*	W.G.Grace	- England	The Oval	1866
224	R.H.Spooner	- Lancashire	The Oval	1911
221	T.C.Middleton	- Hampshire	Southampton	1992
217	E.J.Barlow	- Derbyshire	Ilkeston	1976
217	F.L.Fane	- Essex	The Oval	1911
216*	Zaheer Abbas	- Gloucestershire	The Oval	1976
210	A.V.Avery	- Essex	The Oval	1946
210	J.T.Tyldesley	- Lancashire	The Oval	1913
208	A.H.Dyson	- Glamorgan	The Oval	1932
207	H.T.W.Hardinge	- Kent	Blackheath	1921
207	A.Shrewsbury	- Nottinghamshire	The Oval	1882
206	M.N.Lathwell	- Somerset	Bath	1994
205*	W.R.Hammond	- Gloucestershire	The Oval	1928
204	K.S.Ranjitsinhji	- Sussex	The Oval	1903
204	Majid Khan	- Glamorgan	The Oval	1972
204	I.V.A.Richards	- Somerset	Weston-super-Mare	1977
204	N.R.Taylor	- Kent	Canterbury	1990
203*	N.F.Horner	- Warwickshire	The Oval	1960
203	A.J.Moles	- Warwickshire	Guildford	1994
203	H.Sutcliffe	- Yorkshire	The Oval	1934
202	E.H.Hendren	- MCC	Lord's	1936
201	T.G.Matthews	- Gloucestershire	Clifton	1871
200*	R.T.Simpson	- Nottinghamshire	Nottingham	1949
200*	C.G.Greenidge	- Hampshire	Guildford	1977
200	K.S.Ranjitsinhji	- Sussex	The Oval	1908
200	F.R.Foster	- Warwickshire	Birmingham	1911
200	L.E.G.Ames	- Kent	Blackheath	1928
200	D.A.Livingstone	- Hampshire	Southampton	1962
200	C.B.Fry	- Sussex	Hove	1903

FIRST-CLASS CENTURIONS FOR SURREY

	First	*No*
Abel R.	1886	64
Abel W.J.	1923	1
Alikhan R.I.	1990	2
Atkins P.D.	1988	1
Aworth C.J.	1975	1
Baker A.	1901	5
Baldwin C.	1896	3
Barling H.T.	1927	34
Barrington K.F.	1954	43
Barton M.R.	1948	5
Bedser A.V.	1947	1
Bedser E.A.	1946	9
Berry F.	1938	1
Bicknell D.J.	1987	23
Bird M.C.	1911	4
Block S.A.	1931	1
Bloomfield H.O.	1921	1
Bowden M.P.	1885	2
Brockwell W.	1894	20
Brown A.D.	1992	8
Brown F.R.	1932	9
Burbidge F.	1863	1
Bush H.S.	1902	4
Butcher A.R.	1976	29
Butcher M.A.	1994	1
Caesar J.	1861	2
Caffyn W.	1851	2
Chinnery H.B.	1897	1
Clark T.H.	1950	12
Clarke S.T.	1981	1

	First	No
Clinton G.S.	1979	20
Constable B.	1949	26
Crawford J.N.	1905	8
Crawford V.F.S.	1899	8
Dalmeny Lord	1905	2
Davis W.E.	1904	3
Diver E.J.	1885	1
Dowson E.M.	1902	3
Ducat A.	1909	52
Edrich J.H.	1959	81
Edwards M.J.	1966	12
Falkner N.J.	1984	2
Feltham M.A.	1990	1
Fender P.G.H.	1914	17
Finlay I.W.	1967	1
Fishlock L.B.	1935	50
Fletcher D.G.W.	1947	21
Garland-Wells H.M.	1935	1
Goatly E.G.	1905	3
Greenfield G.P.	1869	1
Gregory R.J.	1926	38
Greig I.A.	1987	4
Griffith G.	1863	2
Harrison H.S.	1913	2
Hayes E.G.	1899	45
Hayward T.W.	1893	88
Henderson R.	1891	1
Hitch J.W.	1911	3
Hobbs J.B.	1905	144
Holland F.C.	1895	12
Hollioake A.J.	1993	4
Holmes E.R.T.	1934	15
Howarth G.P.	1973	18
Humphrey R.	1871	1
Humphrey T.	1865	4
Intikhab Alam	1969	4
Jardine D.R.	1923	14
Jeacocke A.	1921	8
Jefferson R.I.	1963	2
Jephson D.L.A.	1897	9
Jesty T.E.	1985	7
Jupp H.	1864	12
Key K.J.	1887	8
Knight D.J.	1914	9
Knight R.D.V.	1978	15
Laker J.C.	1949	2
Lees W.S.	1905	2
Leveson-Gower H.D.G.	1899	2
Lockwood W.H.	1890	14
Lockyer T.	1864	1

	First	No
Lohmann G.A.	1886	2
Lucas A.P.	1877	2
Lynch M.A.	1981	33
McIntyre A.J.W.	1946	7
Marshal A.	1907	7
May P.B.H.	1950	39
Medlycott K.T.	1984	3
Miller F.P.	1860	1
Miller N.	1899	1
Monkhouse G.	1984	1
Mortlock W.	1863	3
Needham A.	1982	4
Owen-Thomas D.R.	1972	3
Parker J.F.	1938	20
Parsons A.B.D.	1960	3
Pauline D.B.	1983	1
Peach H.A.	1920	4
Pratt R.E.C.	1956	1
Pretty H.C.	1899	1
Raphael J.E.	1904	1
Read J.M.	1883	8
Read W.W.	1876	31
Richards C.J.	1982	7
Roller W.E.	1883	7
Roope G.R.J.	1970	22
Sandham A.	1913	83
Shepherd T.F.	1921	41
Shuter J.	1879	8
Smith A.W.	1994	1
Smith D.M.	1976	11
Smith W.A.	1963	2
Spring W.A.	1908	2
Squires H.S.	1929	36
Stephenson H.H.	1864	2
Stewart A.J.	1983	21
Stewart M.J.	1954	48
Storey S.J.	1962	12
Street A.E.	1895	1
Subba Row R.	1953	3
Thomas D.J.	1983	2
Thorpe G.P.	1988	14
Tindall R.A.E.	1961	2
Ward D.M.	1985	16
Watts E.A.	1934	2
Whitfield E.W.	1932	6
Whittaker G.J.	1946	6
Wilkinson C.T.A.	1914	3
Willett M.D.	1961	8
Wilson E.F.	1929	1
Younis Ahmed	1967	19

HUNDRED IN EACH INNINGS

For Surrey

186	118*	K.F.Barrington	v Warwickshire	Birmingham	1959
117*	114	A.R.Butcher	v Glamorgan	The Oval	1984
112	124	J.H.Edrich	v Nottinghamshire	Nottingham	1959
143	113*	J.H.Edrich	v Worcestershire	Worcester	1970
111	124	J.H.Edrich	v Warwickshire	The Oval	1971
140	115	J.H.Edrich	v Kent	The Oval	1977
131*	100*	L.B.Fishlock	v Sussex	The Oval	1936
113	105	L.B.Fishlock	v Yorkshire	The Oval	1937
129	112	L.B.Fishlock	v Leicestershire	Leicester (GR)	1946
111	118	L.B.Fishlock	v Nottinghamshire	Nottingham	1949
106	112	T.W.Hayward	v Sussex	Hove	1904
144*	100	T.W.Hayward	v Nottinghamshire	Nottingham	1906
143	125	T.W.Hayward	v Leicestershire	Leicester (AR)	1906
	(scored in successive matches)				
160	100	J.B.Hobbs	v Warwickshire	Birmingham	1909
104	143*	J.B.Hobbs	v Cambridge Univ	The Oval	1925
101	101*	J.B.Hobbs	v Somerset	Taunton	1925
112	104	J.B.Hobbs	v Hampshire	The Oval	1927
137	111*	J.B.Hobbs	v Glamorgan	The Oval	1930
113	119*	J.B.Hobbs	v Essex	The Oval	1932
114	101	D.J.Knight	v Yorkshire	The Oval	1919
167	103*	P.B.H.May	v Essex	Southend-on-Sea	1951
109	103*	G.R.J.Roope	v Leicestershire	Leicester (GR)	1971
121	101*	T.F.Shepherd	v Leicestershire	The Oval	1926
131	102	H.S.Squires	v Oxford University	The Oval	1932

Against Surrey

183*	134*	W.E.Alley	- Somerset	Taunton	1961
100	101*	C.Charlesworth	- Warwickshire	Birmingham	1913
125	229	C.B.Fry	- Sussex	Hove	1900
169	185*	G.Gunn	- Nottinghamshire	Nottingham	1919
108	128	W.R.Hammond	- Gloucestershire	The Oval	1927
139	143	W.R.Hammond	- Gloucestershire	Cheltenham	1928
207	102*	H.T.W.Hardinge	- Kent	Blackheath	1921
104	101	E.H.Hendren	- Middlesex	Lord's	1936
108	145	A.J.Hignell	- Cambridge Univ	Cambridge	1978
110	122	J.H.Human	- Cambridge Univ	The Oval	1933
164*	123*	P.N.Kirsten	- Derbyshire	Derby	1982
127*	118*	A.P.E.Knott	- Kent	Maidstone	1972
163	126	H.W.Lee	- Middlesex	The Oval	1919
102	102*	J.A.Newman	- Hampshire	The Oval	1927
147	108*	A.D.Nourse	- South Africans	The Oval	1935
165	100	Nawab of Pataudi, sen.	- Oxford University	The Oval	1931
124	109	W.G.Quaife	- Warwickshire	The Oval	1913
130	104*	A.Ratcliffe	- Cambridge Univ	The Oval	1932
115	118	C.A.G.Russell	- Essex	The Oval	1922
160	103*	G. St A.Sobers	- Nottinghamshire	The Oval	1970
204	142	N.R.Taylor	- Kent	Canterbury	1990
216*	156*	Zaheer Abbas	- Gloucestershire	The Oval	1976

HUNDRED ON DEBUT

For Surrey

114*	P.D.Atkins	v Cambridge University	The Oval	1988
124	M.R.Barton	v MCC	Lord's	1948
107*	H.O.Bloomfield	v Northamptonshire	Northampton	1921
101*	N.J.Falkner	v Cambridge University	Banstead	1984
123	A.J.Hollioake	v Derbyshire	Ilkeston	1993
117*	K.T.Medlycott	v Cambridge University	Banstead	1984
124	N.Miller	v Sussex	Hove	1899
124	H.C.Pretty	v Nottinghamshire	The Oval	1899

M.R. Barton had previously played first-class cricket for Oxford University.
N.J.Falkner and K.T.Medlycott were the first professionals to accomplish this feat for Surrey. It was also the first time that two debut centuries have been scored in the same innings.

Against Surrey

195*	J. Ricketts	- Lancashire	The Oval	1867

THREE OR MORE CENTURIES IN SUCCESSIVE INNINGS

R.Abel	138	v Warwickshire	The Oval	1896
	152	v Leicestershire	The Oval	
	231	v Essex	The Oval	
A.Ducat	290*	v Essex	Leyton	1921
	134	v Northamptonshire	The Oval	
	120	v Warwickshire	Birmingham	
A.Ducat	119	v Lancashire	Manchester	1928
	179*	v Warwickshire	The Oval	
	101*	v Sussex	Horsham	
J.H.Edrich	139	v New Zealanders	The Oval	1965
	121*	v Oxford University	Oxford	
	205*	v Gloucestershire	Bristol	
L.B.Fishlock	113	v Yorkshire	The Oval	1937
	105	v Yorkshire	The Oval	
	127	v Middlesex	Lord's	
T.W.Hayward	144*	v Nottinghamshire	Nottingham	1906
	100	v Nottinghamshire	Nottingham	
	143	v Leicestershire	Leicester (AR)	
	125	v Leicestershire	Leicester (AR)	
J.B.Hobbs	122	v Kent	Blackheath	1914
	226	v Nottinghamshire	The Oval	
	126	v Worcestershire	Worcester	
J.B.Hobbs	110	v Sussex	The Oval	1920
	134	v Leicestershire	Leicester (AR)	
	101	v Warwickshire	Birmingham	
	112	v Yorkshire	Sheffield	
J.B.Hobbs	104	v Cambridge University	The Oval	1925
	143*	v Cambridge University	The Oval	
	111	v Somerset	The Oval	
	215	v Warwickshire	Birmingham	
J.B.Hobbs†	111	v Middlesex	Lord's	1929
	137	v Glamorgan	The Oval	1930
	111*	v Glamorgan	The Oval	

J.B.Hobbs	113	v Essex	The Oval	1932
	119*	v Essex	The Oval	
	123	v Somerset	Taunton	
E.R.T.Holmes†	101	v Lancashire	Manchester	1935
	114	v Worcestershire	The Oval	
	206	v Derbyshire	Chesterfield	
D.R.Jardine†	103	v Middlesex	Lord's	1926
	147	v Leicestershire	Leicester (AR)	1927
	143	v Lancashire	Manchester	
D.J.Knight	114	v Yorkshire	The Oval	1919
	101	v Yorkshire	The Oval	
	146	v Lancashire	Manchester	
W.W.Read†	118	v Oxford University	Oxford	1887
	247	v Lancashire	Manchester	
	244*	v Cambridge University	The Oval	
H.S.Squires	103	v Cambridge University	The Oval	1932
	131	v Oxford University	The Oval	
	102	v Oxford University	The Oval	

† Not successive first-class innings, successive innings for Surrey

MOST FIFTIES IN SUCCESSIVE INNINGS

T.W.Hayward† (9)	87	v Hampshire	The Oval	1899
	137	v Warwickshire	The Oval	
	120*	v London County	The Oval	1900
	55	v London County	Crystal Palace	
	108	v London County	Crystal Palace	
	131*	v Warwickshire	The Oval	
	55	v Hampshire	The Oval	
	193	v Leicestershire	Leicester (GR)	
	120	v Derbyshire	Derby	
T.W.Hayward (9)	61*	v Gloucestershire	The Oval	1906
	70*	v Cambridge University	Cambridge	
	63	v Cambridge University	Cambridge	
	144*	v Nottinghamshire	Nottingham	
	100	v Nottinghamshire	Nottingham	
	143	v Leicestershire	Leicester (AR)	
	125	v Leicestershire	Leicester (AR)	
	54	v Sussex	The Oval	
	69	v Sussex	The Oval	
J.H.Edrich (8)	139	v New Zealanders	The Oval	1965
	121*	v Oxford University	Oxford	
	205*	v Gloucestershire	Bristol	
	55	v Kent	The Oval	
	96	v Essex	The Oval	
	188	v Northamptonshire	Northampton	
	92	v Yorkshire	Bradford	
	105	v Yorkshire	Bradford	

Edrich scored 310 in his next innings for England v New Zealand*

P.B.H.May† (8)	58	v Leicestershire	Leicester (GR)	1957
	96	v Northamptonshire	Northampton	
	83	v Nottinghamshire	Nottingham	
	100	v Lancashire	Manchester	
	56	v Hampshire	Guildford	
	125	v Yorkshire	The Oval	
	68	v Derbyshire	The Oval	
	63	v Yorkshire	Bradford	

A.Ducat (6)	61	v Cambridge University	The Oval	1930
	56	v Oxford University	The Oval	
	87	v Oxford University	The Oval	
	54	v Derbyshire	Derby	
	69*	v Derbyshire	Derby	
	102	v Yorkshire	Sheffield	
L.B.Fishlock† (6)	71	v Lancashire	Manchester	1936
	81	v Glamorgan	The Oval	
	79*	v Sussex	Horsham	
	98	v Indians	The Oval	
	128	v Cambridge University	The Oval	
	63	v Oxford University	The Oval	
E.G.Hayes† (6)	61	v Northamptonshire	Northampton	1905
	69*	v Northamptonshire	Northampton	
	64	v Lancashire	Liverpool	
	63	v Worcestershire	The Oval	
	63	v Worcestershire	The Oval	
	69	v Yorkshire	The Oval	
T.W.Hayward (6)	91	v Worcestershire	The Oval	1908
	69	v Worcestershire	The Oval	
	67	v Oxford University	The Oval	
	50	v Oxford University	The Oval	
	69	v Warwickshire	The Oval	
	124	v Warwickshire	The Oval	
J.B.Hobbs (6)	107	v Essex	The Oval	1925
	87	v Essex	The Oval	
	104	v Cambridge University	The Oval	
	143*	v Cambridge University	The Oval	
	111	v Somerset	The Oval	
	215	v Warwickshire	Birmingham	
J.B.Hobbs† (6)	111	v Middlesex	Lord's	1929
	137	v Glamorgan	The Oval	1930
	111*	v Glamorgan	The Oval	
	66	v Worcestershire	The Oval	
	73	v MCC	Lord's	
	57	v MCC	Lord's	
E.R.T.Holmes† (6)	63	v MCC	Lord's	1936
	74	v MCC	Lord's	
	79	v Gloucestershire	The Oval	
	94	v Gloucestershire	The Oval	
	171*	v Hampshire	The Oval	
	78	v Somerset	The Oval	
A.Sandham† (6)	112	v Middlesex	The Oval	1924
	71	v Sussex	Hove	
	72	v Yorkshire	The Oval	
	60	v Yorkshire	The Oval	
	115	v Leicestershire	The Oval	
	102*	v Middlesex	Lord's	

† Not successive first-class innings, successive innings for Surrey

CARRYING BAT THROUGH BOTH INNINGS OF A MATCH FOR SURREY

H.Jupp	43*	(95)	v Yorkshire	The Oval	1874
	109*	(193)			

CARRYING BAT THROUGH A COMPLETED INNINGS AND LAST OUT IN THE OTHER FOR SURREY

H.Jupp	31 94*	(102) (297)	v Hampshire	The Oval	1866
H.Jupp	53 51*	(102) (113)	v Nottinghamshire	The Oval	1873

CARRYING BAT THROUGH A COMPLETED INNINGS

For Surrey

R.Abel (5)	88*	(198)	v Gloucestershire	Cheltenham	1885
	151*	(425)	v Middlesex	Lord's	1890
	136*	(300)	v Middlesex	The Oval	1894
	357*	(811)	v Somerset	The Oval	1899
	151*	(263)	v Sussex	The Oval	1902
A. Baker	55*	(110)	v Gloucestershire	Bristol	1905
D.J. Bicknell	145*	(268)	v Essex	Chelmsford	1991
W. Brockwell	76*	(158)	v Leicestershire	Leicester (GR)	1898
T.H. Clark	81*	(135)	v Yorkshire	The Oval	1956
G.S. Clinton (2)	113*	(260)	v Derbyshire	The Oval	1984
	84*	(171)	v Yorkshire	Leeds	1986
J.H. Edrich (2)	79*	(122)	v Northamptonshire	The Oval	1963
	61*	(108)	v Essex	Southend-on-Sea	1978
L.B. Fishlock	81*	(141)	v Australians	The Oval	1948
D.G.W. Fletcher	127*	(271)	v Yorkshire	Bradford	1947
T.W. Hayward (7)	156*	(287)	v Philadelphians	The Oval	1903
	188*	(321)	v Kent	Canterbury	1904
	129*	(286)	v Australians	The Oval	1905
	144*	(225)	v Nottinghamshire	Nottingham	1906
	114*	(190)	v Lancashire	The Oval	1907
	90*	(156)	v Somerset	Taunton	1909
	96*	(178)	v Australians	The Oval	1909
J.B. Hobbs (4)	60*	(155)	v Warwickshire	Birmingham	1907
	205*	(344)	v A.I.F.	The Oval	1919
	172*	(294)	v Yorkshire	Leeds	1921
	133*	(300)	v Yorkshire	The Oval	1931
M. Howell	15*	(73)	v Kent	Blackheath	1920
R. Humphrey	30*	(60)	v Nottinghamshire	The Oval	1872
T. Humphrey	43*	(95)	v Sussex	Brighton	1867
H. Jupp (11)	94*	(297)	v Hampshire	The Oval	1866
	90*	(222)	v Yorkshire	Sheffield	1868
	27*	(95)	v Lancashire	Manchester	1870
	50*	(88)	v Gloucestershire	Clifton	1870
	51*	(113)	v Nottinghamshire	The Oval	1873
	43*	(95)	v Yorkshire *(1st inns)*	The Oval	1874
	109*	(193)	v Yorkshire *(2nd inns)*	The Oval	1874
	37*	(74)	v Yorkshire	Sheffield	1876
	73*	(268)	v Kent	The Oval	1876
	91*	(264)	v Kent	The Oval	1877
	117*	(284)	v Yorkshire	Sheffield	1880
A.P. Lucas	36*	(121)	v Gloucestershire	Clifton	1877
A.B.D. Parsons	30*	(71)	v Leicestershire	The Oval	1961
W.W. Read	196*	(413)	v Sussex	The Oval	1892

A. Sandham (6)	123*	(323)	v Hampshire	Portsmouth	1922
	155*	(330)	v Somerset	The Oval	1923
	96*	(158)	v Cambridge University	The Oval	1924
	125*	(282)	v Northamptonshire	Northampton	1930
	113*	(221)	v Hampshire	Bournemouth	1931
	169*	(333)	v Hampshire	The Oval	1933

Against Surrey

H.M.Ackerman	39*	(77)	- Northamptonshire	Kettering	1971
W.H.Ashdown	150*	(303)	- Kent	The Oval	1926
H.Bagshaw	114*	(218)	- Derbyshire	The Oval	1897
R.G.Barlow	29*	(131)	- Lancashire	The Oval	1890
L.T.A.Bates	96*	(207)	- Warwickshire	The Oval	1921
G.Boycott	55*	(131)	- Yorkshire	Sheffield	1985
G.Brown	150*	(294)	- Hampshire	The Oval	1933
C.J.Burnup	103*	(209)	- Kent	The Oval	1899
J.E.Bush	52*	(146)	- Oxford University	Guildford	1952
G.Challenor	155*	(305)	- West Indians	The Oval	1923
H.B.Daft	77*	(240)	- Nottinghamshire	The Oval	1896
J.G.Dewes	101*	(203)	- Middlesex	The Oval	1955
A.E.Fagg	71*	(134)	- Kent	The Oval	1950
W.G.Grace (2)	138*	(215)	- MCC	The Oval	1869
	61*	(105)	- Gloucestershire	The Oval	1893
L.Hall (2)	79*	(285)	- Yorkshire	Sheffield	1885
	34*	(104)	- Yorkshire	The Oval	1888
A.Hamer	112*	(208)	- Derbyshire	The Oval	1957
J.F.Harvey	23*	(67)	- Derbyshire	The Oval	1964
J.Holland	46*	(95)	- Leicestershire	Leicester (GR)	1894
J.T.Ikin	125*	(197)	- Lancashire	The Oval	1951
A.E.Knight (2)	91*	(155)	- Leicestershire	The Oval	1903
	74*	(182)	- Leicestershire	Leicester (AR)	1911
L.J.Lenham	66*	(147)	- Sussex	Hove	1957
T.A.Lloyd	124*	(230)	- Warwickshire	The Oval	1983
F.W.Marlow	43*	(123)	- Sussex	The Oval	1891
J.D.Morley	82*	(237)	- Sussex	Hove	1974
E.Needham	58*	(111)	- Derbyshire	Derby	1908
E.Oscroft	53*	(94)	- Nottinghamshire	Nottingham	1865
L.C.H.Palairet	45*	(126)	- Somerset	Taunton	1902
C.Payne	135*	(367)	- Kent	Gravesend	1866
F.A.Pearson	154*	(342)	- Worcestershire	Dudley	1912
G.Picknell	27*	(64)	- Sussex	The Oval	1850
J.Ricketts	195*	(429)	- Lancashire	The Oval	1867
R.T.Robinson	60*	(248)	- Nottinghamshire	Nottingham	1994
N.H.Rogers	56*	(126)	- MCC	Lord's	1954
W.H.Scotton	110*	(223)	- Nottinghamshire	Nottingham	1886
C.R.Seymour	77*	(154)	- Hampshire	Southampton	1883
C.H.Smith	47*	(129)	- Sussex	The Oval	1868
G.A.T.Vials	62*	(105)	- Northamptonshire	Northampton	1910
I.D.Walker	47*	(126)	- Middlesex	Lord's	1884
P.F.Warner	102*	(201)	- Middlesex	Lord's	1909
A.J.Webbe	83*	(196)	- Middlesex	The Oval	1884
H.Whitfeld	41*	(109)	- Sussex	The Oval	1884

MOST RUNS IN A DAY

For Surrey

306 A.Ducat v Oxford University The Oval 1919
306 runs out of 498 in 280 minutes

Against Surrey

311 N.H.Fairbrother - Lancashire The Oval 1990
311 runs out of 481 in 380 minutes

BATSMEN SCORING OVER 50% OF TOTAL IN EACH INNINGS

L.B.Fishlock	129 out of 244	v Leicestershire	Leicester (GR)	1946
	and 112 out of 212			

MONOPOLISING THE SCORING WHILE AT THE WICKET

J.N.Crawford	39	out of 39	v Somerset	Taunton	1919
P.G.H.Fender	61*	out of 63	v Sussex	Eastbourne	1926
S.T.Clarke	79	out of 85	v Lancashire	Manchester	1981
L.B.Fishlock	93	out of 104	v Australians	The Oval	1938
J.B.Hobbs	183	out of 224	v Warwickshire	The Oval	1914

HUNDRED WITH A RUNNER

117	J.B.Hobbs	v Somerset	The Oval	1933

MOST RUNS ADDED DURING A BATSMAN'S INNINGS

811	R.Abel (357*)	v Somerset	The Oval	1899

FASTEST HUNDREDS

mins				
35	P.G.H.Fender (113*)	v Northamptonshire	Northampton	1920
60	W.S.Lees (130)	v Hampshire	Aldershot	1905

FIFTY WITH FEWEST SCORING STROKES

13	K.F.Barrington (51*)	v Warwickshire	The Oval	1963

(3 sixes, 7 fours, 1 three, 2 singles)

HUNDRED BEFORE LUNCH

For Surrey

FIRST DAY

	Final Score	*Lunch Score*			
R.Abel	152		v Leicestershire	The Oval	1896
W.Brockwell	107	107	v Sussex	Hove	1896
	119		v Oxford University	The Oval	1898
	102	102	v Derbyshire	The Oval	1899
A.R.Butcher	107	107	v Glamorgan	The Oval	1980
V.F.S.Crawford	122	122	v Cambridge University	Cambridge	1901
A.Ducat	115	100*	v Cambridge University	The Oval	1923

E.G.Hayes	121	100*	v Oxford University	The Oval	1901
	108	108*	v Leicestershire	The Oval	1901
T.W.Hayward	135	125*	v Leicestershire	The Oval	1906
	106		v Warwickshire	The Oval	1910
J.B.Hobbs	125		v Worcestershire	Worcester	1906
	205		v Hampshire	The Oval	1909
	119	115*	v Oxford University	The Oval	1910
	113	113	v Gloucestershire	The Oval	1913
	107		v Gloucestershire	Bristol	1913
	100		v Yorkshire	Bradford	1914
	102		v Lancashire	Manchester	1919
	134		v Leicestershire	Leicester (AR)	1920
	145		v Leicestershire	Leicester (AR)	1922
	104		v Gloucestershire	The Oval	1925
	215		v Warwickshire	Birmingham	1925
	131	105*	v Nottinghamshire	The Oval	1927
A.Needham	124	124	v Zimbabweans	The Oval	1985
A.Sandham	195		v Cambridge University	The Oval	1922

AFTER THE FIRST DAY

	Final Score	*Lunch Score*	*Day*			
R.Abel	193	101*	2	v Derbyshire	The Oval	1900
D.J.Bicknell	105*	105*	3	v Essex	The Oval	1989
W.Brockwell	137	102*	3	v Sussex	The Oval	1896
F.R.Brown	212	113*	2	v Middlesex	The Oval	1932
J.N.Crawford	148		2	v Gloucestershire	Bristol	1906
V.F.S.Crawford	159	150*	2	v Worcestershire	The Oval	1901
A.Ducat	204*	109*	2	v Northamptonshire	Northampton	1921
J.H.Edrich	127*	101*	3	v Middlesex	The Oval	1972
E.G.Hayes	104	104	2	v Yorkshire	The Oval	1904
T.W.Hayward	106	101*	2	v Warwickshire	The Oval	1910
J.B.Hobbs	155	137*	2	v Essex	The Oval	1905
(his first century for Surrey)						
E.R.T.Holmes	122*	122*	3	v Nottinghamshire	Nottingham	1947
M.A.Lynch	114	100*	2	v Gloucestershire	Cheltenham	1987
J.F.Parker	108*	108*	3	v Nottinghamshire	Nottingham	1947
T.F.Shepherd	132	109*	2	v Warwickshire	The Oval	1928
M.J.Stewart	110*	110*	3	v Sussex	Guildford	1970

ADDED TO OVERNIGHT SCORE

	Final Score	*Session Scores*	*Day*			
R.Abel	217	19*-131*	2	v Essex	The Oval	1895
	231	89*-200*	2	v Essex	The Oval	1896
	250	105*-205*†	2	v Warwickshire	The Oval	1897
C.Baldwin	234	3*-125*	2	v Kent	The Oval	1897
M.P.Bowden	189*	6*-162*†	2	v Sussex	The Oval	1888
V.F.S.Crawford	129	13*-129	2	v Somerset	The Oval	1899
W.E.Davis	112	11*-112	2	v Derbyshire	Chesterfield	1909
A.Ducat	271	104*-271	2	v Hampshire	Southampton	1919
	290*	184*-290*	3	v Essex	Leyton	1921
I.A.Greig	291	56*-201*	2	v Lancashire	The Oval	1990
E.G.Hayes	218	73*-218	2	v Oxford University	The Oval	1906
	155	49*-155	2	v Middlesex	Lord's	1906
	123	14*-114*†	3	v Lancashire	The Oval	1911
	153	24*-153	2	v Hampshire	Southampton	1919
T.W.Hayward	315*	163*-267*	2	v Lancashire	The Oval	1898
	188*	84*-184*	3	v Kent	Canterbury	1904

	Final Score	Session Scores	Day			
J.B.Hobbs	117	8*-108*†	3	v Lancashire	The Oval	1911
	183	34*-183	2	v Warwickshire	The Oval	1914
	261	142*-261	3	v Oxford University	Oxford	1926
	146	31*-146	2	v New Zealanders	The Oval	1927
A.Marshal	167	58*-167	2	v Kent	The Oval	1908

† at least these scores

Against Surrey

FIRST DAY

	Final Score	Lunch Score			
J.D.Carr	133	111*	- Middlesex	Lord's	1987
K.S.Duleepsinhji	126		- Sussex	Hove	1932
G.A.Gooch	139		- Essex	Chelmsford	1988
L.C.H.Palairet	140	100*	- Somerset	Taunton	1901
C.A.Roach	180		- West Indians	The Oval	1933
G.M.Turner	150	109*	- Worcestershire	Worcester	1978
G.F.Vernon	106	105*	- Middlesex	The Oval	1880
P.F.Warner	149		- Middlesex	The Oval	1907
F.E.Woolley	110		- Kent	Blackheath	1930

AFTER THE FIRST DAY

	Final Score	Lunch Score	Day			
A.W.Carr	115		3	- Nottinghamshire	Nottingham	1926
F.H.B.Champain	149	120*†	2	- Gloucestershire	Bristol	1907
N.H.Fairbrother	366	100*	3	- Lancashire	The Oval	1990
(he scored a hundred in each session)						
C.Hill	104	102*	3	- Australians	The Oval	1905
G.H.Hirst	108		3	- Yorkshire	The Oval	1904
A.I.Kallicharran	149	124*	2	- Warwickshire	Birmingham	1972
M.A.Nash	130	119*	2	- Glamorgan	The Oval	1976
E.H.D.Sewell	106*	106*	2	- Essex	The Oval	1904

ADDED TO OVERNIGHT SCORE

	Final Score	Session Scores	Day			
J.Briggs	186	81*-186	2	- Lancashire	Liverpool	1885
R.O.Butcher	171	12*-137	2	- Middlesex	Uxbridge	1986
R.E.Foster	127	8*-127*	3	- Oxford University	The Oval	1900
C.G.Greenidge	154	52*-154	3	- Hampshire	Southampton	1983
G.H.Hirst	188	84*-188	2	- Yorkshire	The Oval	1899
J.F.Ireland	107*	0*-107*	3	- Cambridge Univ	Cambridge	1910
A.J.Lamb	171	57*-171	2	- Northamptonshire	Northampton	1989
J.R.Mason	147	40*-147	3	- Kent	The Oval	1900
W.R.D.Payton	149*	23*-149*	2	- Nottinghamshire	The Oval	1907
M.J.Procter	154	11*-154	2	- Gloucestershire	Guildford	1978
K.S.Ranjitsinhji	234*	54*-234*	2	- Sussex	Hastings	1902
B.A.Richards	116	3*-116*	2	- Hampshire	Portsmouth	1973
J.J.Sewell	166	29*-166	2	- Middlesex	The Oval	1866
D.Q.Steel	158	18*-121*	2	- Cambridge Univ	The Oval	1877
L.J.Todd	139	38*-139	3	- Kent	Blackheath	1933
F.B.Watson	300*	104*-205*	3	- Lancashire	Manchester	1928
F.E.Woolley	132	19*-132*	3	- Kent	Blackheath	1934

† at least these scores

HUNDREDS BY TWO BATSMEN IN A PRE-LUNCH SESSION

	Day			
J.B. Hobbs (100*) E.G. Hayes (100*)	3	v Lancashire	The Oval	1911
A. Ducat (167) E.G. Hayes (129)	2	v Hampshire	Southampton	1919
E.R.T. Holmes (122*) J.F. Parker (108*)	3	v Nottinghamshire	Nottingham	1947

2000 RUNS IN A SEASON

	Runs	*Avge*	
T.W.Hayward	3,246	72.12	1906
R.Abel	2,849	52.75	1901
T.W.Hayward	2,734	55.79	1904
J.B.Hobbs	2,499	62.47	1914
A.Sandham	2,417	60.42	1928
T.W.Hayward	2,407	53.48	1901
R.Abel	2,404	55.90	1899
J.B.Hobbs	2,399	54.52	1913
T.W.Hayward	2,349	54.62	1900
A.Sandham	2,348	53.36	1929
J.B.Hobbs	2,331	66.60	1925
L.B.Fishlock	2,322	44.65	1950
R.J.Gregory	2,278	55.66	1934
L.B.Fishlock	2,219	43.50	1949
A.Sandham	2,161	51.45	1930
R.J.Gregory	2,149	46.71	1937
J.H.Edrich	2,142	51.00	1962
L.B.Fishlock	2,130	50.71	1946
R.Abel	2,100	56.75	1900
T.W.Hayward	2,087	48.53	1911
D.M.Ward	2,072	76.74	1990
A.Ducat	2,067	49.21	1930
A.Sandham	2,056	57.11	1925
R.Abel	2,050	45.55	1902
P.B.H.May	2,048	58.51	1953
A.Sandham	2,025	61.36	1927
J.B.Hobbs	2,015	80.60	1928
H.T.Barling	2,014	43.78	1946
J.B.Hobbs	2,005	54.18	1919

1000 RUNS IN A SEASON

		Year	*Runs*	*Year*	*Runs*
Abel, R.	(8)	1895	1953	1896	1816
		1897	1901	1898	1913
		1899	2404	1900	2100
		1901	2849	1902	2050
Alikhan, R.I.		1991	1055		
Baker, A.		1905	1257		
Baldwin, C.		1897	1211		
Barling, H.T.	(9)	1928	1004	1933	1915
		1934	1588	1935	1761
		1936	1722	1937	1354
		1938	1284	1946	2014
		1947	1480		

		Year	*Runs*	*Year*	*Runs*
Barrington, K.F.	(10)	1955	1418	1956	1250
		1957	1642	1959	1993
		1960	1323	1961	1510
		1962	1472	1963	1269
		1964	1341	1967	1257
Barton, M.R.	(2)	1948	1171	1951	1004
Bedser, E.A.	(6)	1947	1259	1949	1599
		1950	1061	1951	1164
		1952	1694	1953	1039
Bicknell, D.J.	(6)	1989	1392	1990	1317
		1991	1844	1992	1225
		1993	1418	1994	1261
Bird, M.C.		1911	1404		
Brockwell, W.	(6)	1894	1091	1896	1269
		1897	1295	1898	1610
		1899	1450	1900	1043
Brown, A.D.	(2)	1993	1382	1994	1049
Butcher, A.R.	(7)	1979	1364	1980	1679
		1981	1444	1982	1452
		1983	1349	1984	1415
		1985	1407		
Clark, T.H.	(6)	1952	1410	1953	1241
		1954	1456	1956	1561
		1957	1546	1959	1144
Clinton, G.S.	(7)	1979	1082	1980	1240
		1981	1191	1985	1225
		1986	1027	1988	1054
		1990	1292		
Constable, B.	(12)	1950	1389	1951	1321
		1952	1677	1953	1538
		1954	1363	1955	1208
		1956	1188	1957	1357
		1958	1064	1959	1001
		1961	1748	1962	1002
Crawford, J.N.	(3)	1906	1064	1907	1061
		1908	1258		
Crawford, V.F.S.	(3)	1900	1112	1901	1511
		1902	1017		
Dalmeny, Lord	(2)	1905	1114	1907	1112
Ducat, A.	(14)	1909	1080	1910	1239
		1911	1045	1914	1370
		1919	1695	1920	1197
		1921	1773	1922	1189
		1923	1626	1926	1245
		1927	1637	1928	1660
		1929	1753	1930	2067
Edrich, J.H.	(18)	1959	1743	1960	1500
		1961	1677	1962	2142
		1963	1714	1964	1477
		1965	1951	1966	1913
		1967	1859	1968	1390
		1969	1491	1970	1490
		1971	1742	1972	1087
		1973	1039	1975	1141
		1976	1381	1977	1044
Edwards, M.J.	(5)	1966	1064	1967	1413
		1968	1408	1969	1428
		1970	1281		

		Year	Runs	Year	Runs
Fender, P.G.H.	(4)	1922	1114	1923	1136
		1928	1192	1929	1307
Fishlock, L.B.	(12)	1935	1466	1936	1995
		1937	1784	1938	1950
		1939	1950	1946	2130
		1947	1088	1948	1939
		1949	2219	1950	2322
		1951	1559	1952	1032
Fletcher, D.G.W.	(4)	1947	1394	1952	1886
		1953	1696	1960	1371
Gregory, R.J.	(9)	1928	1144	1929	1101
		1933	1558	1934	2278
		1936	1344	1937	2149
		1938	1686	1939	1775
		1946	1440		
Greig, I.A.	(2)	1989	1013	1990	1259
Harrison, H.S.		1913	1293		
Hayes, E.G.	(16)	1899	1058	1900	1248
		1901	1400	1902	1155
		1903	1760	1904	1873
		1905	1794	1906	1972
		1907	1857	1908	1039
		1909	1911	1910	1008
		1911	1827	1912	1672
		1913	1377	1914	1139
Hayward, T.W.	(20)	1895	1026	1896	1349
		1897	1211	1898	1373
		1899	1910	1900	2349
		1901	2407	1902	1355
		1903	1963	1904	2734
		1905	1916	1906	3246
		1907	1869	1908	1991
		1909	1262	1910	1110
		1911	2087	1912	1294
		1913	1326	1914	1124
Hobbs, J.B.	(24)	1905	1317	1906	1913
		1907	1982	1908	1663
		1909	1819	1910	1683
		1911	1802	1912	1266
		1913	2399	1914	2499
		1919	2005	1920	1976
		1922	1968	1923	1595
		1924	1321	1925	2331
		1926	1960	1927	1383
		1928	2015	1929	1766
		1930	1477	1931	1980
		1932	1561	1933	1105
Holland, F.C.	(4)	1898	1072	1903	1129
		1905	1079	1907	1081
Holmes, E.R.T.	(5)	1934	1301	1935	1746
		1936	1554	1937	1061
		1947	1106		
Howarth, G.P.	(3)	1976	1554	1979	1238
		1982	1158		
Jardine, D.R.	(3)	1924	1186	1926	1096
		1932	1009		
Jeacocke, A.		1921	1016		
Jephson, D.L.A.	(2)	1900	1649	1901	1385
Jesty, T.E.	(2)	1985	1216	1987	1074

		Year	Runs	Year	Runs
Key, K.J.		1897	1083		
Knight, R.D.V.	(6)	1978	1233	1980	1224
		1981	1041	1982	1114
		1983	1235	1984	1254
Lockwood, W.H.	(2)	1899	1113	1900	1266
Lynch, M.A.	(8)	1982	1155	1983	1558
		1984	1546	1985	1714
		1986	1234	1987	1127
		1990	1227	1992	1465
McIntyre, A.J.W.	(2)	1949	1188	1950	1101
Marshal, A.	(3)	1907	1065	1908	1884
		1909	1118		
May, P.B.H.	(7)	1953	2048	1954	1212
		1955	1320	1956	1178
		1957	1718	1958	1670
		1962	1352		
Needham, A.		1985	1223		
Parker, J.F.	(9)	1938	1167	1939	1549
		1946	1131	1947	1346
		1948	1299	1949	1701
		1950	1563	1951	1106
		1952	1204		
Parsons, A.B.D.	(3)	1960	1264	1961	1415
		1962	1085		
Read, J.M.	(2)	1886	1050	1895	1000
Read, W.W.	(5)	1883	1544	1885	1630
		1886	1211	1887	1450
		1888	1032		
Richards, C.J.		1986	1006		
Roope, G.R.J.	(7)	1969	1112	1970	1289
		1971	1641	1972	1140
		1975	1200	1976	1190
		1977	1359		
Sandham, A.	(18)	1920	1563	1921	1914
		1922	1843	1923	1619
		1924	1733	1925	2056
		1926	1679	1927	2025
		1928	2417	1929	2348
		1930	2161	1931	1952
		1932	1353	1933	1034
		1934	1570	1935	1494
		1936	1559	1937	1448
Shepherd, T.F.	(12)	1921	1907	1922	1121
		1923	1498	1924	1301
		1925	1288	1926	1429
		1927	1922	1928	1606
		1929	1866	1930	1771
		1931	1182	1932	1163
Smith, D.M.		1982	1065		
Smith, W.A.		1968	1002		
Squires, H.S.	(11)	1933	1656	1934	1631
		1935	1361	1936	1337
		1937	1312	1938	1377
		1939	1580	1946	1032
		1947	1662	1948	1602
		1949	1663		
Stewart, A.J.	(5)	1985	1009	1986	1665
		1987	1219	1988	1006
		1989	1637		

		Year	Runs	Year	Runs
Stewart, M.J.	(14)	1955	1085	1956	1537
		1957	1801	1958	1178
		1959	1849	1960	1810
		1961	1415	1962	1883
		1964	1980	1965	1587
		1967	1184	1968	1145
		1969	1317	1970	1246
Storey, S.J.	(5)	1964	1050	1965	1009
		1966	1013	1970	1045
		1971	1184		
Tindall, R.A.E.		1963	1063		
Thorpe, G.P.	(3)	1989	1132	1991	1166
		1992	1863		
Ward, D.M.	(2)	1990	2072	1991	1372
Whitfield, E.W.		1938	1005		
Whittaker, G.J.		1951	1439		
Willett, M.D.	(3)	1961	1593	1963	1096
		1964	1789		
Younis Ahmed	(7)	1969	1760	1970	1588
		1971	1485	1972	1232
		1973	1612	1975	1314
		1976	1439		

EARLIEST DATES FOR REACHING MILESTONES

1000 runs	31st May 1900	T.W.Hayward
2000 runs	5th July 1906	T.W.Hayward
3000 runs	20th August 1906	T.W.Hayward

1000 RUNS IN A MONTH

J.B. Hobbs 1112 runs in 14 innings at an average of 85.53 in June 1925

T.W. Hayward scored 997 runs in 12 innings in June 1906 at an average of 90.64, but was rested for the last match in June v Cambridge University which Surrey lost by 8 wickets.

10000 RUNS FOR SURREY

	Career	*M*	*Inn*	*NO*	*Runs*	*Avge*	*HS*	*1000*	*100*	*50*
Hobbs, J.B.	1905-1934	598	956	80	43554	49.71	316*	24	144	186
Hayward, T.W.	1893-1914	593	932	79	36175	42.40	315*	20	88	181
Sandham, A.	1911-1937	525	830	71	33312	43.88	292*	18	83	160
Edrich, J.H.	1958-1978	410	716	80	29305	46.07	226*	18	81	138
Abel, R.	1881-1904	514	813	59	27605	36.61	357*	8	64	120
Hayes, E.G.	1896-1919	500	802	45	25062	33.10	276	16	45	132
Stewart, M.J.	1954-1972	499	844	91	25007	33.20	227*	14	48	125
Ducat, A.	1906-1931	422	657	59	23108	38.64	306*	14	52	107
Fishlock, L.B.	1931-1952	347	588	41	22138	40.47	253	12	50	120
Barrington, K.F.	1953-1968	362	564	99	19197	41.28	207	10	43	100
Barling, H.T.	1927-1948	389	605	54	18995	34.47	269	9	34	96
Gregory, R.J.	1925-1947	415	622	76	18978	34.75	243	9	38	96
Squires, H.S.	1928-1949	402	643	44	18636	31.11	236	11	36	101
Shepherd, T.F.	1919-1932	354	520	60	18254	39.68	277*	12	41	90
Constable, B.	1939-1964	434	681	81	18224	30.37	205*	12	26	91

Read, W.W.	1873-1897	366	580	41	17683	32.80	338	5	31	88
Roope, G.R.J.	1964-1982	342	554	118	16226	37.21	171	7	22	87
Lynch, M.A.	1977-1994	304	491	59	15674	36.28	172*	8	33	76
May, P.B.H.	1950-1963	208	327	46	14168	50.41	211*	7	39	75
Bedser, E.A.	1939-1961	444	669	78	14148	23.93	163	6	9	60
Fender, P.G.H.	1914-1935	414	556	52	14117	28.00	185	4	17	76
Younis Ahmed	1965-1978	262	448	63	14112	36.65	183*	7	19	83
Parker, J.F.	1932-1952	334	512	70	14068	31.82	255	9	20	78
Fletcher, D.G.W.	1946-1961	300	494	40	13646	30.05	194	4	21	72
Butcher, A.R.	1972-1986	283	479	43	14571	33.42	216*	7	29	69
Clinton, G.S.	1979-1990	234	392	50	11838	34.61	192	7	20	66
Brockwell, W.	1886-1903	314	472	45	11830	27.70	225	6	20	49
Stewart, A.J.	1981-1994	207	334	42	11506	39.40	206*	5	21	70
Clark, T.H.	1947-1959	260	421	35	11458	29.68	191	6	12	58
Jupp, H.	1862-1881	252	467	40	11452	26.81	165	-	12	56
McIntyre, A.J.W.	1938-1963	377	544	75	10893	23.22	143*	2	7	50
Read, J.M.	1880-1895	278	450	35	10840	26.12	186*	2	8	59
Edwards, M.J.	1961-1974	235	415	24	10581	27.06	137	5	12	51
Storey, S.J.	1960-1974	315	468	58	10402	25.37	164	5	12	53
Holland, F.C.	1894-1908	282	425	29	10323	26.06	171	4	12	51

P.G.H. Fender is the only player to score 10,000 runs and take 1000 wickets for Surrey

LEADING SURREY BATSMEN

	Most Runs		*Highest Average (qualification: 5 completed innings)*	
1846	A.M.Hoare	59		
1847	N.Wanostrocht (Felix)	221	N.Wanostrocht (Felix)	31.57
1848	W.J.Hammersley	46		
1849	T.Sherman	105	T.Sherman	17.50
1850	G.Brockwell	136	G.Brockwell	27.20
1851	J.Caesar	129	W.Caffyn	20.66
1852	T.Lockyer	215	W.Caffyn	17.90
1853	W.Caffyn	72		
1854	J.Caesar	247	J.Caesar	35.28
1855	W.Caffyn	166	W.Caffyn	27.66
1856	W.Caffyn	134		
1857	T.Lockyer	229	T.Lockyer	20.81
1858	W.Caffyn	340	W.Caffyn	42.50
1859	W.Caffyn	233	W.Caffyn	23.30
1860	W.Caffyn	256	W.Mortlock	24.33
1861	G.Griffith	514	J.Caesar	28.58
1862	H.H.Stephenson	376	H.H.Stephenson	22.11
1863	W.Mortlock	533	H.Jupp	32.28
1864	H.Jupp	594	H.H.Stephenson	40.25
1865	T.Humphrey	812	T.Humphrey	29.00
1866	H.Jupp	922	H.Jupp	40.08
1867	T.Humphrey	735	T.Humphrey	28.26
1868	H.Jupp	780	H.Jupp	28.88
1869	H.Jupp	794	H.Jupp	31.76
1870	E.Pooley	771	E.Pooley	24.87
1871	H.Jupp	763	H.Jupp	25.43
1872	R.G.Humphrey	669	R.G.Humphrey	26.76
1873	H.Jupp	760	H.Jupp	28.14
1874	H.Jupp	900	H.Jupp	45.00
1875	G.F.Elliott	412	W.W.Read	30.87
1876	H.Jupp	736	W.W.Read	42.00
1877	H.Jupp	544	A.P.Lucas	40.77

	Most Runs		*Highest Average (qualification: 5 completed innings)*	
1878	J.Shuter	502	J.Shuter	25.10
1879	J.Shuter	342	A.P.Lucas	29.22
1880	H.Jupp	572	W.W.Read	25.50
1881	W.W.Read	931	W.W.Read	32.10
1882	W.W.Read	820	W.W.Read	27.33
1883	W.W.Read	1544	W.W.Read	49.80
1884	W.W.Read	889	W.W.Read	29.63
1885	W.W.Read	1630	W.W.Read	47.94
1886	W.W.Read	1211	W.W.Read	44.85
1887	W.W.Read	1450	W.W.Read	53.70
1888	W.W.Read	1032	W.W.Read	43.00
1889	K.J.Key	890	K.J.Key	37.08
1890	R.Abel	761	R.Abel	33.08
1891	R.Abel	963	R.Abel	41.86
1892	W.W.Read	942	W.W.Read	36.23
1893	W.W.Read	993	W.W.Read	32.03
1894	W.Brockwell	1091	W.Brockwell	35.19
1895	R.Abel	1953	R.Abel	51.39
1896	R.Abel	1816	R.Abel	46.20
1897	R.Abel	1901	R.Abel	47.52
1898	R.Abel	1913	R.Abel	54.65
1899	R.Abel	2404	T.W.Hayward	57.87
1900	T.W.Hayward	2349	R.Abel	56.75
1901	R.Abel	2849	T.W.Hayward	53.48
1902	R.Abel	2050	R.Abel	45.55
1903	T.W.Hayward	1963	T.W.Hayward	37.75
1904	T.W.Hayward	2734	T.W.Hayward	55.79
1905	T.W.Hayward	1916	T.W.Hayward	46.73
1906	T.W.Hayward	3246	T.W.Hayward	72.12
1907	J.B.Hobbs	1982	T.W.Hayward	47.92
1908	T.W.Hayward	1991	T.W.Hayward	46.30
1909	E.G.Hayes	1911	T.W.Hayward	46.74
1910	J.B.Hobbs	1683	J.B.Hobbs	33.00
1911	T.W.Hayward	2087	T.W.Hayward	48.53
1912	E.G.Hayes	1672	E.G.Hayes	44.00
1913	J.B.Hobbs	2399	J.B.Hobbs	54.52
1914	J.B.Hobbs	2499	J.B.Hobbs	62.47
1919	J.B.Hobbs	2005	D.J.Knight	54.35
1920	J.B.Hobbs	1976	J.B.Hobbs	52.00
1921	A.Sandham	1914	T.F.Shepherd	52.97
1922	J.B.Hobbs	1968	J.B.Hobbs	63.48
1923	A.Ducat	1626	D.J.Knight	53.00
1924	A.Sandham	1733	A.Sandham	64.18
1925	J.B.Hobbs	2331	J.B.Hobbs	66.60
1926	J.B.Hobbs	1960	J.B.Hobbs	85.21
1927	A.Sandham	2025	D.R.Jardine	102.80
1928	A.Sandham	2417	J.B.Hobbs	80.60
1929	A.Sandham	2348	J.B.Hobbs	70.64
1930	A.Sandham	2161	J.B.Hobbs	59.08
1931	J.B.Hobbs	1980	J.B.Hobbs	50.76
1932	J.B.Hobbs	1561	J.B.Hobbs	53.82
1933	H.T.Barling	1915	J.B.Hobbs	61.38
1934	R.J.Gregory	2278	R.J.Gregory	55.56
1935	H.T.Barling	1761	E.R.T.Holmes	48.50
1936	L.B.Fishlock	1995	L.B.Fishlock	53.91
1937	R.J.Gregory	2149	R.J.Gregory	46.71
1938	L.B.Fishlock	1950	L.B.Fishlock	39.00
1939	L.B.Fishlock	1950	R.J.Gregory	38.58

	Most Runs		*Highest Average (qualification: 5 completed innings)*	
1946	L.B.Fishlock	2130	L.B.Fishlock	50.71
1947	H.S.Squires	1662	L.B.Fishlock	40.29
1948	L.B.Fishlock	1939	L.B.Fishlock	39.57
1949	L.B.Fishlock	2219	L.B.Fishlock	43.50
1950	L.B.Fishlock	2322	L.B.Fishlock	44.65
1951	L.B.Fishlock	1559	P.B.H.May	76.75
1952	D.G.W.Fletcher	1886	P.B.H.May	68.00
1953	P.B.H.May	2048	P.B.H.May	58.51
1954	T.H.Clark	1456	P.B.H.May	57.71
1955	K.F.Barrington	1418	P.B.H.May	45.52
1956	T.H.Clark	1561	M.J.Stewart	34.15
1957	M.J.Stewart	1801	P.B.H.May	59.24
1958	P.B.H.May	1670	P.B.H.May	64.23
1959	K.F.Barrington	1993	K.F.Barrington	58.61
1960	M.J.Stewart	1810	K.F.Barrington	45.62
1961	B.Constable	1748	K.F.Barrington	65.65
1962	J.H.Edrich	2142	P.B.H.May	52.00
1963	J.H.Edrich	1714	K.F.Barrington	48.80
1964	M.J.Stewart	1980	K.F.Barrington	58.30
1965	J.H.Edrich	1951	J.H.Edrich	55.74
1966	J.H.Edrich	1913	J.H.Edrich	46.65
1967	J.H.Edrich	1859	K.F.Barrington	66.15
1968	M.J.Edwards	1408	J.H.Edrich	39.71
1969	Younis Ahmed	1760	J.H.Edrich	71.00
1970	Younis Ahmed	1588	J.H.Edrich	49.64
1971	J.H.Edrich	1742	J.H.Edrich	56.19
1972	Younis Ahmed	1232	J.H.Edrich	54.35
1973	Younis Ahmed	1612	Younis Ahmed	55.58
1974	G.R.J.Roope	907	J.H.Edrich	44.46
	Younis Ahmed	907		
1975	Younis Ahmed	1314	J.H.Edrich	45.64
1976	G.P.Howarth	1554	J.H.Edrich	46.03
1977	G.R.J.Roope	1359	G.R.J.Roope	56.62
1978	R.D.V.Knight	1233	G.R.J.Roope	41.77
1979	A.R.Butcher	1364	G.P.Howarth	47.61
1980	A.R.Butcher	1679	A.R.Butcher	47.97
1981	A.R.Butcher	1444	A.R.Butcher	45.12
1982	A.R.Butcher	1452	D.M.Smith	50.71
1983	M.A.Lynch	1558	M.A.Lynch	53.72
1984	M.A.Lynch	1546	G.S.Clinton	43.09
1985	M.A.Lynch	1714	M.A.Lynch	53.56
1986	A.J.Stewart	1665	A.J.Stewart	46.25
1987	A.J.Stewart	1219	A.J.Stewart	38.09
1988	G.S.Clinton	1054	C.J.Richards	50.65
1989	A.J.Stewart	1637	M.A.Lynch	54.71
1990	D.M.Ward	2072	D.M.Ward	76.74
1991	D.J.Bicknell	1844	D.J.Bicknell	47.28
1992	G.P.Thorpe	1863	G.P.Thorpe	51.75
1993	D.J.Bicknell	1418	A.J.Stewart	47.73
1994	D.J.Bicknell	1261	D.J.Bicknell	50.44

J.B.Hobbs

Most Runs for Surrey, 43554
Most Centuries for Surrey, 144
Hundred in Each Innings 6 times
Four Centuries in Successive Innings in 1920 and 1925
Hundred Before Lunch on 17 occasions
1,000 Runs in a Season 24 times

SECTION 3 - PARTNERSHIP RECORDS

HIGHEST WICKET PARTNERSHIPS FOR SURREY

First Wicket

(Qualification 250)

428	J.B.Hobbs & A.Sandham	v Oxford University	The Oval	1926
379	R.Abel & W.Brockwell	v Hampshire	The Oval	1897
364	R.Abel & D.L.A.Jephson	v Derbyshire	The Oval	1900
352	T.W.Hayward & J.B.Hobbs	v Warwickshire	The Oval	1909
321	D.J.Bicknell & G.S.Clinton	v Northamptonshire	The Oval	1990
313	T.W.Hayward & J.B.Hobbs	v Worcestershire	Worcester	1913
290	J.B.Hobbs & T.W.Hayward	v Yorkshire	Lord's	1914
277	G.S.Clinton & A.R.Butcher	v Yorkshire	The Oval	1984
270*	R.Abel & W.Brockwell	v Kent	The Oval	1900
266	A.Sandham & A.Jeacocke	v Northamptonshire	The Oval	1921
266	A.R.Butcher & G.S.Clinton	v Cambridge Univ	Cambridge	1980
265	R.Abel & W.Brockwell	v Warwickshire	The Oval	1898
264	J.B.Hobbs & A.Sandham	v Somerset	Taunton	1932
260	L.B.Fishlock & E.A.Bedser	v Somerset	The Oval	1949
256	D.J.Bicknell & D.M.Ward	v Oxford University	Oxford	1990
255	R.E.C.Pratt & M.J.Stewart	v Cambridge Univ	Guildford	1956
253*	J.B.Hobbs & A.Sandham	v West Indians	The Oval	1928

Second Wicket

(Qualification 250)

371	J.B.Hobbs & E.G.Hayes	v Hampshire	The Oval	1909
344	A.Sandham & R.J.Gregory	v Glamorgan	The Oval	1937
316*	M.J.Stewart & K.F.Barrington	v Essex	The Oval	1962
316*	A.R.Butcher & D.M.Smith	v Warwickshire	Birmingham	1982
299	A.Sandham & A.Ducat	v Lancashire	Manchester	1928
299	D.J.Bicknell & G.P.Thorpe	v Worcestershire	Worcester	1993
291	A.Sandham & H.S.Squires	v Yorkshire	The Oval	1933
281	A.Sandham & A.Ducat	v Nottinghamshire	Nottingham	1930
276	J.B.Hobbs & R.J.Gregory	v Hampshire	Southampton	1926
272	R.Abel & E.G.Hayes	v Worcestershire	The Oval	1900
259	T.W.Hayward & E.G.Hayes	v Yorkshire	The Oval	1911
256*	G.P.Howarth & R.D.V.Knight	v Cambridge Univ	Cambridge	1978

Third Wicket

(Qualification 250)

413	D.J.Bicknell & D.M.Ward	v Kent	Canterbury	1990
353	A.Ducat & E.G.Hayes	v Hampshire	Southampton	1919
317	A.Ducat & T.F.Shepherd	v Essex	Leyton	1928
306	R.Abel & F.C.Holland	v Cambridge Univ	The Oval	1895
305	W.E.Roller & W.W.Read	v Lancashire	Manchester	1887
301	G.P.Thorpe & D.M.Ward	v Derbyshire	The Oval	1994
297	J.H.Edrich & K.F.Barrington	v Middlesex	The Oval	1967
279	D.G.W.Fletcher & H.S.Squires	v Nottinghamshire	Nottingham	1947
267	R.J.Gregory & H.T.Barling	v Nottinghamshire	The Oval	1946
261	A.Ducat & T.F.Shepherd	v Leicestershire	The Oval	1926
261	B.Constable & P.B.H.May	v Nottinghamshire	Nottingham	1958

Fourth Wicket
(Qualification 250)

448	R.Abel & T.W.Hayward	v Yorkshire	The Oval	1899
334	R.Abel & T.W.Hayward	v Somerset	The Oval	1899
293	H.T.Barling & H.S.Squires	v Oxford University	The Oval	1932
289	A.Ducat & T.F.Shepherd	v Gloucestershire	The Oval	1927
270	J.B.Hobbs & D.R.Jardine	v Middlesex	Lord's	1926
256	R.Abel & F.C.Holland	v Essex	The Oval	1895
253*	D.J.Bicknell & A.D.Brown	v Nottinghamshire	Nottingham	1994
250	T.H.Clark & R.E.C.Pratt	v Kent	The Oval	1953

Fifth Wicket
(Qualification 225)

308	J.N.Crawford & F.C.Holland	v Somerset	The Oval	1908
288	H.A.Peach & A.Ducat	v Northamptonshire	Northampton	1920
287	R.Abel & W.H.Lockwood	v Lancashire	The Oval	1899
262	A.Jeacocke & W.J.Abel	v Cambridge Univ	The Oval	1923
256*	R.Abel & D.L.A.Jephson	v Gloucestershire	The Oval	1898
253*	D.J.Bicknell & A.D.Brown	v Nottinghamshire	Nottingham	1994
252	A.J.Stewart & M.A.Lynch	v Kent	Canterbury	1985
250	T.W.Hayward & D.L.A.Jephson	v Derbyshire	The Oval	1901
247*	J.F.Parker & E.R.T.Holmes	v Nottinghamshire	Nottingham	1947
230	C.Baldwin & D.L.A.Jephson	v Kent	The Oval	1897

Sixth Wicket
(Qualification 225)

298	A.Sandham & H.S.Harrison	v Sussex	The Oval	1913
294	D.R.Jardine & P.G.H.Fender	v Yorkshire	Bradford	1928
260	J.N.Crawford & Lord Dalmeny	v Leicestershire	The Oval	1905

Seventh Wicket
(Qualification 200)

262	C.J.Richards & K.T.Medlycott	v Kent	The Oval	1987
200	T.F.Shepherd & J.W.Hitch	v Kent	Blackheath	1921

Eighth Wicket
(Qualification 175)

205	I.A.Greig & M.P.Bicknell	v Lancashire	The Oval	1990
204	T.W.Hayward & L.C.Braund	v Lancashire	The Oval	1898
198	K.F.Barrington & J.C.Laker	v Gloucestershire	The Oval	1954
197	H.T.Barling & A.V.Bedser	v Somerset	Taunton	1947
189*	N.J.Falkner & K.T.Medlycott	v Cambridge Univ	Banstead	1984
188	H.S.Bush & V.F.S.Crawford	v Lancashire	Manchester	1902
182	W.E.Roller & R.Abel	v Kent	The Oval	1883
175	E.Pooley & J.Southerton	v MCC	The Oval	1871

Ninth Wicket

(Qualification 150)

168	E.R.T.Holmes & E.W.J.Brooks	v Hampshire	The Oval	1936
161	G.J.Whittaker & W.S.Surridge	v Glamorgan	The Oval	1951
156	A.E.Street & F.E.Smith	v Leicestershire	Leicester (GR)	1895
155	F.R.Brown & M.J.C.Allom	v Middlesex	The Oval	1932
155	S.J.Storey & R.D.Jackman	v Glamorgan	Cardiff (SG)	1973

Tenth Wicket

(Qualification 100)

173	A.Ducat & A.Sandham	v Essex	Leyton	1921
172	A.Needham & R.D.Jackman	v Lancashire	Manchester	1982
138	R.I.Jefferson & D.A.D.Sydenham	v Northamptonshire	Northampton	1963
133*	A.Sandham & W.J.Abel	v Middlesex	The Oval	1919
131	D.L.A.Jephson & F.Stedman	v Lancashire	The Oval	1900
130	H.Strudwick & J.W.Hitch	v Warwickshire	Birmingham	1911
129	E.G.Goatly & F.Stedman	v South Africans	The Oval	1904
128	W.Mudie & T.Sewell, jun.	v Kent and Sussex	The Oval	1859
119*	E.A.Watts & J.V.Daley	v Hampshire	Bournemouth	1936
118	C.Calvert & T.Sewell, jun.	v Sussex	Brighton	1868
113*	E.W.Whitfield & J.F.Parker	v Indians	The Oval	1932
111	J.F.Parker & A.R.Gover	v Indians	The Oval	1936
105	W.Brockwell & T.Richardson	v Gloucestershire	The Oval	1893
104	F.R.Brown & J.F.Parker	v Kent	Blackheath	1932

HIGHEST WICKET PARTNERSHIPS AGAINST SURREY

First Wicket

(Qualification 250)

377*	N.F.Horner & Khalid Ibadulla	- Warwickshire	The Oval	1960
330	B.Mitchell & E.A.B.Rowan	- South Africans	The Oval	1935
299	M.J.K.Smith & D.V.Smith	- MCC	Lord's	1958
270	A.V.Avery & T.C.Dodds	- Essex	The Oval	1946
267	V.P.Terry & T.C.Middleton	- Hampshire	Southampton	1992
265*	P.Holmes & H.Sutcliffe	- Yorkshire	The Oval	1926
258	J.G.Langridge & J.H.Parks	- Sussex	Horsham	1934
254	G.M.Turner & J.A.Ormrod	- Worcestershire	Worcester	1978

Second Wicket

(Qualification 250)

371	F.B.Watson & G.E.Tyldesley	- Lancashire	Manchester	1928
325	G.Brann & K.S.Ranjitsinhji	- Sussex	The Oval	1899
319	H.W.Lee & G.O.B.Allen	- Middlesex	The Oval	1929
289	A.Shrewsbury & W.Barnes	- Nottinghamshire	The Oval	1882
277	C.J.B.Wood & G.W.Beldam	- London County	The Oval	1901

Third Wicket
(Qualification 250)

364	M.A.Atherton & N.H.Fairbrother	- Lancashire	The Oval	1990
328	H.A.Carpenter & C.P.McGahey	- Essex	The Oval	1904
297	P.B.Wight & W.E.Alley	- Somerset	Taunton	1961
296	W.J.Edrich & E.H.Hendren	- MCC	Lord's	1936
296	W.J.Edrich & D.C.S.Compton	- Middlesex	Lord's	1946
287*	W.J.Edrich & D.C.S.Compton	- Middlesex	The Oval	1947
255*	W.G.Grace & E.N.Knapp	- Gloucestershire	Clifton	1873
250	E.H.Bowley & K.S.Duleepsinhji	- Sussex	The Oval	1931

Fourth Wicket
(Qualification 250)

314	Salim Malik & N.Hussain	- Essex	The Oval	1991
304	D.C.S.Compton & F.G.Mann	- Middlesex	Lord's	1947
281	T.E.R.Cook & James Langridge	- Sussex	The Oval	1930
279	R.E.Marshall & C.L.Walcott	- West Indians	The Oval	1950
276	P.G.T.Kingsley & N.M.Ford	- Oxford University	The Oval	1930
251	I.V.A.Richards & P.M.Roebuck	- Somerset	Weston-s-Mare	1977

Fifth Wicket
(Qualification 225)

340	E.Wainwright & G.H.Hirst	- Yorkshire	The Oval	1899
287	J.O'Connor & C.T.Ashton	- Essex	Brentford	1934
285	E.H.Hendren & J.H.Human	- Middlesex	The Oval	1935
230	J.Iddon & T.M.Halliday	- Lancashire	The Oval	1928
227	T.S.Curtis & M.J.Weston	- Worcestershire	Worcester	1985

Sixth Wicket
(Qualification 225)

376	R.Subba Row & A.Lightfoot	- Northamptonshire	The Oval	1958
285	W.R.Hammond & B.H.Lyon	- Gloucestershire	The Oval	1928
245	J.L.Bryan & C.T.Ashton	- Cambridge Univ	The Oval	1921
237*	R.W.Tolchard & B.J.Booth	- Leicestershire	Leicester (GR)	1971

Seventh Wicket
(Qualification 200)

257	J.T.Morgan & F.R.Brown	- Cambridge Univ	The Oval	1930
204	M.J.Smedley & R.A.White	- Nottinghamshire	The Oval	1967

Eighth Wicket
(Qualification 150)

167	A.Staples & F.Barratt	- Nottinghamshire	Nottingham	1928
165	S.Haigh & Lord Hawke	- Yorkshire	The Oval	1902
150	G.Geary & T.E.Sidwell	- Leicestershire	The Oval	1926

Ninth Wicket

(Qualification 150)

230	D.A.Livingstone & A.T.Castell	- Hampshire	Southampton	1962
192	G.H.Hirst & S.Haigh	- Yorkshire	Bradford	1898
160	K.S.Ranjitsinhji & F.W.Tate	- Sussex	Hastings	1902

Tenth Wicket

(Qualification 100)

249	C.T.Sarwate & S.N.Banerjee	- Indians	The Oval	1946
173	J.Briggs & R.Pilling	- Lancashire	Liverpool	1885
141	J.R.Mason & C.Blythe	- Kent	The Oval	1909
139	P.R.Johnson & R.C.Robertson-Glasgow	- Somerset	The Oval	1926
136	G.Challenor & G.N.Francis	- West Indians	The Oval	1923
130	G.W.Beldam & C.Headlam	- Middlesex	Lord's	1902
126	R.E.S.Wyatt & J.H.Mayer	- Warwickshire	The Oval	1927
122	W.Reeves & G.M.Louden	- Essex	Leyton	1919
120	G.Lavis & J.Mercer	- Glamorgan	The Oval	1934
106	H.Wrathall & J.H.Board	- Gloucestershire	The Oval	1899

TWO HUNDRED AND FIFTY RUN PARTNERSHIPS

For Surrey

448	4th	R.Abel (193) & T.W.Hayward (273)	v Yorkshire	The Oval	1899
428	1st	J.B.Hobbs (261) & A.Sandham (183)	v Oxford Univ	The Oval	1926
413	3rd	D.J.Bicknell (186) & D.M.Ward (263)	v Kent	Canterbury	1990
379	1st	R.Abel (173) & W.Brockwell (225)	v Hampshire	The Oval	1897
371	2nd	J.B.Hobbs (205) & E.G.Hayes (276)	v Hampshire	The Oval	1909
364	1st	R.Abel (193) & D.L.A.Jephson (213)	v Derbyshire	The Oval	1900
353	3rd	A.Ducat (271) & E.G.Hayes (153)	v Hampshire	Southampton	1919
352	1st	T.W.Hayward (204*) & J.B.Hobbs (159)	v Warwickshire	The Oval	1909
344	2nd	A.Sandham (239) & R.J.Gregory (154)	v Glamorgan	The Oval	1937
334	4th	R.Abel (357*) & T.W.Hayward (158)	v Somerset	The Oval	1899
321	1st	D.J.Bicknell (169) & G.S.Clinton (146)	v Northamptonshire	The Oval	1990
317	3rd	A.Ducat (208) & T.F.Shepherd (145*)	v Essex	Leyton	1928
316*	2nd	M.J.Stewart (200*) & K.F.Barrington (130*)	v Essex	The Oval	1962
316*	2nd	A.R.Butcher (187*) & D.M.Smith (105*)	v Warwickshire	Birmingham	1982
313	1st	J.B.Hobbs (184) & T.W.Hayward (146)	v Worcestershire	Worcester	1913
308	5th	J.N.Crawford (232) & F.C.Holland (87)	v Somerset	The Oval	1908
306	3rd	R.Abel (165) & F.C.Holland (171)	v Cambridge Univ	The Oval	1895
305	3rd	W.E.Roller (120) & W.W.Read (247)	v Lancashire	Manchester	1887
301	3rd	G.P.Thorpe (114) & D.M.Ward (294*)	v Derbyshire	The Oval	1994
299	2nd	A.Sandham (282*) & A.Ducat (119)	v Lancashire	Manchester	1928
299	2nd	D.J.Bicknell (130) & G.P.Thorpe (171)	v Worcestershire	Worcester	1993
298	6th	A.Sandham (196) & H.S.Harrison (138*)	v Sussex	The Oval	1913
297	3rd	J.H.Edrich (226*) & K.F.Barrington (113)	v Middlesex	The Oval	1967
294	6th	D.R.Jardine (157) & P.G.H.Fender (177)	v Yorkshire	Bradford	1928
293	4th	H.T.Barling (171) & H.S.Squires (131)	v Oxford Univ	The Oval	1932
291	2nd	A.Sandham (96) & H.S.Squires (178)	v Yorkshire	The Oval	1933
290	1st	J.B.Hobbs (202) & T.W.Hayward (116)	v Yorkshire	Lord's	1914

289	4th	A.Ducat (142) & T.F.Shepherd (277*)	v Gloucestershire	The Oval	1927
288	5th	H.A.Peach (200*) & A.Ducat (149)	v Northants	Northampton	1920
287	5th	R.Abel (178) & W.H.Lockwood (131)	v Lancashire	The Oval	1899
281	2nd	A.Sandham (152) & A.Ducat (218)	v Nottinghamshire	Nottingham	1930
279	3rd	D.G.W.Fletcher (194) & H.S.Squires (154)	v Nottinghamshire	Nottingham	1947
277	1st	G.S.Clinton (192) & A.R.Butcher (118)	v Yorkshire	The Oval	1984
276	2nd	J.B.Hobbs (200) & R.J.Gregory (134*)	v Hampshire	Southampton	1926
272	2nd	R.Abel (221) & E.G.Hayes (150)	v Worcestershire	The Oval	1900
270*	1st	R.Abel (120*) & W.Brockwell (132*)	v Kent	The Oval	1900
270	4th	J.B.Hobbs (316*) & D.R.Jardine (103)	v Middlesex	Lord's	1926
267	3rd	R.J.Gregory (164) & H.T.Barling (233)	v Nottinghamshire	The Oval	1946
266	1st	A.Sandham (292*) & A.Jeacocke (138)	v Northamptonshire	The Oval	1921
266	1st	A.R.Butcher (216*) & G.S.Clinton (89)	v Cambridge Univ	Cambridge	1980
265	1st	R.Abel (135) & W.Brockwell (152)	v Warwickshire	The Oval	1898
264	1st	J.B.Hobbs (123) & A.Sandham (215)	v Somerset	Taunton	1932
262	5th	A.Jeacocke (156) & W.J.Abel (117)	v Cambridge Univ	The Oval	1923
262	7th	C.J.Richards (172*) & K.T.Medlycott (153)	v Kent	The Oval	1987
261	3rd	A.Ducat (235) & T.F.Shepherd (121)	v Leicestershire	The Oval	1926
261	3rd	B.Constable (96) & P.B.H.May (163)	v Nottinghamshire	Nottingham	1958
260	6th	J.N.Crawford (152*) & Lord Dalmeny (138)	v Leicestershire	The Oval	1905
260	1st	L.B.Fishlock (210) & E.A.Bedser (154)	v Somerset	The Oval	1949
259	2nd	T.W.Hayward (177) & E.G.Hayes (89)	v Yorkshire	The Oval	1911
256*	5th	R.Abel (104*) & D.L.A.Jephson (166*)	v Gloucestershire	The Oval	1898
256*	2nd	G.P.Howarth (179*) & R.D.V.Knight (103*)	v Cambridge Univ	Cambridge	1978
256	4th	R.Abel (217) & F.C.Holland (123)	v Essex	The Oval	1895
256	1st	D.J.Bicknell (63) & D.M.Ward (181)	v Oxford Univ	Oxford	1990
254	1st	R.E.C.Pratt (120) & M.J.Stewart (155*)	v Cambridge Univ	Guildford	1956
		(255 were added for this wicket, D.J.W.Fletcher (0) retired not out when the score was 1)*			
253*	1st	J.B.Hobbs (123*) & A.Sandham (108*)	v West Indians	The Oval	1928
253*	5th	D.J.Bicknell (235*) & A.D.Brown (134*)	v Nottinghamshire	Nottingham	1994
252	5th	A.J.Stewart (158) & M.A.Lynch (115)	v Kent	Canterbury	1985
250	5th	T.W.Hayward (158) & D.L.A.Jephson (133)	v Derbyshire	The Oval	1901
250	4th	T.H.Clark (165) & R.E.C.Pratt (90)	v Kent	The Oval	1953

Against Surrey

377*	1st	N.F.Horner (203*) & Khalid Ibadulla (170*)	- Warwickshire	The Oval	1960
376	6th	R.Subba Row (300) & A.Lightfoot (119)	- Northants	The Oval	1958
371	2nd	F.B.Watson (300*) & G.E.Tyldesley (187)	- Lancashire	Manchester	1928
364	3rd	M.A.Atherton (191) & N.H.Fairbrother (366)	- Lancashire	The Oval	1990
340	5th	E.Wainwright (228) & G.H.Hirst (186)	- Yorkshire	The Oval	1899
330	1st	B.Mitchell (195) & E.A.B.Rowan (171)	- South Africans	The Oval	1935
328	3rd	H.A.Carpenter (199) & C.P.McGahey (173)	- Essex	The Oval	1904
325	2nd	G.Brann (157) & K.S.Ranjitsinhji (197)	- Sussex	The Oval	1899
319	2nd	H.W.Lee (225) & G.O.B.Allen (155)	- Middlesex	The Oval	1929
314	4th	Salim Malik (185*) & N.Hussain (128)	- Essex	The Oval	1991
304	4th	D.C.S.Compton (178) & F.G.Mann (106)	- Middlesex	Lord's	1947
299	1st	M.J.K.Smith (160) & D.V.Smith (173)	- MCC	Lord's	1958
297	3rd	P.B.Wight (125) & W.E.Alley (183*)	- Somerset	Taunton	1961
296	3rd	W.J.Edrich (114) & E.H.Hendren (202)	- MCC	Lord's	1936
296	3rd	W.J.Edrich (147) & D.C.S.Compton (235)	- Middlesex	Lord's	1946

289	2nd	A.Shewsbury (207) & W.Barnes (130)	- Nottinghamshire	The Oval	1882
287*	3rd	W.J.Edrich (157*) & D.C.S.Compton (137*)	- Middlesex	The Oval	1947
287	5th	J.O'Connor (248) & C.T.Ashton (118)	- Essex	Brentwood	1934
285	6th	W.R.Hammond (205*) & B.H.Lyon (131)	- Gloucestershire	The Oval	1928
285	5th	E.H.Hendren (195) & J.H.Human (144)	- Middlesex	The Oval	1935
281	4th	T.E.R.Cook (122) & James Langridge (159*)	- Sussex	The Oval	1930
279	4th	R.E.Marshall (143) & C.L.Walcott (149)	- West Indians	The Oval	1950
277	2nd	C.J.B.Wood (137) & G.W.Beldam (150*)	- London County	The Oval	1901
276	4th	P.G.T.Kingsley (176) & N.M.Ford (180)	- Oxford Univ	The Oval	1930
270	1st	A.V.Avery (210) & T.C.Dodds (103)	- Essex	The Oval	1946
267	1st	V.P.Terry (131) & T.C.Middleton (221)	- Hampshire	Southampton	1992
265*	1st	P.Holmes (127*) & H.Sutcliffe (131*)	- Yorkshire	The Oval	1926
258	1st	J.G.Langridge (160) & J.H.Parks (122)	- Sussex	Horsham	1934
257	7th	J.T.Morgan (110) & F.R.Brown (150)	- Cambridge Univ	The Oval	1930
255*	3rd	W.G.Grace (160*) & E.M.Knapp (90*)	- Gloucestershire	Clifton	1873
254	1st	G.M.Turner (150) & J.A.Ormrod (173)	- Worcestershire	Worcester	1978
251	4th	I.V.A.Richards (204) & P.M.Roebuck (112)	- Somerset	Weston-s-M	1977
250	3rd	E.H.Bowley (144) & K.S.Duleepsinhji (162)	- Sussex	The Oval	1931

SECTION 4 - INDIVIDUAL BOWLING RECORDS

NINE OR MORE WICKETS IN AN INNINGS

For Surrey

10-43	T.Rushby	v Somerset	Taunton	1921
10-45	T.Richardson	v Essex	The Oval	1894
10-54	G.A.R.Lock	v Kent	Blackheath	1956
10-67	E.A.Watts	v Warwickshire	Birmingham	1939
10-88	J.C.Laker	v Australians	The Oval	1956
9-17	P.J.Loader	v Warwickshire	The Oval	1958
9-28	P.J.Loader	v Kent	Blackheath	1953
9-31	W.C.Smith	v Hampshire	The Oval	1904
9-45	M.P.Bicknell	v Cambridge University	The Oval	1988
9-47	J.W.Sharpe	v Middlesex	The Oval	1891
9-47	T.Richardson	v Yorkshire	Sheffield	1893
9-49	T.Richardson	v Sussex	The Oval	1895
9-57	P.I.Pocock	v Glamorgan	Cardiff (SG)	1979
9-59	W.H.Lockwood	v Essex	Leyton	1902
9-67	G.A.Lohmann	v Sussex	Hove	1889
9-70	T.Richardson	v Hampshire	The Oval	1895
9-70	D.A.D.Sydenham	v Gloucestershire	The Oval	1964
9-77	G.A.R.Lock	v Oxford University	Guildford	1960
9-81	W.S.Lees	v Sussex	Eastbourne	1905
9-94	W.H.Lockwood	v Essex	The Oval	1900
9-105	W.H.Lockwood	v Gloucestershire	Cheltenham	1899
9-130	G.Griffith	v Lancashire	The Oval	1867

Against Surrey

10-28	W.P.Howell	- Australians	The Oval	1899
10-49	E.J.Tyler	- Somerset	Taunton	1895
10-59	G.Burton	- Middlesex	The Oval	1888
10-74	V.E.Walker	- England	The Oval	1859
9-32	D.L.Underwood	- Kent	The Oval	1978
9-33	M.McIntyre	- Nottinghamshire	The Oval	1872
9-34	A.D.Pougher	- England	The Oval	1895
9-35	S.Hargreave	- Warwickshire	The Oval	1903
9-49	J.Jackson	- Nottinghamshire	The Oval	1860
9-63	E.G.Dennett	- Gloucestershire	Bristol	1913
9-78	M.Flanagan	- MCC	Lord's	1876
9-82	T.W.J.Goddard	- Gloucestershire	Cheltenham	1946
9-82	J.W.Hearne	- Middlesex	Lord's	1911
9-83	A.W.Shipman	- Leicestershire	The Oval	1910
9-91	T.G.Wass	- Nottinghamshire	The Oval	1902
9-93	F.G.Bull	- Essex	The Oval	1897
9-97	C.Blythe	- Kent	Lord's	1914
9-97	B.L.Muncer	- Glamorgan	Cardiff (AP)	1947
9-105	G.Wells	- Sussex	Brighton	1860
9-118	C.W.L.Parker	- Gloucestershire	Gloucester	1925

FIFTEEN OR MORE WICKETS IN A MATCH

For Surrey

16-83	G.A.R.Lock	v Kent	Blackheath	1956
15-83	T.Richardson	v Warwickshire	The Oval	1898
15-95	T.Richardson	v Essex	The Oval	1894
15-97	J.C.Laker	v MCC	Lord's	1954
15-98	G.A.Lohmann	v Sussex	Hove	1889
15-113	T.Richardson	v Leicestershire	The Oval	1896
15-154	T.Richardson	v Yorkshire	Leeds	1897
15-155	T.Richardson	v Hampshire	The Oval	1895
15-182	G.A.R.Lock	v Kent	Blackheath	1958
15-184	W.H.Lockwood	v Gloucestershire	Cheltenham	1899

Against Surrey

15-57	W.P.Howell	- Australians	The Oval	1899
15-73	J.Jackson	- Nottinghamshire	The Oval	1860
15-76	S.Hargreave	- Warwickshire	The Oval	1903
15-91	C.W.L.Parker	- Gloucestershire	Cheltenham	1930
15-116	W.G.Grace	- Gloucestershire	Cirencester	1879
15-138	H.C.McDonell	- Cambridge University	Cambridge	1904
15-195	E.G.Dennett	- Gloucestershire	Bristol	1913
15-297	C.H.Ellis	- Sussex	Brighton	1863

HAT-TRICKS

For Surrey

J.Street	v Middlesex	The Oval	1868
W.E.Roller	v Sussex	The Oval	1885
W.H.Lockwood	v Cambridge University	Cambridge	1893
T.Richardson	v Gloucestershire	The Oval	1893
T.Richardson	v Leicestershire	The Oval	1896
W.S.Lees	v Hampshire	Southampton	1897
T.Richardson	v Warwickshire	The Oval	1898
T.Richardson	v Sussex	Hove	1898
T.W.Hayward	v Gloucestershire	The Oval	1899
T.W.Hayward	v Derbyshire	Chesterfield	1899
W.Brockwell	v Yorkshire	Sheffield	1900
W.H.Lockwood	v Derbyshire	The Oval	1901
W.H.Lockwood	v Yorkshire	Sheffield	1903
D.L.A.Jephson	v Middlesex	The Oval	1904
W.C.Smith	v Hampshire	The Oval	1908
W.C.Smith	v Northamptonshire	The Oval	1910
J.W.Hitch	v Cambridge University	The Oval	1911
(four wickets in five balls)			
J.W.Hitch	v Warwickshire	The Oval	1914
P.G.H.Fender	v Somerset	The Oval	1914
W.C.H.Sadler	v Cambridge University	The Oval	1923
P.G.H.Fender	v Gloucestershire	The Oval	1924
H.A.Peach	v Sussex	The Oval	1924
(four wickets in four balls)			
T.F.Shepherd	v Gloucestershire	The Oval	1926
A.R.Gover	v Worcestershire	Worcester	1935
(four wickets in four balls)			
J.C.Laker	v Gloucestershire	Gloucester	1951
J.C.Laker	v Warwickshire	The Oval	1953

J.C.Laker	v Cambridge University	Guildford	1953
A.V.Bedser	v Essex	The Oval	1953
G.A.R.Lock	v Somerset	Weston-super-Mare	1955
D.Gibson	v Northamptonshire	Northampton	1961
P.J.Loader	v Leicestershire	The Oval	1963
R.Harman	v Kent	Blackheath	1963
(four wickets in five balls)			
S.J.Storey	v Glamorgan	Swansea	1965
R.Harman	v Derbyshire	Ilkeston	1968
R.D.Jackman	v Kent	Canterbury	1971
P.I.Pocock	v Worcestershire	Guildford	1971
Intikhab Alam	v Yorkshire	The Oval	1972
P.I.Pocock	v Sussex	Eastbourne	1972
(five wickets in six balls)			
R.D.Jackman	v Yorkshire	Leeds	1973
G.G.Arnold	v Leicestershire	Leicester (GR)	1974
S.T.Clarke	v Nottinghamshire	The Oval	1980
A.H.Gray	v Yorkshire	Sheffield	1985
(four wickets in five balls)			
S.T.Clarke	v Essex	Colchester	1987
(four wickets in five balls)			

Against Surrey

W.H.R.Andrews	- Somerset	The Oval	1937
W.Blackman	- Sussex	Hove	1881
C.Blythe	- Kent	Blackheath	1910
(four wickets in five balls)			
G.S.Boyes	- Hampshire	Portsmouth	1925
H.J.Butler	- Nottinghamshire	Nottingham	1937
W.H.Cotton	- Leicestershire	The Oval	1965
J.Crossland	- Lancashire	The Oval	1881
E.G.Dennett	- Gloucestershire	Bristol	1913
G.R.Dilley	- Kent	The Oval	1985
R.V.Divecha	- Indians	The Oval	1952
M.Flanagan	- MCC	Lord's	1876
A.P.Freeman	- Kent	Blackheath	1934
A.E.R.Gilligan	- Sussex	The Oval	1923
W.J.Hammersley	- MCC	The Oval	1848
A.Hill	- Yorkshire	The Oval	1880
R.Illingworth	- Leicestershire	The Oval	1975
V.E.Jackson	- Leicestershire	Leicester (GR)	1950
R.O.Jenkins	- Worcestershire	The Oval	1948
R.O.Jenkins *(1st inn)*	- Worcestershire	Worcester	1949
R.O.Jenkins *(2nd inn)*	- Worcestershire	Worcester	1949
V.W.C.Jupp	- Sussex	Hove	1911
M.Leyland	- Yorkshire	Sheffield	1935
F.Martin	- Kent	The Oval	1890
J.Mercer	- Glamorgan	The Oval	1932
C.S.Nayudu	- Indians	The Oval	1946
C.W.L.Parker	- Gloucestershire	The Oval	1924
F.A.Pearson	- Worcestershire	Worcester	1914
A.C.S.Pigott	- Sussex	Hove	1978
(his first wickets in first-class cricket)			
A.E.G.Rhodes	- MCC	Lord's	1948
K.Shuttleworth	- Leicestershire	The Oval	1977
F.A.Tarrant	- Middlesex	Lord's	1909
F.W.Tate	- Sussex	The Oval	1901
S.Turner	- Essex	The Oval	1971
Wasim Akram	- Lancashire	Southport	1988

R.Whitehead	- Lancashire	Manchester	1912
G.A.Wilson	- Worcestershire	Worcester	1901
F.E.Woolley	- Kent	Blackheath	1919

WICKET WITH FIRST BALL

For Surrey

J.J.Parfitt	v Yorkshire	The Oval	1881
E.C.Streatfeild	v Lancashire	The Oval	1890
J.G.O'Gorman	v Glamorgan	The Oval	1927

Against Surrey

H.Stubberfield	- Sussex	Brighton	1857
G.McCanlis	- Kent	The Oval	1873
W.H.Copson	- Derbyshire	The Oval	1932
W.G.Davies	- Glamorgan	The Oval	1957

FIVE WICKETS IN A INNINGS ON DEBUT FOR SURREY

5-26	E.C.Streatfeild	v Lancashire	The Oval	1890

BOWLING UNCHANGED THROUGH BOTH INNINGS OF A COMPLETED MATCH

For Surrey

D.Day (12-?) & W.Martingell (8-?)	v Kent	The Oval	1846
W.Martingell (10-69) & T.Sherman (7-82)	v Sussex	The Oval	1856
W.Martingell (10-67) & G.Griffith (9-35)	v Kent	Tunbridge W	1856
W.Caffyn (9-28) & G.Griffith (10-34)	v Sussex	The Oval	1857
W.Caffyn (8-71) & G.Griffith (7-56)	v North	Sheffield	1857
J.Southerton (9-108) & J.Street (11-61)	v Kent	Maidstone	1872
J.Beaumont (10-49) & G.A.Lohmann (10-49)	v Kent	The Oval	1889
G.A.Lohmann (13-54) & J.W.Sharpe (7-50)	v Lancashire	Manchester	1890
G.A.Lohmann (11-40) & J.W.Sharpe (9-31)	v Somerset	The Oval	1891
T.Richardson (9-99) & F.E.Smith (10-71)	v Gloucestershire	The Oval	1894
T.Richardson (11-60) & G.A.Lohmann (8-59)	v Derbyshire	Derby	1895
T.Richardson (12-20) & T.W.Hayward (7-43)	v Leicestershire	Leicester (GR)	1897
J.N.Crawford (10-78) & H.C.McDonell (10-89)	v Gloucestershire	Cheltenham	1904
J.N.Crawford (11-63) & T.Rushby (6-67)	v Sussex	The Oval	1907
J.N.Crawford (6-52) & W.C.Smith (11-65)	v Derbyshire	Derby	1907
W.S.Lees (8-104) & T.Rushby (9-90)	v Lancashire	Manchester	1908

Against Surrey

J.Jackson (7-57) & R.C.Tinley (12-93)	- North	The Oval	1860
I.Hodgson (9-88) & G.R.Atkinson (10-115)	- Yorkshire	Sheffield	1861
L.Greenwood (11-71) & G.Freeman (8-73)	- Yorkshire	The Oval	1867
G.Freeman (13-60) & T.Emmett (5-55)	- Yorkshire	Sheffield	1869
A.Shaw (13-58) & G.Wootton (6-71)	- MCC	The Oval	1870
G.Freeman (10-43) & T.Emmett (9-92)	- Yorkshire	The Oval	1870
J.Southerton (14-99) & James Lillywhite (5-84)	- Sussex	The Oval	1871
T.Emmett (8-113) & A.Hill (12-57)	- Yorkshire	The Oval	1871
James Lillywhite (7-101) & R.Fillery (13-123)	- Sussex	The Oval	1873
T.Emmett (12-84) & A.Hill (8-55)	- Yorkshire	Sheffield	1873
W.McIntyre (11-70) & A.Watson (8-79)	- Lancashire	Manchester	1873

W.McIntyre (11-54) & A.Watson (8-47)	- Lancashire	The Oval	1873
A.Shaw (7-56) & F.Morley (12-70)	- Nottinghamshire	Nottingham	1878
A.Hill (6-85) & E.Peate (14-77)	- Yorkshire	Huddersfield	1881
W.Hearne (13-98) & F.Martin (6-65)	- Kent	Catford	1894
J.T.Hearne (12-90) & J.T.Rawlin (7-69)	- Middlesex	The Oval	1896
S.Hargreave (15-76) & S.Santall (5-66)	- Warwickshire	The Oval	1903
G.H.Hirst (10-67) & W.Rhodes (10-81)	- Yorkshire	The Oval	1903
C.Blythe (12-67) & A.Hearne (7-61)	- Kent	The Oval	1903
F.G.Roberts (11-93) & E.G.Dennett (9-99)	- Gloucestershire	Bristol	1903
H.Dean (7-84) & W.Huddleston (12-82)	- Lancashire	Manchester	1907
J.W.H.T.Douglas (11-98) & B.Tremlin (9-115)	- Essex	The Oval	1914

125 WICKETS IN A SEASON (100 SINCE 1969)

T.Richardson	(6)	1894 - 196	1895 - 252	1896 - 202	1897 - 238
		1898 - 136	1901 - 159		
G.A.Lohmann	(5)	1885 - 138	1888 - 163	1889 - 143	1890 - 129
		1891 - 138			
A.R.Gover	(5)	1934 - 126	1935 - 133	1936 - 179	1937 - 168
		1939 - 129			
G.A.R.Lock	(5)	1952 - 126	1955 - 183	1956 - 138	1957 - 187
		1960 - 126			
W.S.Lees	(4)	1905 - 184	1906 - 154	1907 - 135	1909 - 128
J.W.Hitch	(4)	1911 - 137	1913 - 162	1914 - 126	1919 - 131
J.C.Laker	(3)	1950 - 155	1951 - 128	1954 - 132	
W.C.Smith	(2)	1910 - 225	1911 - 156		
P.G.H.Fender	(2)	1922 - 143	1923 - 140		
A.V.Bedser	(2)	1955 - 131	1957 - 131		
W.H.Lockwood		1892 - 134			
T.Rushby		1911 - 132			
P.J.Loader		1962 - 131			
E.Barratt		1883 - 144			
N.A.Knox		1906 - 129			
E.A.Watts		1938 - 129			
R.Harman		1964 - 127			
R.D.Jackman		1980 - 121			
Waqar Younis		1991 - 113			

MOST WICKETS IN A SEASON

(Qualification: 100 wickets)

		Wkts	*Avge*			*Wkts*	*Avge*
1895	T.Richardson	252	13.94	1906	W.S.Lees	154	20.25
1897	T.Richardson	238	14.23	1883	E.Barratt	144	15.83
1910	W.C.Smith	225	12.83	1889	G.A.Lohmann	143	11.85
1896	T.Richardson	202	15.70	1922	P.G.H.Fender	143	19.49
1894	T.Richardson	196	10.32	1923	P.G.H.Fender	140	18.56
1957	G.A.R.Lock	187	12.09	1891	G.A.Lohmann	138	10.84
1905	W.S.Lees	184	17.65	1956	G.A.R.Lock	138	11.22
1955	G.A.R.Lock	183	12.22	1885	G.A.Lohmann	138	14.21
1936	A.R.Gover	179	16.50	1911	J.W.Hitch	137	22.92
1937	A.R.Gover	168	18.70	1898	T.Richardson	136	20.63
1888	G.A.Lohmann	163	9.94	1907	W.S.Lees	135	17.90
1913	J.W.Hitch	162	18.96	1892	W.H.Lockwood	134	13.51
1901	T.Richardson	159	23.25	1935	A.R.Gover	133	26.88
1911	W.C.Smith	156	19.55	1954	J.C.Laker	132	14.07
1950	J.C.Laker	155	15.56	1911	T.Rushby	132	20.98

		Wkts	Avge			Wkts	Avge
1957	A.V.Bedser	131	16.56	1952	A.V.Bedser	117	16.11
1955	A.V.Bedser	131	17.61	1900	T.Richardson	117	23.81
1962	P.J.Loader	131	18.51	1949	J.C.Laker	116	19.02
1919	J.W.Hitch	131	22.98	1947	A.V.Bedser	116	22.93
1890	G.A.Lohmann	129	13.80	1933	A.R.Gover	116	25.99
1938	E.A.Watts	129	18.47	1953	J.C.Laker	115	17.06
1906	N.A.Knox	129	19.00	1962	D.A.D.Sydenham	115	17.65
1939	A.R.Gover	129	24.11	1959	P.J.Loader	115	19.09
1951	J.C.Laker	128	18.92	1903	T.Richardson	115	22.57
1909	W.S.Lees	128	21.29	1919	T.Rushby	114	22.05
1964	R.Harman	127	21.12	1904	W.S.Lees	114	24.90
1952	G.A.R.Lock	126	17.16	1870	J.Southerton	113	12.69
1914	J.W.Hitch	126	19.76	1991	Waqar Younis	113	14.65
1960	G.A.R.Lock	126	20.68	1967	P.I.Pocock	111	17.91
1934	A.R.Gover	126	25.93	1906	J.N.Crawford	111	19.54
1893	T.Richardson	124	14.65	1921	P.G.H.Fender	111	25.58
1955	J.C.Laker	124	17.63	1912	W.C.Smith	109	16.81
1900	W.H.Lockwood	124	19.41	1920	P.G.H.Fender	109	20.55
1925	P.G.H.Fender	124	20.32	1961	G.A.R.Lock	109	26.66
1894	W.H.Lockwood	123	13.86	1897	T.W.Hayward	108	17.92
1886	G.A.Lohmann	122	14.16	1908	W.S.Lees	108	20.47
1956	P.J.Loader	122	15.14	1963	D.A.D.Sydenham	107	15.85
1957	P.J.Loader	122	15.82	1899	W.H.Lockwood	106	19.26
1980	R.D.Jackman	121	15.40	1950	A.V.Bedser	106	20.89
1884	E.Barratt	121	18.17	1959	G.A.R.Lock	106	21.04
1905	N.A.Knox	121	20.62	1939	E.A.Watts	106	22.66
1958	G.A.R.Lock	120	12.70	1926	P.G.H.Fender	106	23.09
1885	J.Beaumont	119	15.50	1902	T.Richardson	106	24.59
1909	T.Rushby	119	16.08	1957	J.C.Laker	104	13.27
1873	J.Southerton	118	12.27	1966	S.J.Storey	104	18.39
1954	G.A.R.Lock	118	13.86	1920	J.W.Hitch	104	22.03
1887	G.A.Lohmann	118	15.69	1884	C.E.Horner	103	15.36
1907	J.N.Crawford	118	16.02	1914	T.Rushby	103	19.14
1898	W.H.Lockwood	118	16.69	1910	J.W.Hitch	103	20.42
1947	A.R.Gover	118	23.54	1952	J.C.Laker	102	16.49
1946	A.R.Gover	118	23.65	1932	F.R.Brown	102	16.89
1890	J.W.Sharpe	117	13.05	1903	W.S.Lees	102	20.80
1892	G.A.Lohmann	117	14.11	1878	E.Barratt	100	14.81

BEST AVERAGE FOR A HUNDRED WICKETS IN A SEASON

		Wkts	Avge			Wkts	Avge
1888	G.A.Lohmann	163	9.94	1894	W.H.Lockwood	123	13.86
1894	T.Richardson	196	10.32	1954	G.A.R.Lock	118	13.86
1891	G.A.Lohmann	138	10.84	1895	T.Richardson	252	13.94
1956	G.A.R.Lock	138	11.22	1954	J.C.Laker	132	14.07
1889	G.A.Lohmann	143	11.85	1892	G.A.Lohmann	117	14.11
1957	G.A.R.Lock	187	12.09	1886	G.A.Lohmann	122	14.16
1955	G.A.R.Lock	183	12.22	1885	G.A.Lohmann	138	14.21
1873	J.Southerton	118	12.27	1897	T.Richardson	238	14.23
1870	J.Southerton	113	12.69	1893	T.Richardson	124	14.65
1958	G.A.R.Lock	120	12.70	1991	Waqar Younis	113	14.65
1910	W.C.Smith	225	12.83	1878	E.Barratt	100	14.81
1890	J.W.Sharpe	117	13.05	1956	P.J.Loader	122	15.14
1957	J.C.Laker	104	13.27	1884	C.E.Horner	103	15.36
1892	W.H.Lockwood	134	13.51	1980	R.D.Jackman	121	15.40
1890	G.A.Lohmann	129	13.80	1885	J.Beaumont	119	15.50

		Wkts	Avge			Wkts	Avge
1950	J.C.Laker	155	15.56	1922	P.G.H.Fender	143	19.49
1887	G.A.Lohmann	118	15.69	1906	J.N.Crawford	111	19.54
1896	T.Richardson	202	15.70	1911	W.C.Smith	156	19.55
1957	P.J.Loader	122	15.82	1914	J.W.Hitch	126	19.76
1883	E.Barratt	144	15.83	1959	G.A.R.Lock	121	20.17
1963	D.A.D.Sydenham	107	15.85	1906	W.S.Lees	154	20.25
1907	J.N.Crawford	118	16.02	1925	P.G.H.Fender	124	20.32
1909	T.Rushby	119	16.08	1910	J.W.Hitch	103	20.42
1952	A.V.Bedser	117	16.11	1908	W.S.Lees	108	20.47
1952	J.C.Laker	102	16.49	1920	P.G.H.Fender	109	20.55
1936	A.R.Gover	179	16.50	1905	N.A.Knox	121	20.62
1957	A.V.Bedser	131	16.56	1898	T.Richardson	136	20.63
1898	W.H.Lockwood	118	16.69	1960	G.A.R.Lock	126	20.68
1912	W.C.Smith	109	16.81	1903	W.S.Lees	102	20.80
1932	F.R.Brown	102	16.89	1950	A.V.Bedser	106	20.89
1953	J.C.Laker	115	17.06	1911	T.Rushby	132	20.98
1952	G.A.R.Lock	126	17.16	1964	R.Harman	127	21.12
1955	A.V.Bedser	131	17.61	1909	W.S.Lees	128	21.29
1955	J.C.Laker	124	17.63	1920	J.W.Hitch	104	22.03
1905	W.S.Lees	184	17.65	1919	T.Rushby	114	22.05
1962	D.A.D.Sydenham	115	17.65	1903	T.Richardson	115	22.57
1907	W.S.Lees	135	17.90	1939	E.A.Watts	106	22.66
1967	P.I.Pocock	111	17.91	1911	J.W.Hitch	137	22.92
1897	T.W.Hayward	108	17.92	1947	A.V.Bedser	116	22.93
1884	E.Barratt	121	18.17	1919	J.W.Hitch	131	22.98
1966	S.J.Storey	104	18.39	1926	P.G.H.Fender	106	23.09
1938	E.A.Watts	129	18.47	1901	T.Richardson	159	23.25
1962	P.J.Loader	131	18.51	1947	A.R.Gover	118	23.54
1923	P.G.H.Fender	140	18.56	1946	A.R.Gover	118	23.65
1937	A.R.Gover	168	18.70	1900	T.Richardson	117	23.81
1951	J.C.Laker	128	18.92	1939	A.R.Gover	129	24.11
1913	J.W.Hitch	162	18.96	1902	T.Richardson	106	24.59
1906	N.A.Knox	129	19.00	1904	W.S.Lees	114	24.90
1949	J.C.Laker	116	19.02	1921	P.G.H.Fender	111	25.58
1959	P.J.Loader	115	19.09	1934	A.R.Gover	126	25.93
1914	T.Rushby	103	19.14	1933	A.R.Gover	116	25.99
1899	W.H.Lockwood	106	19.26	1961	G.A.R.Lock	109	26.66
1900	W.H.Lockwood	124	19.41	1935	A.R.Gover	133	26.88

MOST BALLS BOWLED IN AN INNINGS FOR SURREY

Balls	*O*	*M*	*R*	*W*				
476	119	40	152	5	J.Southerton	v Gloucestershire	Clifton	1871

MOST RUNS CONCEDED IN AN INNINGS AGAINST SURREY

Runs	*O*	*M*	*R*	*W*				
226	59	11	226	6	E.B.Shine	- Kent	The Oval	1897

SOME EXPENSIVE ANALYSES FOR SURREY

(Qualification: five overs)

R/O	*O*	*M*	*R*	*W*				
17.6	5	0	88	1	N.F.Sargeant	v Gloucestershire	Guildford	1991
9.62	8	0	77	2	G.S.Clinton	v Warwickshire	Birmingham	1980
9.55	9	0	86	0	D.J.Bicknell	v Derbyshire	The Oval	1992
8.6	5	0	43	0	N.M.Kendrick	v Sussex	Guildford	1990
8.6	5	0	43	1	M.A.Lynch	v Middlesex	The Oval	1990
8.42	7.5	0	66	2	D.M.Ward	v Gloucestershire	Guildford	1991
8.42	7	0	59	0	K.T.Medlycott	v Kent	Guildford	1990

MOST EXPENSIVE ANALYSIS AGAINST SURREY

R/O	*O*	*M*	*R*	*W*				
9.09	11	0	100	2	T.E.S.Francis	- Cambridge Univ	The Oval	1923

OUTSTANDING SPELLS OF WICKET-TAKING

For Surrey

Wkts	*Balls*				
7	11	P.I.Pocock	v Sussex	Eastbourne	1972
6	9	P.I.Pocock	v Sussex	Eastbourne	1972
5	6	P.I.Pocock	v Sussex	Eastbourne	1972
7	19	P.G.H.Fender	v Middlesex	Lord's	1927
6	11	P.G.H.Fender	v Middlesex	Lord's	1927
5	7	P.G.H.Fender	v Middlesex	Lord's	1927

Against Surrey

Wkts	*Balls*				
8	39	W.H.R.Andrews	- Somerset	The Oval	1937
7	24	F.E.Woolley	- Kent	The Oval	1911
5	10	C.Blythe	- Kent	Blackheath	1910

BOWLERS TAKING FIVE WICKETS IN AN INNINGS MOST TIMES

	Career	*5wi*	*10wm*
Richardson, T.	1892-1904	169	60
Lohmann, G.A.	1884-1896	128	41
Southerton, J.	1854-1879	115	29
Lockwood, W.H.	1889-1904	105	27
Lock, G.A.R.	1946-1963	123	31
Laker, J.C.	1946-1959	93	24
Lees, W.S.	1896-1911	92	20
Smith, W.C.	1900-1914	92	27
Hitch, J.W.	1907-1925	90	21
Gover, A.R.	1928-1947	87	15
Fender, P.G.H.	1914-1935	86	14
Bedser, A.V.	1939-1960	72	11
Loader, P.J.	1951-1963	65	13
Barrett, E.	1876-1885	62	16
Jackman, R.D.	1966-1982	61	7
Rushby, T.	1903-1921	58	9
Pocock, P.I.	1964-1986	53	7

500 WICKETS IN A CAREER FOR SURREY

	Career	*Runs*	*Wkts*	*Ave*	*B-B*	*5wi*	*10wm*	*100W*
T.Richardson	1892-1904	31732	1775	17.87	10-45	169	60	10
G.A.R.Lock	1946-1963	29835	1713	17.41	10-54	123	31	9
P.G.H.Fender	1914-1935	38200	1586	24.08	8-24	86	14	6
A.V.Bedser	1939-1960	27918	1459	19.13	8-18	72	11	5
A.R.Gover	1928-1947	34101	1437	23.73	8-34	87	15	8
P.I.Pocock	1964-1986	35577	1399	25.43	9-57	53	7	1
J.C.Laker	1946-1959	24236	1395	17.37	10-88	93	24	8
W.S.Lees	1896-1911	28542	1331	21.44	9-81	92	20	7
J.W.Hitch	1907-1925	26550	1232	21.55	8-38	90	21	6
G.A.Lohmann	1884-1896	16108	1221	13.19	9-67	128	41	8
R.D.Jackman	1966-1982	26969	1206	22.36	8-58	61	7	1
W.H.Lockwood	1889-1904	21266	1182	17.99	9-59	105	27	5
P.J.Loader	1951-1963	20685	1108	18.66	9-17	65	13	4
W.C.Smith	1900-1914	17616	1036	17.00	9-31	92	27	3
J.Southerton	1854-1879	13793	994	13.87	8-34	115	29	2
T.Rushby	1903-1921	19544	954	20.48	10-43	58	9	4
E.A.Bedser	1939-1961	19831	797	24.88	7-33	24	4	-
H.A.Peach	1919-1931	20261	778	26.04	8-60	30	1	-
G.G.Arnold	1963-1977	14857	745	19.94	8-41	32	2	-
E.A.Watts	1933-1949	18757	722	25.97	10-67	24	2	2
E.Barratt	1876-1885	12227	706	17.31	8-28	62	16	3
Intikhab Alam	1969-1981	18871	629	30.00	8-74	25	2	-
D.Gibson	1957-1969	12213	550	22.20	7-26	26	1	-
G.Griffith	1856-1871	9122	549	16.61	9-130	45	7	-
J.F.Parker	1932-1952	15387	538	28.60	6-34	8	-	-
J.Street	1863-1878	11435	534	21.41	7-141	36	6	-
W.Brockwell	1886-1903	12273	500	24.54	8-22	21	-	-

LEADING SURREY BOWLERS

	Most Wickets		*Best Average (Qualification: 10 wickets)*	
1846	D.Day	20		
1847	T.Sherman	24		
	D.Day	24		
1848	E.Hinckley	8		
1849	W.R.Hillyer	18		
1850	T.Sherman	44		
1851	T.Sherman	60	T.Sherman	8.31
1852	T.Sherman	28	D.Day	15.95
1853	T.Sherman	10		
1854	H.H.Stephenson	27	H.H.Stephenson	7.62
1855	W.Martingell	21	W.Martingell	7.80
1856	W.Martingell	28	W.Martingell	6.89
1857	W.Caffyn	61	W.Caffyn	7.39
1858	W.Caffyn	44	W.Caffyn	11.29
	H.H.Stephenson	44		
1859	W.Caffyn	34	T.Sewell, jun.	10.50
1860	W.Caffyn	31	H.H.Stephenson	10.00
1861	W.Caffyn	38	G.Griffith	11.90
1862	W.Caffyn	48	W.Caffyn	10.06
1863	T.Sewell, jun.	37	W.Mortlock	13.48
1864	G.Griffith	57	G.Griffith	14.64
1865	G.Griffith	55	T.Humphrey	15.60

1866	G.Griffith	56	G.Griffith	18.53
1867	G.Griffith	56	J.Bristow	13.91
1868	J.Southerton	94	J.Southerton	13.67
1869	J.Southerton	71	J.Southerton	14.07
1870	J.Southerton	113	W.H.Anstead	10.87
1871	J.Southerton	67	E.Bray	13.94
1872	J.Southerton	65	J.Southerton	12.61
1873	J.Southerton	118	J.Southerton	12.27
1874	J.Southerton	91	G.Strachan	11.80
1875	J.Southerton	89	J.Southerton	14.74
1876	J.Southerton	90	J.Southerton	15.11
1877	E.Barratt	78	A.P.Lucas	8.36
1878	E.Barratt	100	E.Barratt	14.81
1879	E.Blamires	57	J.Southerton	12.35
1880	J.Potter	78	J.Potter	16.84
1881	E.Barratt	82	G.G.Jones	14.75
1882	E.Barratt	93	C.E.Horner	14.02
1883	E.Barratt	144	E.Barratt	15.83
1884	E.Barratt	121	C.E.Horner	15.36
1885	G.A.Lohmann	138	G.A.Lohmann	14.21
1886	G.A.Lohmann	122	T.Bowley	13.35
1887	G.A.Lohmann	118	G.G.Jones	11.75
1888	G.A.Lohmann	163	G.A.Lohmann	9.94
1889	G.A.Lohmann	143	G.A.Lohmann	11.85
1890	G.A.Lohmann	129	E.C.Streatfeild	9.06
1891	G.A.Lohmann	138	G.A.Lohmann	10.84
1892	W.H.Lockwood	134	R.Abel	13.03
1893	T.Richardson	124	C.M.Wells	14.13
1894	T.Richardson	196	T.Richardson	10.32
1895	T.Richardson	252	T.Richardson	13.94
1896	T.Richardson	202	G.A.Lohmann	15.65
1897	T.Richardson	238	T.Richardson	14.23
1898	T.Richardson	136	W.H.Lockwood	16.62
1899	W.H.Lockwood	106	W.H.Lockwood	19.26
1900	W.H.Lockwood	124	W.H.Lockwood	19.41
1901	T.Richardson	159	T.W.Hayward	19.86
1902	T.Richardson	106	W.H.Lockwood	18.56
1903	T.Richardson	115	H.C.McDonell	17.87
1904	W.S.Lees	114	J.N.Crawford	16.93
1905	W.S.Lees	184	W.C.Smith	16.91
1906	W.S.Lees	154	N.A.Knox	19.00
1907	W.S.Lees	135	J.N.Crawford	16.02
1908	W.S.Lees	108	E.C.Kirk	15.66
1909	W.S.Lees	128	W.C.Smith	12.43
1910	W.C.Smith	225	E.C.Kirk	7.28
1911	W.C.Smith	156	J.B.Hobbs	18.20
1912	W.C.Smith	109	W.C.Smith	16.81
1913	J.W.Hitch	162	W.C.Smith	17.33
1914	J.W.Hitch	126	T.Rushby	19.14
1919	J.W.Hitch	131	T.Rushby	22.05
1920	P.G.H.Fender	109	J.B.Hobbs	11.82
1921	P.G.H.Fender	111	T.Rushby	20.18
1922	P.G.H.Fender	143	P.G.H.Fender	19.49
1923	P.G.H.Fender	140	P.G.H.Fender	18.56
1924	S.Fenley	84	T.S.Jennings	18.52
1925	P.G.H.Fender	124	J.H.Lockton	14.00
1926	P.G.H.Fender	106	P.G.H.Fender	23.09
1927	P.G.H.Fender	89	A.C.T.Geary	25.15
1928	P.G.H.Fender	99	H.A.Peach	28.24
1929	H.A.Peach	81	A.G.Penfold	15.46

1930	M.J.C.Allom	88	E.G.Stroud	22.86
1931	P.G.H.Fender	83	E.J.Sheffield	19.64
1932	F.R.Brown	102	F.R.Brown	16.89
1933	A.R.Gover	116	M.J.C.Allom	24.00
1934	A.R.Gover	126	A.R.Gover	25.93
1935	A.R.Gover	133	A.R.Gover	26.88
1936	A.R.Gover	179	A.R.Gover	16.50
1937	A.R.Gover	168	A.R.Gover	18.70
1938	E.A.Watts	129	E.A.Watts	18.47
1939	A.R.Gover	129	E.A.Watts	22.66
1946	A.R.Gover	118	J.F.Parker	15.59
1947	A.R.Gover	118	J.C.Laker	17.43
1948	J.W.McMahon	91	A.V.Bedser	19.44
1949	J.C.Laker	116	A.V.Bedser	18.95
1950	J.C.Laker	155	J.C.Laker	15.56
1951	J.C.Laker	128	A.V.Bedser	15.01
1952	G.A.R.Lock	126	A.V.Bedser	16.12
1953	J.C.Laker	115	G.A.R.Lock	13.82
1954	J.C.Laker	132	G.A.R.Lock	13.87
1955	G.A.R.Lock	183	D.F.Cox	12.07
1956	G.A.R.Lock	138	G.A.R.Lock	11.22
1957	G.A.R.Lock	187	G.A.R.Lock	12.09
1958	G.A.R.Lock	120	G.A.R.Lock	12.70
1959	P.J.Loader	115	D.A.D.Sydenham	15.96
1960	G.A.R.Lock	126	D.Gibson	17.60
1961	G.A.R.Lock	109	D.Gibson	22.30
1962	P.J.Loader	131	D.A.D.Sydenham	17.65
1963	D.A.D.Sydenham	107	D.A.D.Sydenham	15.85
1964	R.Harman	127	D.A.D.Sydenham	17.68
1965	D.Gibson	85	G.G.Arnold	17.89
1966	S.J.Storey	104	S.J.Storey	18.39
1967	P.I.Pocock	111	G.G.Arnold	17.83
1968	P.I.Pocock	89	J.Cumbes	17.68
1969	P.I.Pocock	73	R.G.D.Willis	17.22
1970	Intikhab Alam	72	R.D.Jackman	23.55
1971	G.G.Arnold	83	G.G.Arnold	17.12
1972	R.D.Jackman	84	P.I.Pocock	24.21
1973	R.D.Jackman	89	R.D.Jackman	19.95
1974	R.D.Jackman	81	G.G.Arnold	10.09
1975	R.D.Jackman	72	G.G.Arnold	19.86
1976	R.D.Jackman	85	R.D.Jackman	20.70
1977	R.D.Jackman	75	R.D.Jackman	25.09
1978	R.D.Jackman	70	P.I.Pocock	24.10
1979	R.D.Jackman	93	R.D.Jackman	17.15
1980	R.D.Jackman	121	R.D.Jackman	15.40
1981	Intikhab Alam	65	S.T.Clarke	14.97
1982	S.T.Clarke	85	S.T.Clarke	19.95
1983	S.T.Clarke	79	G.Monkhouse	22.12
1984	S.T.Clarke	78	S.T.Clarke	21.62
1985	A.H.Gray	79	A.H.Gray	22.98
1986	A.H.Gray	51	S.T.Clarke	16.79
1987	S.T.Clarke	58	A.H.Gray	15.16
1988	K.T.Medlycott	69	S.T.Clarke	14.49
1989	M.P.Bicknell	65	M.P.Bicknell	26.41
	A.J.Murphy	65		
1990	M.P.Bicknell	64	Waqar Younis	23.80
1991	Waqar Younis	113	Waqar Younis	14.65
1992	M.P.Bicknell	71	M.P.Bicknell	25.67
1993	J.E.Benjamin	64	M.P.Bicknell	17.11
1994	J.E.Benjamin	76	J.E.Benjamin	20.76

SECTION 5 - ALL-ROUND RECORDS

100 RUNS AND 10 WICKETS IN A MATCH

For Surrey

E.A.Bedser	71 & 30	7-142 & 3-89	v Gloucestershire	The Oval	1951
J.N.Crawford	148	7-85 & 4-63	v Gloucestershire	Bristol	1906
P.G.H.Fender	104	3-48 & 7-76	v Essex	Leyton	1926
R.J.Gregory	171	5-36 & 5-66	v Middlesex	Lord's	1930
W.H.Lockwood	63 & 37	6-48 & 6-48	v Lancashire	The Oval	1902
K.T.Medlycott	2 & 109	5-36 & 6-98	v Cambridge Univ	Cambridge	1991

Against Surrey

R.G.Barlow	71 & 39*	5-27 & 5-92	- Lancashire	Manchester	1883
J.Briggs	112	5-51 & 6-64	- Lancashire	The Oval	1893
D.C.S.Compton	137*	6-94 & 6-80	- Middlesex	The Oval	1947
E.R.Dexter	27 & 94	7-38 & 3-58	- Sussex	The Oval	1962
E.M.Dowson	71* & 50	3-47 & 8-68	- Cambridge Univ	The Oval	1903
M.McIntyre	88* & 27	9-33 & 3-66	- Nottinghamshire	The Oval	1872
W.B.Money	89 & 13	6-66 & 6-104	- Cambridge Univ	The Oval	1868
V.E.Walker	20* & 108	10-74 & 4-17	- England	The Oval	1859

SEASON DOUBLE

Player	*No Times*	*Year*	*Runs*	*Ave*	*Wkts*	*Ave*
W.H.Lockwood	2	1899	1,113	37.10	106	19.26
		1900	1,266	32.46	124	19.41
J.N.Crawford	2	1906	1,064	29.55	111	19.54
		1907	1,061	35.36	118	16.02
P.G.H.Fender	2	1922	1,114	39.78	143	19.49
		1923	1,136	31.55	140	18.56
T.W.Hayward	1	1897	1,211	36.69	108	17.92
S.J.Storey	1	1966	1,013	24.70	104	18.39

10000 RUNS AND 1000 WICKETS IN A CAREER

	Career	*Runs*	*Wkts*
P.G.H.Fender	1914-1935	14117	1586

SECTION 6 - WICKET-KEEPING RECORDS

MOST DISMISSALS IN AN INNINGS

For Surrey

		Ct	St			
A. Long	7	7	0	v Sussex	Hove	1964
E.Pooley	6	5	1	v Sussex	The Oval	1868
E.Pooley	6	3	3	v Sussex	The Oval	1868
E.Pooley	6	4	2	v Yorkshire	The Oval	1870
E.Pooley	6	1	5	v Kent	The Oval	1878
H.Strudwick	6	6	0	v Sussex	The Oval	1914
E.W.J.Brooks	6	6	0	v Kent	Blackheath	1935
G.N.G.Kirby	6	6	0	v Cambridge University	Guildford	1949
R.Swetman	6	6	0	v Kent	The Oval	1960
R.Swetman	6	6	0	v Somerset	Taunton	1960
A.J.Stewart	6	6	0	v Leicestershire	Leicester (GR)	1989
A.J.Stewart	6	6	0	v Glamorgan	The Oval	1993

Against Surrey

T.J.Zoehrer	8	6	2	- Australians	The Oval	1993
F.M.Engineer	6	6	0	- Lancashire	The Oval	1970
T.Foster	6	6	0	- Derbyshire	The Oval	1883
F.H.Huish	6	1	5	- Kent	The Oval	1911
D.Hunter	6	5	1	- Yorkshire	Sheffield	1891
M.H.Matthews	6	4	2	- Oxford University	The Oval	1937
H.Phillips	6	3	3	- Sussex	The Oval	1872
G.Ubsdell	6	1	5	- Hampshire	Southampton	1865
K.J.Wadsworth	6	5	1	- New Zealanders	The Oval	1973

MOST DISMISSALS IN A MATCH

For Surrey

		Ct	St			
E.Pooley	12	8	4	v Sussex	The Oval	1868
A.Long	11	11	0	v Sussex	Hove	1964
A.J.Stewart	11	11	0	v Leicestershire	Leicester (GR)	1989
E.Pooley	10	2	8	v Kent	The Oval	1878
C.J.Richards	10	9	1	v Sussex	Guildford	1987
C.J.Richards	9	6	3	v Glamorgan	Cardiff (SG)	1987
A.J.Stewart	9	9	0	v Glamorgan	The Oval	1993
E.Pooley	8	4	4	v Kent	Gravesend	1868
E.Pooley	8	6	2	v Middlesex	The Oval	1875
E.Pooley	8	4	4	v MCC	Lord's	1876
H.Strudwick	8	7	1	v Essex	Leyton	1904
E.W.J.Brooks	8	7	1	v Somerset	The Oval	1933
C.J.Richards	8	8	0	v Derbyshire	The Oval	1987

Against Surrey

F.H.Huish	10	1	9	- Kent	The Oval	1911
H.Phillips	10	5	5	- Sussex	The Oval	1872
T.J.Zoehrer	9	7	2	- Australians	The Oval	1993

MOST DISMISSALS IN A SEASON

	Ct	*St*		
90	73	17	A.Long	1962
87	71	16	F.Stedman	1901
87	66	21	A.J.W.McIntyre	1949
81	73	8	E.W.J.Brooks	1933
81	61	20	A.J.W.McIntyre	1955
80	63	17	H.Strudwick	1903
80	74	6	E.W.J.Brooks	1937
80	68	12	R.Swetman	1961
79	70	9	E.W.J.Brooks	1938
78	72	6	E.W.J.Brooks	1934
78	69	9	A.Long	1964
76	69	7	E.W.J.Brooks	1929
76	69	7	E.W.J.Brooks	1936
75	62	13	A.J.W.McIntyre	1950

HIGHEST TOTALS WITHOUT BYES

Scored by Opponents

557-7	H.Smith	v Gloucestershire	The Oval	1927
557	N.D.Burns	v Somerset	The Oval	1992
553	P.Moores	v Sussex	Hove	1988
551-7	D.Hunter	v Yorkshire	The Oval	1899

Scored by Surrey

570-8	E.W.J.Brooks	- Essex	Brentwood	1934

MOST DISMISSALS IN A CAREER

	Total	*Ct*	*St*	*Career*
H.Strudwick	1,223	1,040	183	1902-1927
E.W.J.Brooks	808	712	96	1925-1939
A.Long	805	702	103	1960-1975
A.J.W.McIntyre	762	617	145	1938-1963
H.Wood	619	523	96	1884-1900
E.Pooley	607	357	250	1861-1883
C.J.Richards	600	534	66	1976-1988

SECTION 7 - FIELDING RECORDS

MOST CATCHES IN AN INNINGS

For Surrey

7	M.J.Stewart	v Northamptonshire	Northampton	1957
5	R.Abel	v Hampshire	Portsmouth	1898
5	E.G.Hayes	v London County	The Oval	1901
5	G.A.R.Lock	v Lancashire	Manchester	1953
5	W.S.Surridge	v Lancashire	The Oval	1955
5	G.R.J.Roope	v Cambridge University	Cambridge	1980

Against Surrey

6	W.R.Hammond	- Gloucestershire	Cheltenham	1928
5	F.W.Wright	- Oxford University	The Oval	1865
5	V.E.Walker	- Middlesex	The Oval	1865
5	G.Gunn	- Nottinghamshire	Nottingham	1909
5	F.H.Gillingham	- Essex	The Oval	1919
5	H.Ashton	- Cambridge University	The Oval	1922
5	A.F.Wensley	- Sussex	Horsham	1934
5	F.H.Vigar	- Essex	The Oval	1951
5	D.Wilson	- Yorkshire	The Oval	1969

MOST CATCHES IN A MATCH

For Surrey

8	G.A.R.Lock	v Warwickshire	The Oval	1957
7	J.F.Parker	v Kent	Blackheath	1952
7	G.A.R.Lock	v Lancashire	Manchester	1953
7	W.S.Surridge	v Leicestershire	The Oval	1955
7	M.J Stewart	v Northamptonshire	Northampton	1957
6	R.Abel	v Derbyshire	Derby	1884
6	J.M.Read	v Hampshire	Southampton	1884
6	R.Abel	v Hampshire	Portsmouth	1898
6	E.G.Hayes	v Leicestershire	Leicester (AR)	1906
6	F.C.Holland	v Leicestershire	Leicester (AR)	1908
6	P.G.H.Fender	v Leicestershire	Leicester (AR)	1928
6	T.F.Shepherd	v Kent	The Oval	1929
6	W.S.Surridge	v Glamorgan	Cardiff (AP)	1956
6	R.E.C.Pratt	v Sussex	Hastings	1956
6	M.J.Stewart	v Sussex	Hove	1961
6	G.A.R.Lock	v Australians	The Oval	1961
6	M.J.Edwards	v Kent	Maidstone	1967
6	M.J.Edwards	v Essex	Colchester	1970
6	G.R.J.Roope	v Nottinghamshire	Nottingham	1970

Against Surrey

10	W.R. Hammond	- Gloucestershire	Cheltenham	1928
	(8 off the bowling of C.W.L.Parker)			
7	H. Ashton	- Cambridge University	The Oval	1922
7	C.H. Ellis	- Sussex	Brighton	1863
7	J.R. Mason	- Kent	The Oval	1905
7	A.F. Wensley	- Sussex	Horsham	1934

MOST CATCHES IN A SEASON

77	M.J.Stewart	1957
64	K.F.Barrington	1957
59	G.R.J.Roope	1971
58	G.A.R.Lock	1957
58	M.J.Stewart	1958
55	W.S.Surridge	1955
54	W.S.Surridge	1956
54	K.F.Barrington	1958
53	M.J.Edwards	1967
52	M.J.Stewart	1955
52	M.J.Stewart	1959
51	W.S.Surridge	1952
50	E.G.Hayes	1906
50	G.A.R.Lock	1952

MOST CATCHES IN A CAREER

604	M.J.Stewart	1954-1972
561	E.G.Hayes	1896-1919
532	G.A.R.Lock	1946-1963
513	G.R.J.Roope	1964-1982
492	R.Abel	1881-1904
470	P.G.H.Fender	1914-1935
420	T.W.Hayward	1893-1914
381	K.F.Barrington	1953-1968
360	W.S.Surridge	1947-1956
318	S.J.Storey	1960-1974
316	J.F.Parker	1932-1952
314	M.A.Lynch	1977-1994
300	W.W.Read	1873-1897

H.Strudwick

1223 victims for Surrey

T.Richardson

Most wickets, 1775, for Surrey

SECTION 8 - GROUND RECORDS

SUMMARY OF RESULTS OF ALL FIRST-CLASS MATCHES BY GROUND

	First	*W*	*D*	*L*	*T*	*A*	*Total*
Banstead Recreation Ground, Avenue Road	1984	-	1	-	-	-	1
Godalming Broadwater Park	1854	1	-	-	-	-	1
Guildford Sports Ground, Woodbridge Road	1938-1994	35	27	10	-	-	72
Kennington The Oval	1846-1994	691	625	313	6	14	1649
Kingston-on-Thames Leighton Motors Ground, Lower Ham Rd	1946	-	2	-	-	-	2
Reigate Priory Ground, Bell Street	1909	-	-	1	-	-	1
St.John's Wood Lord's Cricket Ground	1914	2	-	-	-	-	2
TOTAL HOME RESULTS		729	655	324	6	14	1728

	First	*W*	*D*	*L*	*T*	*A*	*Total*
Aldershot Officers Club Services Ground	1905-1906	2	-	-	-	-	2
Arundel Chichester Road, Arundel Castle Park	1991	-	1	-	-	-	1
Ashby de-la-Zouch Bath Grounds	1951-1964	-	1	1	-	1	3
Aylesford Preston Hall Ground	1846-1847	-	1	1	-	-	2
Basingstoke May's Bounty Ground, Fairfields Road	1935-1989	1	2	2	-	-	5
Bath The Recreation Ground, William Street	1914-1994	4	3	5	-	-	12
Beckenham Foxglove Road	1886-1905	4	-	1	-	-	5
Birmingham County Ground, Edgbaston	1894-1993	17	36	10	-	2	65
Birmingham Mitchell and Butler's Ground	1934-1936	1	1	-	-	-	2
Blackheath The Rectory Field, Charlton Road	1889-1970	16	23	16	-	-	55
Blackpool Stanley (Wingate) Park, West Park Road	1978-1990	-	2	-	-	-	2
Bournemouth Dean Park, Cavendish Road	1900-1991	10	7	3	-	-	20
Bournville Bournville Cricket Ground, Linden Road	1911	-	-	1	-	-	1
Bradford Horton Park Avenue	1888-1992	8	9	10	-	-	27
Brentwood Old County Ground, Shenfield Road	1934-1960	1	2	1	-	-	4
Brighton Royal Brunswick Ground, Brunswick Rd	1851-1871	9	6	4	-	-	19
Bristol Durdham Downs, Clifton	1870	-	-	1	-	-	1

Bristol Clifton College, Close Ground	1871-1898	2	7	7	-	-	16
Bristol Green Bank (Packer's Ground)	1924	-	1	-	-	-	1
Bristol The Phoenix Ground, Ashley Down	1890-1992	11	11	10	-	-	32
Bulawayo (Rhodesia) Queen's Ground	1959	-	1	-	-	-	1
Burton-on-Trent Allied Breweries, Belvedere Road	1970	-	1	-	-	-	1
Buxton Park Road Ground	1964	-	1	-	-	-	1
Cambridge Fenner's, Mortimer Road	1857-1992	24	21	4	-	-	49
Canterbury St.Lawrence Ground, Old Dover Road	1862-1993	4	8	6	-	-	18
Catford Private Banks Sports Ground	1893-1896	1	-	3	-	-	4
Cardiff Cardiff Arms Park, Westgate Street	1923-1966	7	3	6	-	-	16
Cardiff Sophia Gardens	1970-1990	4	3	-	-	-	7
Chelsea Prince's Ground, Hans Place	1872-1876	3	-	2	-	-	5
Chelmsford County Ground, New Writtle Street	1937-1991	2	9	7	-	-	18
Cheltenham College Ground	1872-1990	14	9	11	-	1	35
Chesterfield Queens Park, Park Road	1898-1987	9	8	3	-	1	21
Clacton-on-Sea Vista Road Recreation Ground	1935-1963	1	1	2	-	-	4
Cirencester Cirencester C.C.(Park) Ground	1879	-	1	-	-	-	1
Colchester Lower Castle Park, Catchpole Road	1939-1994	1	2	2	-	-	5
Colchester Garrison "A" Cricket Ground, Napier Road	1970	-	1	-	-	-	1
Coventry Courtauld's Ground, Lockhurst Lane	1947-1966	2	-	3	-	-	5
Darlington Feetham's Cricket Ground	1994	1	-	-	-	-	1
Dartford Hesketh Park, Hesketh Road	1986	-	1	-	-	-	1
Derby County Ground (Racecourse), Nottingham Rd	1883-1991	19	7	7	-	-	33
Dewsbury Dewsbury and Savile Ground, Savile Town	1884	-	1	-	-	-	1
Dudley Tipton Road	1912-1951	-	2	-	-	-	2
Durham Durham University Ground (Racecourse)	1991	1	-	-	-	-	1
Eastbourne The Saffrons, Compton Place Road	1905-1972	1	4	-	-	-	5
Ebbw Vale Eugene Cross Park	1961	-	-	1	-	-	1
Eccles Western Cricket Club	1857	-	-	1	-	-	1

Ground	Years						
Folkestone Sports Ground, Cheriton Road	1975-1981	1	2	-	-	-	3
Glasgow Hamilton Crescent	1923	-	1	-	-	-	1
Glossop North Road Ground	1902	-	1	-	-	-	1
Gloucester King's School	1994	1	-	-	-	-	1
Gloucester Spa Ground	1902	-	1	-	-	-	1
Gloucester Wagon Works Ground	1925-1970	6	1	2	-	-	9
Gravesend Bat and Ball Country Ground, Wrotham Rd	1864-1964	4	1	2	-	-	7
Harrogate St.George's Road	1981-1990	-	2	1	-	-	3
Hastings Central Ground, Queens Road,	1902-1956	4	4	3	-	-	11
Hinckley Leicester Road	1986	-	-	1	-	-	1
Hove New County Ground, Eaton Road	1872-1993	38	30	10	-	1	79
Horsham Cricket Field Road Ground, Worthing Rd	1909-1985	4	4	3	-	-	11
Huddersfield St. John's Ground, Fartown	1881	-	-	1	-	-	1
Hull Hull Town C.C. Ground, Argyle Street	1879-1968	1	-	2	-	-	3
Ilford Valentine's Park, Cranbrook Road	1948-1974	2	4	1	-	-	7
Ilkeston Rutland Recreation Ground, Oakwell Drive	1934-1993	2	1	2	-	-	5
Islington Cattle Market	1865-1868	1	1	2	-	-	4
Kettering Town Ground, Northampton Road	1929-1971	4	-	1	-	-	5
Kidderminster Chester Road North Ground	1938-1952	1	1	-	-	-	2
Leeds Recreation Ground, Holbeck	1883	-	-	1	-	-	1
Leeds Headingley Ground, St. Michael's Lane	1892-1986	4	7	12	-	-	23
Leicester Aylestone Road	1901-1936	14	10	2	-	1	27
Leicester Grace Road	1894-1993	16	17	4	-	-	37
Leyton County Ground, Crawley Road	1894-1969	23	9	5	-	-	37
Liverpool Wavertree Road Ground, Edge Hill	1866	1	-	-	-	-	1
Liverpool Aigburth Road	1884-1905	2	1	1	-	-	4
Llanelli Stradey Park	1952-1962	-	2	-	-	-	2
Loughborough Park Road	1914	1	-	-	-	-	1
Loughborough Brush Sports Ground, Forest Road	1953	-	1	-	-	-	1
Lydney Recreational Trust Ground, Lyefield Road	1963	-	1	-	-	-	1

Lytham St. Anne's							
Church Road Ground	1992	-	-	1	-	-	1
Maidstone							
Mote Park	1861-1982	4	10	6	-	-	20
Manchester							
Old Trafford, Stretford	1867-1994	21	38	29	-	2	90
Moreton-in-Marsh							
Moreton-in-Marsh CC, Batsford Rd	1887	1	-	-	-	-	1
Neath							
The Gnoll	1937-1992	1	1	1	-	-	3
Northampton							
County Ground, Wantage Road	1906-1993	18	17	9	-	-	44
Nottingham							
Trent Bridge Ground	1852-1994	33	37	42	-	-	112
Nuneaton							
Griff and Coton Ground	1967	-	1	-	-	-	1
Oxford							
The University Parks, Parks Road	1885-1990	12	9	4	-	-	25
Peterborough							
Town Ground	1947	-	1	-	-	-	1
Petworth							
New Ground, Petworth Park	1849	-	-	1	-	-	1
Pontypridd							
Ynysangharad Park	1954	-	1	-	-	-	1
Portsmouth							
United Services Recreation, Burnaby Road	1898-1982	12	4	5	-	-	21
Romford							
Gidea Park Sports Ground, Gallons Corner	1959-1968	1	1	-	-	-	2
Rushden							
Town Ground	1952	1	-	-	-	-	1
Scarborough							
North Marine Road Ground, formerly Queens	1892-1994	2	3	1	-	-	6
Salford							
Broughton Ground	1859-1863	1	2	2	-	-	5
Salisbury (Rhodesia)							
Police Ground	1959	-	-	1	-	-	1
Sheffield							
Hyde Park Ground	1851	1	-	-	-	-	1
Sheffield							
Bramall Lane (New) Ground	1862-1985	15	11	25	-	1	52
Southampton							
Antelope (Day's) Ground	1865-1884	2	-	2	-	-	4
Southampton							
County Ground, Northlands Road	1885-1994	8	15	7	-	-	30
Southend-on-Sea							
Southchurch Park, Kensington Road	1907-1978	3	2	2	-	-	7
Southport							
Trafalgar Road Ground, Birkdale	1964-1988	-	3	-	-	-	3
St.John's Wood							
Lord's Cricket Ground	1847-1993	49	53	52	-	-	154
Stourbridge							
Amblecote	1910-1932	-	1	1	-	-	2
Stroud							
Erinoid Ground	1960	-	1	-	-	-	1
Sydenham							
Crystal Palace Park	1869-1904	-	3	3	-	-	6
Swansea							
St.Helen's Ground, Mumbles Road	1927-1994	5	8	3	-	-	16

Ground	Years						
Taunton							
Athletic (County) Ground, St.James Street	1883-1987	15	20	10	-	-	45
Tonbridge							
Angel Ground	1892	1	-	-	-	-	1
Tunbridge Wells							
Higher Common Ground, Fir Tree Road	1856-1880	3	-	1	-	-	4
Tunbridge Wells							
Nevill Ground, Warwick Park	1978-1987	-	1	1	-	-	2
Uxbridge							
Uxbridge CC Ground, Park Road	1981-1986	1	-	1	-	-	2
West Brompton							
Lillie Bridge	1871	-	1	-	-	-	1
Westcliff-on-Sea							
Chalkwell Park, London Road	1938	-	-	1	-	-	1
Wells							
Rowden Road	1950	1	-	-	-	-	1
Weston-super-Mare							
Clarence Park, Clarence Road North	1926-1990	8	4	4	-	-	16
Worcester							
County Ground, New Road	1900-1993	12	24	11	-	-	47
Worksop							
Town Ground, Central Avenue	1973	-	1	-	-	-	1
Yeovil							
West Hendford	1935	1	-	-	-	-	1
TOTAL AWAY RESULTS		542	572	413	-	10	1537
TOTAL		1271	1227	737	6	24	3265

HOME GROUND RECORDS

THE OVAL, KENNINGTON

Record					
Highest Innings Total	Surrey 811		v Somerset	1899
	Against 863		- Lancashire	1990
Lowest Innings Total	Surrey 16		v Nottinghamshire	1880
	Against 20		- Kent	1870
Highest Individual innings	Surrey 357*	R Abel	v Somerset	1899
	Against 366	N.H.Fairbrother	- Lancashire	1990
Best Bowling in an innings	Surrey 10-45	T.Richardson	v Essex	1894
	Against 10-59	G.E.Burton	- Middlesex	1888
Best bowling in a match	Surrey 15-83	T.Richardson	v Warwickshire	1898
	Against 15-57	W.P.Howell	- Australians	1899
Highest Match Aggregate	1650-19 wkts		v Lancashire	1990
Lowest Match Aggregate	157-22 wkts		v Worcestershire	1954

Best Wickets Partnerships - Surrey:-

Wkt	Runs	Partners	Opponents	Year
1st	428	J.B.Hobbs & A.Sandham	v Oxford University	1926
2nd	371	J.B.Hobbs & E.G.Hayes	v Hampshire	1909
3rd	306	R.Abel & F.C.Holland	v Cambridge University	1895
4th	448	R.Abel & T.W.Hayward	v Yorkshire	1899
5th	308	J.N.Crawford & F.C.Holland	v Somerset	1908
6th	298	A.Sandham & H.S.Harrison	v Sussex	1913
7th	262	C.J.Richards & K.T.Medlycott	v Kent	1987
8th	205	I.A.Greig & M.P.Bicknell	v Lancashire	1990
9th	168	E.R.T.Holmes & E.W.J.Brooks	v Hampshire	1936
10th	133*	A.Sandham & W.J.Abel	v Middlesex	1919

Best Wicket Partnerships - Opponents:-

1st	377*	N.F.Horner & K.Ibadulla	- Warwickshire	1960
2nd	325	G.Brann & K.S.Ranjitsinhji	- Sussex	1899
3rd	364	M.A.Atherton & N.H.Fairbrother	- Lancashire	1990
4th	314	Salim Malik & N.Hussain	- Essex	1991
5th	340	E.Wainwright & G.H.Hirst	- Yorkshire	1899
6th	376	R.Subba Row & A.Lightfoot	- Northamptonshire	1958
7th	257	J.T.Morgan & F.R.Brown	- Cambridge University	1930
8th	165	S.Haigh & Lord Hawke	- Yorkshire	1902
9th	149	F.S.Lucas & J.Phillips	- Middlesex	1894
10th	249	C.T.Sarwate & S.N.Banerjee	- Indians	1946

WOODBRIDGE ROAD, GUILDFORD

Highest Innings Total	Surrey	504		v Hampshire	1948
	Against	446-7d		- Worcestershire	1979
Lowest Innings Total	Surrey	76		v Kent	1992
	Against	48		- Hampshire	1946
Highest Individual innings	Surrey	172	T.H.Barling	v Hampshire	1946
	Against	203	A.J.Moles	- Warwickshire	1994
Best Bowling in an innings	Surrey	9-77	G.A.R.Lock	v Oxford University	1960
	Against	7-34	D.Shackleton	- Hampshire	1958
Best bowling in a match	Surrey	12-148	G.A.R.Lock	v Oxford University	1960
	Against	9-125	A.C.S.Pigott	- Sussex	1987
Highest Match Aggregate	1356-26 wkts			v Glamorgan	1982
Lowest Match Aggregate	382-22 wkts			v Hampshire	1954

Best Wickets Partnerships - Surrey:-

1st	256	R.E.C.Pratt & M.J.Stewart	v Cambridge University	1956
2nd	185	A.R.Butcher & A.J.Stewart	v Worcestershire	1983
3rd	205	J.H.Edrich & R.D.V.Knight	v Gloucestershire	1978
4th	162	B.Constable & R.A.E.Tindall	v Sussex	1961
5th	155	J.F.Parker & E.W.Whitfield	v Hampshire	1938
6th	145*	G.P.Howarth & D.J.Thomas	v Glamorgan	1982
7th	99	M.J.Stewart & A.Long	v Leicestershire	1969
8th	173	B.Constable & J.C.Laker	v Cambridge University	1949
9th	81	R.D.Jackman & P.I.Pocock	v Hampshire	1977
10th	68	R.D.Jackman & G.G.Arnold	v Hampshire	1977

Best Wicket Partnerships - Opponents:-

1st	161	D.S.Sheppard & K.P.A.Matthews	- Cambridge University	1951
2nd	160	V.P.Terry & M.C.J.Nicholas	- Hampshire	1988
3rd	190	D.A.Reeve & J.R.T.Barclay	- Sussex	1984
4th	201	R.C.Ontong & J.A.Hopkins	- Glamorgan	1982
5th	214	D.P.Ostler & T.L.Penney	- Warwickshire	1992
6th	106*	A.J.Moles & N.M.K.Smith	- Warwickshire	1994
		(Smith retired not out with the score on 106 - a further 25 were added by Moles and D.R.Brown)		
7th	148	J.Birkenshaw & B.Dudleston	- Leicestershire	1969
8th	73	J.M.Mills & P.B.Datta	- Cambridge University	1947
9th	110	G.Welch & D.R.Brown	- Warwickshire	1994
10th	51	R.E.East & J.K.Lever	- Essex	1968

SECTION 9 - RECORDS AGAINST EACH OPPONENT

RESULTS OF FIRST-CLASS MATCHES 1846-1994

		HOME						*AWAY*						*ALL*
	First Played	*W*	*D*	*L*	*T*	*A*	*Tot*	*W*	*D*	*L*	*T*	*A*	*Tot*	*Total*
Derbyshire	1883	35	24	5	-	1	65	30	19	12	-	1	62	127
Durham	1992	1	-	-	-	-	1	2	-	-	-	-	2	3
Essex	1894	33	36	15	-	3	87	34	31	21	-	-	86	173
Glamorgan	1923	18	22	6	-	-	46	17	18	11	-	-	46	92
Gloucestershire	1870	54	26	17	-	-	97	35	33	31	-	1	100	197
Hampshire	1865	40	34	7	-	2	83	35	28	19	-	-	82	165
Kent	1846	58	47	20	2	-	127	38	47	38	-	-	123	250
Lancashire	1866	33	38	22	1	2	96	24	44	31	-	2	101	197
Leicestershire	1894	32	29	8	-	1	70	31	29	8	-	2	70	140
Middlesex	1850	47	45	30	2	-	124	41	39	39	-	-	119	243
Northamptonshire	1905	20	21	9	-	1	51	23	18	10	-	-	51	102
Nottinghamshire	1851	43	48	25	-	-	116	33	38	42	-	-	113	229
Somerset	1883	45	21	9	-	-	75	29	27	19	-	-	75	150
Sussex	1849	61	45	18	-	-	124	54	49	21	-	1	125	249
Warwickshire	1894	34	27	11	-	1	73	20	38	13	-	2	73	146
Worcestershire	1900	28	22	6	-	-	56	13	28	13	-	-	54	110
Yorkshire	1851	37	48	31	-	1	117	29	32	53	-	1	115	232
MCC	1847	1	-	6	1	-	8	12	16	17	-	-	45	53
Cambridge University	1865	34	25	18	-	1	78	23	20	3	-	-	46	124
Oxford University	1864	29	24	13	-	-	66	12	9	4	-	-	25	91
Australians	1878	9	21	20	-	-	50	-	-	-	-	-	-	50
Indians	1911	3	6	3	-	-	12	-	-	-	-	-	-	12
New Zealanders	1927	2	6	2	-	-	10	-	-	-	-	-	-	10
Pakistanis	1954	-	4	3	-	-	7	-	-	-	-	-	-	7
South Africans	1901	3	8	5	-	-	16	-	-	-	-	-	-	16
Sri Lankans	1984	1	1	-	-	-	2	-	-	-	-	-	-	2
West Indians	1906	2	8	4	-	1	15	-	-	-	-	-	-	15
Zimbabweans	1985	-	2	-	-	-	2	-	-	-	-	-	-	2
Cambridgeshire	1857	3	1	1	-	-	5	1	1	1	-	-	3	8
Combined Services	1946	1	4	-	-	-	5	-	-	-	-	-	-	5
England	1848	6	6	4	-	-	16	1	1	1	-	-	3	19
Gentlemen of England	1905	3	1	-	-	-	4	-	-	-	-	-	-	4
Kent & Sussex	1858	1	1	-	-	-	2	2	-	-	-	-	2	4
London County	1900	3	1	1	-	-	5	-	3	2	-	-	5	10
Manchester	1857	-	-	-	-	-	-	-	-	1	-	-	1	1
North of England	1857	5	-	2	-	-	7	2	2	2	-	-	6	13
Philadelphians	1897	2	-	1	-	-	3	-	-	-	-	-	-	3
Rest of England	1955	-	-	2	-	-	2	1	-	-	-	-	1	3
Rhodesia	1959	-	-	-	-	-	-	-	1	1	-	-	2	2
Scotland	1913	2	1	-	-	-	3	-	1	-	-	-	1	4
South of England	1864	-	2	-	-	-	2	-	-	-	-	-	-	2
Total		729	655	324	6	14	1728	542	572	413	-	10	1537	3265

COUNTY MATCHES

SURREY v DERBYSHIRE

Home		P	W	L	D	T	A
Guildford	1939	1	-	1	-	-	-
The Oval	1883-1994	63	35	4	24	-	1
HOME TOTAL		64	35	5	24	-	1

Away		P	W	L	D	T	A
Burton-on-Trent (Ind Coope)	1970	1	-	-	1	-	-
Buxton	1964	1	-	-	1	-	-
Chesterfield	1898-1987	20	9	3	8	-	1
Derby	1883-1991	33	19	7	7	-	-
Glossop	1902	1	-	-	1	-	-
Ilkeston	1934-1993	5	2	2	1	-	-
AWAY TOTAL		61	30	12	19	-	1

	P	W	L	D	T	A
GRAND TOTAL	125	65	17	43	-	2

Highest Innings Total	Surrey:	611-9d		The Oval	1904
	Derbyshire:	438-9d		Ilkeston	1993
Lowest Innings Total	Surrey:	60		The Oval	1935
	Derbyshire:	42		The Oval	1887
Highest Individual Innings	Surrey:	294*	D.M.Ward	The Oval	1994
	Derbyshire:	217	E.J.Barlow	Ilkeston	1976
Best Bowling in an innings	Surrey:	8-16	R.Harman	Ilkeston	1968
	Derbyshire:	8-50	C.Gladwin	The Oval	1953
Best Bowling in a match	Surrey:	14-113	R.Harman	Ilkeston	1968
	Derbyshire:	13-107	C.Gladwin	The Oval	1956

Highest Wicket Partnerships - for Surrey:-

1st	364	R.Abel & D.L.A.Jephson	The Oval	1900
2nd	144	T.W.Hayward & E.G.Hayes	The Oval	1911
3rd	301	G.P.Thorpe & D.M.Ward	The Oval	1994
4th	156	H.S.Squires & J.F.Parker	Derby	1937
5th	250	T.W.Hayward & D.L.A.Jephson	The Oval	1901
6th	177	R.Henderson & R.Abel	The Oval	1887
7th	179	F.C.Holland & K.J.Key	Derby	1897
8th	109	G.S.Clinton & M.A.Feltham	The Oval	1984
9th	99	E.G.Goatly & H.Strudwick	The Oval	1911
10th	93	C.J.Richards & P.I.Pocock	Chesterfield	1984

Highest Wicket Partnerships - for Derbyshire:-

1st	192	P.D.Bowler & J.E.Morris	Ilkeston	1993
2nd	198	K.J.Barnett & A.Hill	The Oval	1983
3rd	196	P.N.Kirsten & J.H.Hampshire	Derby	1982
4th	123	A.Hill & K.J.Barnett	The Oval	1979
5th	114	D.Smith & T.S.Worthington	The Oval	1934
6th	136	D.Smith & N.M.Ford	The Oval	1934
7th	102	P.G.Newman & A.E.Warner	Derby	1985
8th	95	A.H.J.Cochrane & G.G.Walker	The Oval	1884
9th	80	W.Evershed & J.Marlow	The Oval	1883
10th	68	S.H.Wood & W.Bestwick	The Oval	1900

SURREY v DURHAM

Home		P	W	L	D	T	A	Away		P	W	L	D	T	A
The Oval	1993	1	1	-	-	-	-	Darlington	1994	1	1	-	-	-	-
HOME TOTAL		1	1	-	-	-	-	Durham Univ	1992	1	1	-	-	-	-
								AWAY TOTAL		2	2	-	-	-	-
GRAND TOTAL		3	3	-	-	-	-								

Highest Innings Total	Surrey:	538-6d		Darlington	1994
	Durham:	357		Durham Univ	1992
Lowest Innings Total	Surrey:	236		Darlington	1994
	Durham:	120		The Oval	1993
Highest Individual innings	Surrey:	190	D.J.Bicknell	Darlington	1994
	Durham:	108	C.W.Scott	Darlington	1994
Best Bowling in an innings	Surrey:	6-30	J.E.Benjamin	Durham Univ	1992
	Durham:	5-90	P.Bainbridge	The Oval	1993
Best Bowling in a match	Surrey:	9-128	J.E.Benjamin	Durham Univ	1992
	Durham:	7-163	S.J.E.Brown	Darlington	1994

Highest Wicket Partnerships - for Surrey:-

1st	165	D.J.Bicknell & P.D.Atkins	The Oval	1993
2nd	96	D.J.Bicknell & G.P.Thorpe	Darlington	1994
3rd	99	D.J.Bicknell & G.P.Thorpe	Durham Univ	1992
4th	222	D.J.Bicknell & A.D.Brown	Darlington	1994
5th	119	A.D.Brown & P.D.Atkins	Durham Univ	1992
6th	70	A.D.Brown & R.E.Bryson	Durham Univ	1992
7th	83	A.D.Brown & N.F.Sargeant	Durham Univ	1992
8th	64	G.J.Kersey & J.Boiling	Darlington	1994
9th	40	N.F.Sargeant & J.Boiling	Durham Univ	1992
10th	34*	A.D.Brown & A.J.Murphy	The Oval	1993

Highest Wicket Partnerships - for Durham:-

1st	37	W.Larkins & M.Saxelby	Darlington	1994
2nd	40	W.Larkins & I.T.Botham	Durham Univ	1992
3rd	38	I.T.Botham & P.Bainbridge	Durham Univ	1992
4th	69	S.Hutton & I.Smith	Durham Univ	1992
5th	89	I.T.Botham & I.Smith	Durham Univ	1992
6th	26	J.I.Longley & A.C.Cummins	Darlington	1994
7th	87	J.I.Longley & C.W.Scott	Darlington	1994
8th	18	S.M.McEwan & C.W.Scott	Durham Univ	1992
9th	88	C.W.Scott & D.A.Graveney	Darlington	1994
10th	70	D.A.Graveney & S.J.E.Brown	Durham Univ	1992

SURREY v ESSEX

Home		P	W	L	D	T	A
Guildford	1968	1	-	-	1	-	-
The Oval	1894-1993	83	33	15	35	-	3
HOME TOTAL		84	33	15	36	-	3

Away		P	W	L	D	T	A
Brentwood	1934-1960	4	1	1	2	-	-
Chelmsford	1937-1991	18	2	7	9	-	-
Clacton-on-Sea	1935-1963	4	1	2	1	-	-
Colchester (Castle Park)	1939-1994	5	1	2	2	-	-
Colchester (Garrison)	1970	1	-	-	1	-	-
Ilford	1948-1974	7	2	1	4	-	-
Leyton	1894-1969	37	23	5	9	-	-
Romford	1959-1968	2	1	-	1	-	-
Southend-on-Sea	1907-1978	7	3	2	2	-	-
Westcliff-on-Sea	1938	1	-	1	-	-	-
AWAY TOTAL		86	34	21	31	-	-

	P	W	L	D	T	A
GRAND TOTAL	170	67	36	67	-	3

Highest Innings Total	Surrey:	613-6d		The Oval	1990
	Essex:	616-5d		The Oval	1904
Lowest Innings Total	Surrey:	14		Chelmsford	1983
	Essex:	37		Leyton	1899
Highest Individual innings	Surrey:	290*	A.Ducat	Leyton	1921
	Essex:	248	J.O'Connor	Brentwood	1934
Best Bowling in an innings	Surrey:	10-45	T.Richardson	The Oval	1894
	Essex:	9-93	F.G.Bull	The Oval	1897
Best Bowling in a match	Surrey:	15-95	T.Richardson	The Oval	1894
	Essex:	13-113	T.P.B.Smith	The Oval	1950

Highest Wicket Partnerships - for Surrey:-

1st	216	J.B.Hobbs & A.Sandham	Leyton	1925
2nd	316*	M.J.Stewart & K.F.Barrington	The Oval	1962
3rd	317	A.Ducat & T.F.Shepherd	Leyton	1928
4th	256	R.Abel & F.C.Holland	The Oval	1895
5th	128	R.A.E.Tindall & B.Constable	Clacton-on-Sea	1963
6th	151	S.J.Storey & D.Gibson	Chelmsford	1967
7th	166	A.Ducat & H.Strudwick	Leyton	1921
8th	137	A.Sandham & J.W.Hitch	Leyton	1923
9th	106	A.Sandham & H.A.Peach	Leyton	1923
10th	173	A.Ducat & A.Sandham	Leyton	1921

Highest Wicket Partnerships - for Essex:-

1st	270	A.V.Avery & T.C.Dodds	The Oval	1946
2nd	206	J.A.Cutmore & J.O'Connor	The Oval	1929
3rd	328	H.A.Carpenter & C.P.McGahey	The Oval	1904
4th	314	Salim Malik & N.Hussain	The Oval	1991
5th	287	J.O'Connor & C.T.Ashton	Brentwood	1934
6th	194	N.Hussain & J.J.B.Lewis	The Oval	1990
7th	124	J.W.H.T.Douglas & C.P.McGahey	Leyton	1910
8th	87	K.D.Boyce & R.N.S.Hobbs	The Oval	1973
9th	123	L.C.Eastman & A.B.Hipkin	Southend-on-Sea	1924
10th	122	W.Reeves & G.M.Louden	Leyton	1919

SURREY v GLAMORGAN

Home		P	W	L	D	T	A
Guildford	1982	1	1	-	-	-	-
The Oval	1924-1993	45	17	6	22	-	-
HOME TOTAL		46	18	6	22	-	-

Away		P	W	L	D	T	A
Cardiff (Arms Park)	1923-1966	16	7	6	3	-	-
Cardiff (Sophia Gardens)	1970-1990	7	4	-	3	-	-
Ebbw Vale	1961	1	-	1	-	-	-
Llanelli	1952-1962	2	-	-	2	-	-
Neath	1937-1992	3	1	1	1	-	-
Pontypridd	1954	1	-	-	1	-	-
Swansea	1927-1994	16	5	3	8	-	-
AWAY TOTAL		46	17	11	18	-	-

	P	W	L	D	T	A
GRAND TOTAL	92	35	17	40	-	-

Highest Innings Total	Surrey:	560-8d		The Oval	1947
	Glamorgan:	550-6d		The Oval	1936
Lowest Innings Total	Surrey:	50		Cardiff (AP)	1948
	Glamorgan:	31		The Oval	1957
Highest Individual innings	Surrey:	248*	A.Sandham	Cardiff (AP)	1928
	Glamorgan:	280*	R.G.Duckfield	The Oval	1936
Best Bowling in an innings	Surrey:	9-57	P.I.Pocock	Cardiff (SG)	1979
	Glamorgan:	9-97	B.L.Muncer	Cardiff (AP)	1947
Best Bowling in a match	Surrey:	14-69	A.V.Bedser	Cardiff (AP)	1956
	Glamorgan:	12-84	J.C.Clay	The Oval	1934

Highest Wicket Partnerships - for Surrey:-

1st	212	J.H.Edrich & A.R.Butcher	Cardiff (SG)	1977
2nd	344	A.Sandham & R.J.Gregory	The Oval	1937
3rd	244	A.Sandham & T.H.Barling	Cardiff (AP)	1936
4th	211	D.M.Ward & G.P.Thorpe	Neath	1992
5th	183	A.Sandham & R.J.Gregory	Cardiff (AP)	1928
6th	183	A.J.W.McIntyre & E.R.T.Holmes	The Oval	1947
7th	127	M.A.Lynch & G.Monkhouse	Swansea	1983
8th	147	C.J.Richards & S.T.Clarke	Swansea	1981
9th	161	G.J.Whittaker & W.S.Surridge	The Oval	1951
10th	54	J.C.Laker & A.V.Bedser	Swansea	1955

Highest Wicket Partnerships - for Glamorgan:-

1st	233	D.E.Davies & W.G.A.Parkhouse	Swansea	1950
2nd	164	A.Jones & R.C.Ontong	The Oval	1978
3rd	111	R.C.Ontong & S.P.Henderson	Swansea	1983
4th	217	W.E.Bates & J.J.Hills	The Oval	1930
5th	172	A.H.Dyson & V.G.J.Jenkins	The Oval	1932
6th	186	R.G.Duckfield & D.Davies	The Oval	1936
7th	171	M.J.Llewellyn & M.A.Nash	The Oval	1976
8th	116	P.M.Walker & D.G.L.Evans	Swansea	1958
9th	74	M.A.Nash & A.E.Cordle	The Oval	1978
10th	120	G.Lavis & J.Mercer	The Oval	1934

SURREY v GLOUCESTERSHIRE

Home		P	W	L	D	T	A
Guildford	1978-1993	4	2	1	1	-	-
The Oval	1894-1990	93	52	16	25	-	-
HOME TOTAL		97	54	17	26	-	-

Away		P	W	L	D	T	A
Bristol (Durdham)	1870	1	-	1	-	-	-
Bristol (Clifton)	1871-1898	16	2	7	7	-	-
Bristol (Packer's)	1922	1	-	-	1	-	-
Bristol (Phoenix)	1890-1992	32	11	10	11	-	-
Cheltenham (College)	1872-1990	34	14	11	9	-	1
Cirencester	1879	1	-	-	1	-	-
Gloucester (Spa)	1902	1	-	-	1	-	-
Gloucester (Wagon Works)	1925-1970	9	6	2	1	-	-
Gloucester (Kings)	1994	1	1	-	-	-	-
Lydney	1963	1	-	-	1	-	-
Moreton-in-Marsh	1887	1	1	-	-	-	-
Stroud	1960	1	-	-	1	-	-
AWAY TOTAL		99	35	31	33	-	1

	P	W	L	D	T	A
GRAND TOTAL	196	89	48	59	-	1

Highest Innings Total	Surrey:	579		Bristol	1901
	Glos:	544		The Oval	1928
Lowest Innings Total	Surrey:	27		Cheltenham	1874
	Glos:	39		Clifton	1888
Highest Individual innings	Surrey:	277*	T.F.Shepherd	The Oval	1927
	Glos:	216*	Zaheer Abbas	The Oval	1976
Best Bowling in an innings	Surrey:	9-70	D.A.D.Sydenham	The Oval	1964
	Glos:	9-63	E.G.Dennett	Bristol	1913
Best Bowling in a match	Surrey:	15-184	W.H.Lockwood	Cheltenham	1899
	Glos:	15-91	C.W.L Parker	Cheltenham	1930

Highest Wicket Partnerships - for Surrey:-

1st	233	J.B.Hobbs & A.Sandham	The Oval	1922
2nd	203*	M.J.Edwards & Younis Ahmed	The Oval	1969
3rd	205	J.H.Edrich & R.D.V.Knight	Guildford	1978
4th	289	A.Ducat & T.F.Shepherd	The Oval	1927
5th	256*	R.Abel & D.L.A.Jephson	The Oval	1898
6th	135	Younis Ahmed & Intikhab Alam	The Oval	1973
7th	166	W.H.Lockwood & W.Brockwell	The Oval	1894
8th	198	K.F.Barrington & J.C.Laker	The Oval	1954
9th	96	W.E.Davis & H.Strudwick	The Oval	1910
10th	105	W.Brockwell & T.Richardson	The Oval	1893

Highest Wicket Partnerships - for Gloucestershire:-

1st	219	Sadiq Mohammad & A.W.Stovold	Bristol	1975
2nd	234	W.G.Grace & F.Townsend	The Oval	1870
3rd	255*	W.G.Grace & E.M.Knapp	Clifton	1873
4th	196	A.W.Stovold & M.J.Procter	Guildford	1978
5th	145	J.H.Brain & J.R.Painter	Clifton	1884
6th	285	W.R.Hammond & B.H.Lyon	The Oval	1928
7th	112	G.F.Grace & F.G.Monkland	Clifton	1875
8th	111	C.I.Monks & V.Hopkins	Bristol	1937
9th	111	K.M.Curran & T.M.Alderman	Cheltenham	1988
10th	106	H.Wrathall & J.H.Board	The Oval	1899

SURREY v HAMPSHIRE

Home		P	W	L	D	T	A	Away		P	W	L	D	T	A
Kingston	1946	1	-	-	1	-	-	Aldershot	1905-1906	2	2	-	-	-	-
Guildford	1938-1988	15	9	1	5	-	-	Basingstoke	1935-1989	5	1	2	2	-	-
The Oval	1865-1993	65	31	6	28	-	2	Bournemouth	1900-1991	20	10	3	7	-	-
HOME TOTAL		81	40	7	34	-	2	Portsmouth	1898-1982	21	12	5	4	-	-
								Southampton (Antelope Ground)	1865-1884	4	2	2	-	-	-
								Southampton (Northlands Road)	1885-1994	30	8	7	15	-	-
								AWAY TOTAL		82	35	19	28	-	-
GRAND TOTAL		163	75	26	62	-	2								

Highest Innings Total	Surrey:	742		The Oval	1909
	Hampshire:	603-7d		Southampton	1994
Lowest Innings Total	Surrey:	64		Basingstoke	1986
	Hampshire:	32		The Oval	1885
Highest Individual innings	Surrey:	276	E.G.Hayes	The Oval	1909
	Hampshire:	221	T.C.Middleton	Southampton	1992
Best Bowling in an innings	Surrey:	9-31	W.C.Smith	The Oval	1904
	Hampshire:	8-85	C.J.Knott	Portsmouth	1939
Best Bowling in a match	Surrey:	15-155	T.Richardson	The Oval	1895
	Hampshire:	12-163	A.R.Wassell	Bournemouth	1961

Highest Wicket Partnerships - for Surrey:-

1st	379	R.Abel & W.Brockwell	The Oval	1897
2nd	371	J.B.Hobbs & E.G.Hayes	The Oval	1909
3rd	353	A.Ducat & E.G.Hayes	Southampton	1919
4th	238	H.S.Squires & J.F.Parker	Bournemouth	1948
5th	159	B.Constable & G.J.Whittaker	Southampton	1951
6th	166	P.G.H.Fender & W.J.Abel	The Oval	1922
7th	145	H.T.Barling & P.G.H.Fender	Southampton	1933
8th	171	A.J.W.McIntyre & E.R.T.Holmes	Guildford	1948
9th	168	E.R.T.Holmes & E.W.J.Brooks	The Oval	1936
10th	119*	E.A.Watts & J.V.Daley	Bournemouth	1936

Highest Wicket Partnerships - for Hampshire:-

1st	267	V.P.Terry & T.C.Middleton	Southampton	1992
2nd	180	R.E.Marshall & H.Horton	The Oval	1961
3rd	209	D.R.Turner & R.M.C.Gilliat	The Oval	1969
4th	160	C.P.Mead & W.G.L.F.Lowndes	The Oval	1934
5th	164	E.A.English & A.S.Webb	The Oval	1898
6th	184	M.C.J.Nicholas & A.N.Aymes	Southampton	1994
7th	122	C.P.Mead & W.L.C.Creese	Bournemouth	1931
8th	121	A.E.Pothecary & G.S.Boyes	The Oval	1935
9th	230	D.A.Livingstone & A.T.Castell	Southampton	1962
10th	73	W.L.Budd & G.E.M.Heath	The Oval	1937

SURREY v KENT

Home		P	W	L	D	T	A
Guildford	1988-1992	3	-	1	2	-	-
Lord's†	1914	1	1	-	-	-	-
The Oval	1846-1994	123	57	19	45	2	-
HOME TOTAL		127	58	20	47	2	-

Away		P	W	L	D	T	A
Aylesford	1846-1847	2	-	1	1	-	-
Beckenham	1886-1905	5	4	1	-	-	-
Blackheath	1889-1970	55	16	16	23	-	-
Canterbury (St.Lawrence)	1862-1993	18	4	6	8	-	-
Catford	1893-1896	4	1	3	-	-	-
Crystal Palace	1896	1	-	1	-	-	-
Dartford	1986	1	-	-	1	-	-
Folkestone	1975-1981	3	1	-	2	-	-
Gravesend	1864-1964	7	4	2	1	-	-
Maidstone	1861-1982	20	4	6	10	-	-
Tonbridge	1892	1	1	-	-	-	-
Tunbridge Wells (Common)	1856-1880	4	3	1	-	-	-
Tunbridge Wells (Nevill)	1978-1987	2	-	1	1	-	-
AWAY TOTAL		123	38	38	47	-	-

	P	W	L	D	T	A
GRAND TOTAL	250	96	58	94	2	-

† transferred from The Oval which had been requisitioned by the military

Highest Innings Total	Surrey:	648		Canterbury	1990
	Kent:	579-8d		The Oval	1935
Lowest Innings Total	Surrey:	44		Maidstone	1884
	Kent:	20		The Oval	1870
Highest Individual innings	Surrey:	263	D.M.Ward	Canterbury	1990
	Kent:	229	F.E.Woolley	The Oval	1935
Best Bowling in an innings	Surrey:	10-54	G.A.R.Lock	Blackheath	1956
	Kent:	9-32	D.L.Underwood	The Oval	1978
Best Bowling in a match	Surrey:	16-83	G.A.R.Lock	Blackheath	1956
	Kent:	14-?	W.R.Hillyer	Aylesford	1847

Highest Wicket Partnerships - for Surrey:-

1st	270*	R.Abel & W.Brockwell	The Oval	1900
2nd	241	K.J.Key & W.W.Read	The Oval	1887
3rd	413	D.J.Bicknell & D.M.Ward	Canterbury	1990
4th	250	T.H.Clark & R.E.C.Pratt	The Oval	1953
5th	252	A.J.Stewart & M.A.Lynch	Canterbury	1985
6th	162	M.Howell & P.G.H.Fender	The Oval	1922
7th	262	C.J.Richards & K.T.Medlycott	The Oval	1987
8th	182	W.E.Roller & R.Abel	The Oval	1883
9th	59	A.J.W.McIntyre & G.A.R.Lock	Blackheath	1949
10th	104	F.R.Brown & J.F.Parker	Blackheath	1932

Highest Wicket Partnerships - for Kent:-

1st	212	M.R.Benson & N.R.Taylor	Dartford	1986
2nd	219	A.E.Fagg & F.E.Woolley	Blackheath	1934
3rd	239	H.T.W.Hardinge & L.E.G.Ames	Blackheath	1929
4th	248	W.L.Knowles & J.R.Mason	The Oval	1900
5th	202	H.T.W.Hardinge & L.P.Hedges	Blackheath	1921
6th	217	D.G.Aslett & C.S.Cowdrey	Canterbury	1985
7th	132	G.C.Collins & J.C.Hubble	Maidstone	1926
8th	143	E.G.Witherden & W.Murray-Wood	Blackheath	1953
9th	87	M.C.Kemp & A.Penn	Maidstone	1883
10th	141	J.R.Mason & C.Blythe	The Oval	1909

SURREY v LANCASHIRE

Home		P	W	L	D	T	A
The Oval	1866-1993	94	33	22	38	1	2
HOME TOTAL		94	33	22	38	1	2

Away		P	W	L	D	T	A
Blackpool	1978-1990	2	-	-	2	-	-
Liverpool (Wavertree)	1866	1	1	-	-	-	-
Liverpool (Aigburth)	1884-1905	4	2	1	1	-	-
Lytham St Anne's	1993	1	-	1	-	-	-
Manchester	1867-1994	88	21	29	38	-	2
Southport	1964-1988	3	-	-	3	-	-
AWAY TOTAL		99	24	31	44	-	2

		P	W	L	D	T	A
GRAND TOTAL		194	57	53	82	1	4

Highest Innings Total	Surrey:	707-9d		The Oval	1990
	Lancashire:	863		The Oval	1990
Lowest Innings Total	Surrey:	33		The Oval	1873
	Lancashire:	27		Manchester	1958
Highest Individual innings	Surrey:	315*	T.W.Hayward	The Oval	1898
	Lancashire:	366	N.H.Fairbrother	The Oval	1990
Best Bowling in an innings	Surrey:	9-130	G.Griffith	The Oval	1867
	Lancashire:	8-33	A.Mold	Manchester	1896
Best Bowling in a match	Surrey:	14-130	J.Southerton	The Oval	1868
	Lancashire:	12-82	W.Huddleston	Manchester	1907

Highest Wicket Records - for Surrey:-

1st	242	J.B.Hobbs & E.G.Hayes	The Oval	1911
2nd	299	A.Sandham & A.Ducat	Manchester	1928
3rd	305	W.E.Roller & W.W.Read	Manchester	1887
4th	218*	P.B.H.May & K.F.Barrington	The Oval	1955
5th	287	R.Abel & W.H.Lockwood	The Oval	1899
6th	116	W.J.Abel & P.G.H.Fender	The Oval	1923
7th	151	T.F.Shepherd & H.A.Peach	The Oval	1921
8th	205	I.A.Greig & M.P.Bicknell	The Oval	1990
9th	106	H.D.G.Leveson-Gower & H.Strudwick	Manchester	1908
10th	172	A.Needham & R.D.Jackman	Manchester	1982

Highest Wicket Records - for Lancashire:-

1st	208	F.B.Watson & C.Hallows	Manchester	1927
2nd	371	F.B.Watson & G.E.Tyldesley	Manchester	1928
3rd	364	M.A.Atherton & N.H.Fairbrother	The Oval	1990
4th	177	J.T.Tyldesley & G.E.Tyldesley	The Oval	1913
5th	230	J.Iddon & T.M.Halliday	The Oval	1928
6th	184	C.Hopwood & M.L.Taylor	Manchester	1931
7th	198	A.Eccles & J.I'Anson	Manchester	1902
8th	115	A.Eccles & J.Sharp	Manchester	1899
9th	83	J.Ricketts & E.Whittaker	The Oval	1867
10th	173	J.Briggs & R.Pilling	Liverpool	1885

SURREY v LEICESTERSHIRE

Home		P	W	L	D	T	A
Guildford	1949-1969	3	2	-	1	-	-
The Oval	1894-1994	66	30	8	28	-	1
HOME TOTAL		69	32	8	29	-	1

Away		P	W	L	D	T	A
Ashby-de-la-Zouch	1951-1963	2	-	1	1	-	1
Hinckley (Leicester Road)	1986	1	-	1	-	-	-
Leicester (Aylestone Road)	1901-1936	26	14	2	10	-	1
Leicester (Grace Road)	1894-1993	37	16	4	17	-	-
Loughborough (Brush Sports)	1953	1	-	-	1	-	-
Loughborough (Park Road)	1914	1	1	-	-	-	-
AWAY TOTAL		68	31	8	29	-	2

	P	W	L	D	T	A
GRAND TOTAL	137	63	16	58	-	3

Highest Innings Total	Surrey:	576		The Oval	1947
	Leics:	516-8d		The Oval	1929
Lowest Innings Total	Surrey:	35		Leicester (GR)	1894
	Leics:	35 (1st inns)		Leicester (GR)	1897
		35 (2nd inns)		Leicester (GR)	1897
Highest Individual innings	Surrey:	253	L.B.Fishlock	Leicester (GR)	1948
	Leics:	175*	M.Tompkin	The Oval	1951
Best Bowling in an innings	Surrey:	8-44	W.H.Lockwood	Leicester (GR)	1898
		8-44	J.W.Hitch	Leicester (AR)	1913
	Leics:	9-83	A.W Shipman	The Oval	1910
Best Bowling in a match	Surrey:	15-113	T.Richardson	The Oval	1896
	Leics:	12-178	W.E.Astill	Leicester (AR)	1929

Highest Wicket Partnerships - for Surrey:-

1st	208	T.W.Hayward & J.B.Hobbs	The Oval	1906
2nd	220	R.Abel & F.C.Holland	The Oval	1896
3rd	261	A.Ducat & T.F.Shepherd	The Oval	1926
4th	244	L.B.Fishlock & M.R.Barton	Leicester (GR)	1948
5th	196	R.Subba Row & E.A.Bedser	Loughborough	1953
6th	260	J.N.Crawford & Lord Dalmeny	The Oval	1905
7th	158	Younis Ahmed & R.D.Jackman	Leicester (GR)	1974
8th	139	A.J.W.McIntyre & J.C.Laker	The Oval	1958
9th	156	A.E.Street & F.E.Smith	Leicester (GR)	1895
10th	59	R.Swetman & A.V.Bedser	Leicester (GR)	1956

Highest Wicket Partnerships - for Leicestershire:-

1st	179	M.R.Hallam & W.Watson	The Oval	1959
2nd	239	C.J.B.Wood & H.Whitehead	The Oval	1911
3rd	236	M.Tompkin & C.H.Palmer	The Oval	1951
4th	143	W.Watson & J.van Geloven	Leicester (GR)	1959
5th	147	J.H.King & V.F.S.Crawford	The Oval	1909
6th	237*	R.W.Tolchard & B.J.Booth	Leicester (GR)	1971
7th	148	J.Birkenshaw & B.Dudleston	Guildford	1969
8th	150	G.Geary & T.E.Sidwell	The Oval	1926
9th	77	S.Coe & A.W.Shipman	Leicester (AR)	1923
10th	45	J.E.Walsh & T.J.Goodwin	The Oval	1950

SURREY v MIDDLESEX

Home		P	W	L	D	T	A
The Oval	1850-1994	124	47	30	45	2	-
HOME TOTAL		124	47	30	45	2	-

Away		P	W	L	D	T	A
Chelsea	1872-1876	5	3	2	-	-	-
Islington	1865-1868	4	1	2	1	-	-
Lord's	1847-1993	107	36	34	37	-	-
Uxbridge	1981-1986	2	1	1	-	-	-
West Brompton	1871	1	-	-	1	-	-
AWAY TOTAL		119	41	39	39	-	-

	P	W	L	D	T	A
GRAND TOTAL	243	88	69	84	2	-

Highest Innings Total	Surrey:	582-9d		The Oval	1919
	Middlesex:	568-9d		The Oval	1919
Lowest Innings Total	Surrey:	35		Islington	1868
	Middlesex:	25		The Oval	1885
Highest Individual innings	Surrey:	316*	J.B.Hobbs	Lord's	1926
	Middlesex:	235	D.C.S.Compton	Lord's	1946
Best Bowling in an innings	Surrey:	9-47	J.W.Sharpe	The Oval	1891
	Middlesex:	10-59	G.Burton	The Oval	1888
Best Bowling in a match	Surrey:	14-92	J.Southerton	The Oval	1877
	Middlesex:	14-97	J.A.Young	The Oval	1948

Highest Wicket Partnerships - for Surrey:-

1st	244	J.B.Hobbs & A.Sandham	The Oval	1923
2nd	161	W.A.Smith & G.R.J.Roope	The Oval	1968
3rd	297	J.H.Edrich & K.F.Barrington	The Oval	1967
4th	270	J.B.Hobbs & D.R.Jardine	Lord's	1926
5th	182	G.P.Howarth & G.R.J.Roope	The Oval	1974
6th	198	E.W.Whitfield & F.R.Brown	Lord's	1932
7th	180*	M.A.Lynch & C.J.Richards	The Oval	1985
8th	157	W.Mortlock & J.W.Noble	The Oval	1866
9th	155	F.R.Brown & M.J.C.Allom	The Oval	1932
10th	133*	A.Sandham & W.J.Abel	The Oval	1919

Highest Wicket Partnerships - for Middlesex:-

1st	232	P.F.Warner & J.Douglas	The Oval	1907
2nd	319	H.W.Lee & G.O.B.Allen	The Oval	1929
3rd	296	W.J.Edrich & D.C.S.Compton	Lord's	1946
4th	304	D.C.S.Compton & F.G.Mann	Lord's	1947
5th	285	E.H.Hendren & J.H.Human	The Oval	1935
6th	161	T.Hearne & V.E.Walker	Islington	1866
7th	179*	C.T.Radley & J.E.Emburey	The Oval	1979
8th	119	E.H.Hendren & J.M.Sims	Lord's	1935
9th	149	F.S.Lucas & J.Phillips	The Oval	1894
10th	130	G.W.Beldam & C.Headlam	Lord's	1902

SURREY v NORTHAMPTONSHIRE

Home		P	W	L	D	T	A	Away		P	W	L	D	T	A
Guildford	1955-1975	3	3	-	-	-	-	Kettering	1929-1971	5	4	1	-	-	-
The Oval	1905-1994	47	17	9	21	-	1	Northampton	1906-1993	44	18	9	17	-	-
HOME TOTAL		50	20	9	21	-	1	Peterborough	1947	1	-	-	1	-	-
								Rushden	1952	1	1	-	-	-	-
								AWAY TOTAL		51	23	10	18	-	-
GRAND TOTAL		101	43	19	39	-	1								

Highest Innings Total	Surrey:	619-5d		Northampton	1920
	Northants:	529-9		The Oval	1958
Lowest Innings Total	Surrey:	58		The Oval	1913
	Northants:	32		The Oval	1905
Highest Individual innings	Surrey:	292*	A.Sandham	The Oval	1921
	Northants:	300	R.Subba Row	The Oval	1958
Best Bowling in an innings	Surrey:	8-13	W.C.Smith	The Oval	1910
	Northants:	8-60	F.H.Tyson	The Oval	1957
Best Bowling in a match	Surrey:	14-29	W.C.Smith	The Oval	1910
	Northants:	13-112	F.H.Tyson	The Oval	1957

Highest Wicket Partnerships - for Surrey:-

1st	321	D.J.Bicknell & G.S.Clinton	The Oval	1990
2nd	247	A.Sandham & A.Ducat	The Oval	1921
3rd	167	M.J.Stewart & K.F.Barrington	Northampton	1967
4th	232*	A.Ducat & H.O.Bloomfield	Northampton	1921
5th	288	H.A.Peach & A.Ducat	Northampton	1920
6th	171*	H.A.Peach & P.G.H.Fender	Northampton	1920
7th	142	A.J.W.McIntyre & A.V.Bedser	The Oval	1950
8th	87	D.J.Thomas & G.Monkhouse	The Oval	1983
9th	70	J.F.Parker & E.W.J.Brooks	The Oval	1932
10th	138	R.I.Jefferson & D.A.D.Sydenham	Northampton	1963

Highest Wicket Partnerships - for Northamptonshire:-

1st	139	D.Brookes & C.P.Davis	The Oval	1946
2nd	154	G.Cook & D.S.Steele	The Oval	1977
3rd	234	D.S.Steele & Mushtaq Mohammad	Northampton	1972
4th	144*	D.J.Capel & R.G.Williams	The Oval	1988
5th	102	D.J.Capel & K.M.Curran	The Oval	1992
6th	376	R.Subba Row & A.Lightfoot	The Oval	1958
7th	135	A.J.Lamb & K.M.Curran	Northampton	1991
8th	98	J.E.Timms & A.D.G.Matthews	Kettering	1929
9th	111	W.Barron & K.Fiddling	The Oval	1947
10th	81	A.D.G.Matthews & A.E.Thomas	The Oval	1928

SURREY v NOTTINGHAMSHIRE

Home		P	W	L	D	T	A	Away	Played	P	W	L	D	T	A
Godalming	1854	1	1	-	-	-	-	Nottingham	1852-1994	112	33	42	37	-	-
Guildford	1974-1989	2	1	-	1	-	-	Worksop	1973	1	-	-	1	-	-
The Oval	1851-1993	113	41	25	47	-	-	AWAY TOTAL		113	33	42	38	-	-
HOME TOTAL		116	43	25	48	-	-								
GRAND TOTAL		229	76	67	86	-	-								

Highest Innings Total	Surrey:	706-4d		Nottingham	1947
	Notts:	548-9		The Oval	1898
Lowest Innings Total	Surrey:	16		The Oval	1880
	Notts:	40		The Oval	1955
Highest Individual innings	Surrey:	235*	D.J.Bicknell	Nottingham	1994
	Notts:	236*	W.Gunn	The Oval	1898
Best Bowling in an innings	Surrey:	8-37	W.Martingell	The Oval	1853
	Notts:	9-33	M.McIntyre	The Oval	1872
Best Bowling in a match	Surrey:	14-145	T.Richardson	Nottingham	1893
	Notts:	15-73	J.Jackson	The Oval	1860

Highest Wicket Records - for Surrey:-

1st	230	A.R.Butcher & A.Needham	The Oval	1985
		(233 runs were added for this wicket, G.S.Clinton retired injured when the score was 3)		
2nd	281	A.Sandham & A.Ducat	Nottingham	1930
3rd	279	D.G.W.Fletcher & H.S.Squires	Nottingham	1947
4th	224	M.A.Lynch & T.E.Jesty	The Oval	1986
5th	247*	J.F.Parker & E.R.T.Holmes	Nottingham	1947
6th	183	A.Ducat & E.G.Goatly	Nottingham	1914
7th	130	V.F.S.Crawford & E.M.Dowson	The Oval	1901
8th	103	T.W.Hayward & D.L.A.Jephson	The Oval	1899
9th	109	E.W.J.Brooks & P.G.H.Fender	Nottingham	1933
10th	79	K.J.Key & T.Richardson	Nottingham	1895

Highest Wicket Records - for Nottinghamshire:-

1st	159	R.T.Simpson & J.D.Clay	The Oval	1953
2nd	289	A.Shrewsbury & W.Barnes	The Oval	1882
3rd	194	M.J.Harris & M.J.Smedley	Worksop	1973
4th	216*	J.Hardstaff & G.V.Gunn	Nottingham	1939
5th	191	N.W.Hill & C.J.Poole	Nottingham	1960
6th	200	W.R.D.Payton & S.J.Staples	The Oval	1923
7th	204	M.J.Smedley & R.A.White	The Oval	1967
8th	167	A.Staples & F.Barratt	Nottingham	1928
9th	147	J.Selby & E.Mills	The Oval	1883
10th	84	W.R.D.Payton & T.G.Wass	Nottingham	1909

SURREY v SOMERSET

Home		P	W	L	D	T	A
Guildford	1976-1989	2	1	-	1	-	-
The Oval	1883-1993	73	44	9	20	-	-
HOME TOTAL		75	45	9	21	-	-

Away	Played	P	W	L	D	T	A
Bath	1914-1994	12	4	5	3	-	-
Taunton	1883-1987	45	15	10	20	-	-
Wells	1950	1	1	-	-	-	-
Weston-super-Mare	1926-1990	16	8	4	4	-	-
Yeovil	1935	1	1	-	-	-	-
AWAY TOTAL		75	29	19	27	-	-

	P	W	L	D	T	A
GRAND TOTAL	150	74	28	48	-	-

Highest Innings Total	Surrey:	811		The Oval	1899
	Somerset:	507-6d		Weston-s-M	1946
Lowest Innings Total	Surrey:	35		The Oval	1937
	Somerset:	36		Weston-s-M	1955
Highest Individual innings	Surrey:	357*	R.Abel	The Oval	1899
	Somerset:	206	M.N.Lathwell	Bath	1994
Best Bowling in an innings	Surrey:	10-43	T.Rushby	Taunton	1921
	Somerset:	10-49	E.J.Tyler	Taunton	1895
Best Bowling in a match	Surrey:	13-105	E.Barratt	The Oval	1883
	Somerset:	13-91	E.J.Tyler	Taunton	1895

Highest Wicket Records - for Surrey:-

1st	264	J.B.Hobbs & A.Sandham	Taunton	1932
2nd	170	R.J.Gregory & H.S.Squires	Weston-s-Mare	1934
3rd	180	A.Ducat & T.F.Shepherd	The Oval	1925
4th	334	R.Abel & T.W.Hayward	The Oval	1899
5th	308	J.N.Crawford & F.C.Holland	The Oval	1908
6th	211	R.Abel & V.F.S.Crawford	The Oval	1899
7th	180	A.Ducat & J.W.Hitch	Taunton	1911
8th	197	H.T.Barling & A.V.Bedser	Taunton	1947
9th	146	W.Brockwell & H.Wood	The Oval	1895
10th	83	E.W.J.Brooks & A.R.Gover	Yeovil	1935

Highest Wicket Records - for Somerset:-

1st	219	J.W.Lee & F.S.Lee	Weston-s-Mare	1934
2nd	157	R.T.Virgin & S.G.Wilkinson	The Oval	1972
3rd	297	P.B.Wight & W.E.Alley	Taunton	1961
4th	251	I.V.A.Richards & P.M.Roebuck	Weston-s-Mare	1977
5th	121	S.M.J.Woods & H.Martyn	The Oval	1904
6th	128	R.J.Turner & G.D.Rose	The Oval	1992
7th	127	S.M.J.Woods & D.L.Evans	The Oval	1894
8th	106	J.Lawrence & H.W.Stephenson	The Oval	1949
9th	126	V.T.Hill & E.J.Tyler	Taunton	1896
10th	139	P.R.Johnson & R.C.Robertson-Glasgow	The Oval	1926

SURREY v SUSSEX

Home		P	W	L	D	T	A	Away		P	W	L	D	T	A
Guildford	1947-1990	12	5	2	5	-	-	Arundel	1991	1	-	-	1	-	-
The Oval	1849-1994	112	56	16	40	-	-	Brighton (Brunswick)	1851-1871	17	7	4	6	-	-
HOME TOTAL		124	61	18	45	-	-	Eastbourne	1905-1972	5	1	-	4	-	-
								Hastings	1902-1956	11	4	3	4	-	-
								Horsham	1909-1985	11	4	3	4	-	-
								Hove	1872-1993	78	38	10	30	-	1
								Petworth	1849	1	-	1	-	-	-
								AWAY TOTAL		124	54	21	49	-	1
GRAND TOTAL		248	115	39	94	-	1								

Highest Innings Total	Surrey:	698		The Oval	1888
	Sussex:	705-8d		Hastings	1902
Lowest Innings Total	Surrey:	51		Petworth	1849
	Sussex:	31		The Oval	1857
Highest Individual innings	Surrey:	204	W.E.Roller	The Oval	1885
	Sussex:	234*	K.S.Ranjitsinhji	Hastings	1902
Best Bowling in an innings	Surrey:	9-49	T.Richardson	The Oval	1895
	Sussex:	9-105	G.Wells	Brighton	1860
Best Bowling in a match	Surrey:	15-98	G.A.Lohmann	Hove	1889
	Sussex:	15-297	C.H.Ellis	Brighton	1863

Highest Wicket Partnerships - for Surrey:-

1st	231	R.Abel & W.Brockwell	The Oval	1897
2nd	247	T.W.Hayward & E.G.Hayes	The Oval	1908
3rd	240	D.J.Bicknell & A.J.Stewart	Hove	1993
4th	236	A.Sandham & A.Jeacocke	The Oval	1922
5th	181	A.J.Stewart & I.A.Greig	The Oval	1989
6th	298	A.Sandham & H.S.Harrison	The Oval	1913
7th	186	J.N.Crawford & W.S.Lees	The Oval	1906
8th	150	R.D.Jackman & Intikhab Alam	The Oval	1973
9th	86	B.Constable & W.S.Surridge	Hastings	1950
10th	118	C.Calvert & T.Sewell, jun.	Brighton	1868

Highest Wicket Partnerships - for Sussex:-

1st	258	J.G.Langridge & J.H.Parks	Horsham	1934
2nd	325	G.Brann & K.S.Ranjitsinhji	The Oval	1899
3rd	250	E.H.Bowley & K.S.Duleepsinhji	The Oval	1931
4th	281	T.E.R.Cook & James Langridge	The Oval	1930
5th	161	J.Vine & C.L.A.Smith	The Oval	1911
6th	119	W.Newham & G.Brann	Hove	1903
7th	167	C.Oakes & H.E.Hammond	Horsham	1938
8th	115	G.S.Whitfeld & G.Leach	Hove	1908
9th	160	K.S.Ranjitsinhji & F.W.Tate	Hastings	1902
10th	82	E.B.Dwyer & H.R.Butt	Hove	1906

SURREY v WARWICKSHIRE

Home		P	W	L	D	T	A	Away		P	W	L	D	T	A
Guildford	1992-1994	2	-	1	1	-	-	Birmingham (Edgbaston)	1894-1993	63	17	10	36	-	2
The Oval	1894-1990	70	34	10	26	-	1								
HOME TOTAL		72	34	11	27	-	1	Birmingham (M & B)	1934-1936	2	1	-	1	-	-
								Coventry (Courtaulds)	1947-1966	5	2	3	-	-	-
								Nuneaton (Griff & Coton)	1967	1	-	-	1	-	-
								AWAY TOTAL		71	20	13	38	-	2
GRAND TOTAL		143	54	24	65	-	3								

Highest Innings Total	Surrey:	634		The Oval	1906
	Warks:	585-7		The Oval	1905
Lowest Innings Total	Surrey:	61		The Oval	1962
	Warks:	45		The Oval	1953
Highest Individual innings	Surrey:	250	R.Abel	The Oval	1897
	Warks:	255*	W.G.Quaife	The Oval	1905
Best Bowling in an innings	Surrey:	10-67	E.A.Watts	Edgbaston	1939
	Warks:	9-35	S.Hargreave	The Oval	1903
Best Bowling in a match	Surrey:	15-83	T.Richardson	The Oval	1898
	Warks:	15-76	S.Hargreave	The Oval	1903

Highest Wicket Partnerships - for Surrey:-

1st	352	T.W.Hayward & J.B.Hobbs	The Oval	1909
2nd	316*	A.R.Butcher & D.M.Smith	Edgbaston	1982
3rd	199	A.Ducat & T.F.Shepherd	The Oval	1928
4th	213	T.W.Hayward & E.G.Goatly	The Oval	1906
5th	177	T.E.Jesty & D.B.Pauline	Edgbaston	1985
6th	190	H.B.Chinnery & K.J.Key	Edgbaston	1897
7th	145	F.C.Holland & W.S.Lees	Edgbaston	1906
8th	107	W.A.Smith & G.G.Arnold	Edgbaston	1968
9th	107	D.R.Jardine & E.W.J.Brooks	Edgbaston	1926
10th	130	H.Strudwick & J.W.Hitch	Edgbaston	1911

Highest Wicket Partnerships - for Warwickshire:-

1st	377*	N.F.Horner & Khalid Ibadulla	The Oval	1960
2nd	244	N.Kilner & L.T.A.Bates	Edgbaston	1926
3rd	229	N.Kilner & R.E.S.Wyatt	Edgbaston	1929
4th	188	M.J.K.Smith & A.I.Kallicharran	Edgbaston	1972
5th	214	D.P.Ostler & T.L.Penney	Guildford	1992
6th	199	A.F.A.Lilley & C.S.Baker	The Oval	1906
7th	170	T.W.Cartwright & A.C.Smith	The Oval	1961
8th	126*	W.G.Quaife & S.Santall	The Oval	1905
9th	110	G.Welch & D.R.Brown	Guildford	1994
10th	126	R.E.S.Wyatt & J.H.Mayer	The Oval	1927

SURREY v WORCESTERSHIRE

Home		P	W	L	D	T	A	Away		P	W	L	D	T	A
Guildford	1971-1983	3	2	1	-	-	-	Bournville	1911	1	-	1	-	-	-
The Oval	1900-1994	53	26	5	22	-	-	Dudley	1912-1951	2	-	-	2	-	-
HOME TOTAL		56	28	6	22	-	-	Kidderminster	1938-1952	2	1	-	1	-	-
								Stourbridge	1910-1932	2	-	1	1	-	-
								Worcester	1900-1993	47	12	11	24	-	-
								AWAY TOTAL		54	13	13	28	-	-
GRAND TOTAL		110	41	19	50	-	-								

Highest Innings Total	Surrey:	544		Worcester	1904
	Worcs:	446-7d		Guildford	1979
Lowest Innings Total	Surrey:	57		The Oval	1958
	Worcs:	25		The Oval	1954
Highest Individual innings	Surrey:	221	R.Abel	The Oval	1900
	Worcs:	182	G.A.Hick	Worcester	1993
Best Bowling in an innings	Surrey:	8-21	P.J.Loader	The Oval	1953
	Worcs:	8-38	L.J.Coldwell	Worcester	1965
Best Bowling in a match	Surrey:	14-85	A.R.Gover	Kidderminster	1938
	Worcs:	12-145	R.T.D.Perks	The Oval	1938

Highest Wicket Partnerhips - for Surrey:-

1st	313	T.W.Hayward & J.B.Hobbs	Worcester	1913
2nd	299	D.J.Bicknell & G.P.Thorpe	Worcester	1993
3rd	227	R.Abel & V.F.S.Crawford	The Oval	1901
4th	194	Younis Ahmed & G.R.J.Roope	The Oval	1972
5th	193	T.E.Jesty & M.A.Lynch	The Oval	1986
6th	220	G.P.Thorpe & A.J.Hollioake	The Oval	1994
7th	173	Younis Ahmed & Intikhab Alam	Worcester	1975
8th	96	A.Ducat & J.W.Hitch	The Oval	1914
9th	81	R.D.Jackman & P.I.Pocock	Worcester	1973
10th	87	W.S.Lees & T.Rushby	Worcester	1909

Highest Wicket Records - for Worcestershire:-

1st	254	G.M.Turner & J.A.Ormrod	Worcester	1978
2nd	232	T.S.Curtis & G.A.Hick	Worcester	1991
3rd	153	M.S.Scott & Younis Ahmed	The Oval	1981
4th	211	S.H.Martin & B.W.Quaife	The Oval	1935
5th	227	T.S.Curtis & M.J.Weston	Worcester	1985
6th	191*	D.N.Patel & S.J.Rhodes	The Oval	1986
7th	197	H.H.I.H.Gibbons & R.Howorth	The Oval	1938
8th	133*	P.A.Neale & G.A.Hick	The Oval	1984
9th	109	S.J.Rhodes & R.K.Illingworth	Worcester	1989
10th	49	W.B.Burns & E.W.Bale	Worcester	1909

SURREY v YORKSHIRE

Home		P	W	L	D	T	A
Guildford	1991	1	1	-	-	-	-
Lord's	1914	1	1	-	-	-	-
The Oval	1851-1993	114	35	31	48	-	1
HOME TOTAL		116	37	31	48	-	1

Away		P	W	L	D	T	A
Bradford	1888-1992	27	8	10	9	-	-
Dewsbury	1884	1	-	-	1	-	-
Harrogate	1981-1990	3	-	1	2	-	-
Holbeck	1883	1	-	1	-	-	-
Huddersfield	1881	1	-	1	-	-	-
Hull	1879-1968	3	1	2	-	-	-
Leeds (Headingley)	1892-1986	23	4	12	7	-	-
Scarborough	1969-1994	4	1	1	2	-	-
Sheffield (Hyde Park)	1851	1	1	-	-	-	-
Sheffield (Bramall Lane)	1862-1985	50	14	25	11	-	1
AWAY TOTAL		114	29	53	32	-	1

	P	W	L	D	T	A
GRAND TOTAL	230	66	84	80	-	2

Highest Innings Total	Surrey:	560-6d		The Oval	1933
	Yorkshire:	704		The Oval	1899
Lowest Innings Total	Surrey:	31		Holbeck	1883
	Yorkshire:	26		The Oval	1909
Highest Individual innings	Surrey:	273	T.W.Hayward	The Oval	1899
	Yorkshire:	255	W.Barber	Sheffield	1935
Best Bowling in an innings	Surrey:	9-47	T.Richardson	Sheffield	1893
	Yorkshire:	8-5	E.Peate	Holbeck	1883
Best Bowling in a match	Surrey:	15-154	T.Richardson	Leeds	1897
	Yorkshire:	14-77	E.Peate	Huddersfield	1881

Highest Wicket Partnerships - for Surrey:-

1st	290	J.B.Hobbs & T.W.Hayward	Lord's	1914
2nd	291	A.Sandham & H.S.Squires	The Oval	1933
3rd	221	T.W.Hayward & C.Baldwin	The Oval	1896
4th	448	R.Abel & T.W.Hayward	The Oval	1899
5th	208	W.H.Lockwood & D.L.A. Jephson	The Oval	1900
6th	294	D.R.Jardine & P.G.H.Fender	Bradford	1928
7th	135	A.J.Hollioake & M.A.Butcher	The Oval	1993
8th	148	F.R.Brown & E.A.Watts	Leeds	1939
9th	96	G.A.R.Lock & P.J.Loader	Leeds	1955
10th	60	N.M.Kendrick & A.J.Murphy	The Oval	1992

Highest Wicket Partnerships - for Yorkshire:-

1st	265*	P.Holmes & H.Sutcliffe	The Oval	1926
2nd	196	H.Sutcliffe & E.Oldroyd	The Oval	1922
3rd	240	L.Hutton & M.Leyland	Leeds	1939
4th	201*	J.H.Hampshire & D.B.Close	Bradford	1965
5th	340	E.Wainwright & G.H.Hirst	The Oval	1899
6th	134	W.A.I.Washington & G.H.Hirst	Leeds	1902
7th	148	J.Rowbottom & J.Thewlis	The Oval	1873
8th	165	S.Haigh & Lord Hawke	The Oval	1902
9th	192	G.H.Hirst & S.Haigh	Bradford	1898
10th	54	T.F.Smailes & F.Wilkinson	The Oval	1938

UNIVERSITY MATCHES

SURREY v CAMBRIDGE UNIVERSITY

Home		P	W	L	D	T	A	Away		P	W	L	D	T	A
Banstead	1984	1	-	-	1	-	-	Cambridge (Fenner's)	1865-1992	46	23	3	20	-	-
Guildford	1947-1963	9	3	-	6	-	-	AWAY TOTAL		46	23	3	20	-	-
The Oval	1865-1988	67	31	18	18	-	1								
HOME TOTAL		77	34	18	25	-	1								
GRAND TOTAL		123	57	21	45	-	1								

Highest Innings Total	for Surrey:	594-8d		The Oval	1923
	for CU:	572		The Oval	1930
Lowest Innings Total	for Surrey:	40		The Oval	1876
	for CU:	60		Cambridge	1899
		60		Guildford	1961
Highest Individual innings	for Surrey:	244*	W.W.Read	The Oval	1887
	for CU:	231	J.L.Bryan	The Oval	1921
Best Bowling in an innings	for Surrey:	9-45	M.P.Bicknell	The Oval	1988
	for CU:	8-68	E.M.Dowson	The Oval	1902
Best Bowling in a match	for Surrey:	13-75	W.S.Lees	Cambridge	1903
	for CU:	15-138	H.C.McDonell	Cambridge	1904

Best Wicket Partnership for Surrey:-
3rd 306 R.Abel & F.C.Holland The Oval 1895
Best Wicket Partnership for Cambridge University:-
7th 257 J.H.Morgan & F.R.Brown The Oval 1930

SURREY v OXFORD UNIVERSITY

Home		P	W	L	D	T	A	Away		P	W	L	D	T	A
Guildford	1946-1970	10	5	1	4	-	-	Oxford	1885-1990	25	12	4	9	-	-
The Oval	1864-1994	55	24	11	20	-	-	AWAY TOTAL		25	12	4	9	-	-
Reigate	1909	1	-	1	-	-	-								
HOME TOTAL		66	29	13	24	-	-								
GRAND TOTAL		91	41	17	33	-	-								

Highest Innings Total	Surrey:	650		The Oval	1888
	OU:	577		Reigate	1909
Lowest Innings Total	Surrey:	63		Oxford	1886
	OU	50		Oxford	1968
Highest Individual innings	Surrey:	338	W.W.Read	The Oval	1888
	OU:	180	N.M.Ford	The Oval	1930
Best Bowling in an innings	Surrey:	9-77	G.A.R.Lock	Guildford	1960
	OU:	8-26	F.H.E.Cunliffe	Oxford	1896
Best Bowling in a match	Surrey:	14-103	T.W.Hayward	Oxford	1897
	OU:	12-138	W.F.Maitland	The Oval	1864

Best Wicket Partnership for Surrey:-
1st 428 J.B.Hobbs & A.Sandham The Oval 1926
Best Wicket Partnership for Oxford University:-
4th 276 P.G.T.Kingsley & N.M.Ford The Oval 1930

TEST-PLAYING COUNTRIES

SURREY v AUSTRALIANS

Home		P	W	L	D
The Oval	1878-1993	48	9	20	19
HOME TOTAL		48	9	20	19

Highest Innings Total	for Surrey:	501		The Oval	1886
	for Aust:	632		The Oval	1948
Lowest Innings Total	for Surrey:	48		The Oval	1882
	for Aust:	52		The Oval	1888
Highest Individual innings	for Surrey:	219	A.Sandham	The Oval	1934
	for Aust:	252*	D.G.Bradman	The Oval	1930
Best Bowling in an innings	for Surrey:	10-88	J.C.Laker	The Oval	1956
	for Aust:	10-28	W.P.Howell	The Oval	1899
Best Bowling in a match	for Surrey:	12-124	W.C.Smith	The Oval	1905
		12-124	W.C.Smith	The Oval	1909
	for Aust:	15-57	W.P.Howell	The Oval	1899

Best Wicket Partnership for Surrey:-

2nd 242 A.Sandham & R.J.Gregory The Oval 1934

Best Wicket Partnership for Australians:-

1st 239 W.H.Ponsford & S.J.McCabe The Oval 1934

SURREY v INDIANS

Home		P	W	L	D
The Oval	1911-1990	12	3	3	6
HOME TOTAL		12	3	3	6

Highest Innings Total	for Surrey:	452		The Oval	1936
	for Indians:	454		The Oval	1946
Lowest Innings Total	for Surrey:	71		The Oval	1952
	for Indians:	108		The Oval	1952
Highest Individual innings	for Surrey:	143	P.B.H.May	The Oval	1952
	for Indians:	148	V.L.Manjrekar	The Oval	1959
Best Bowling in an innings	for Surrey:	6-64	J.C.Laker	The Oval	1952
	for Indians:	7-111	B.S.Bedi	The Oval	1971
Best Bowling in a match	for Surrey:	10-98	M.C.Bird	The Oval	1911
	for Indians:	9-74	R.Surendranath	The Oval	1959

Best Wicket Partnership for Surrey:-

2nd 155 G.S.Clinton & A.J.Stewart The Oval 1990

Best Wicket Partnership for Indians:-

10th 249 C.T.Sarwate & S.N.Banerjee The Oval 1946

SURREY v NEW ZEALANDERS

Home		P	W	L	D
The Oval	1927-1973	10	2	2	6
HOME TOTAL		10	2	2	6

Highest Innings Total	for Surrey:	645-9d		The Oval	1949
	for NZ:	495		The Oval	1937
Lowest Innings Total	for Surrey:	149		The Oval	1937
	for NZ:	51		The Oval	1958
Highest Individual innings	for Surrey:	255	J.F.Parker	The Oval	1949
	for NZ:	187	B.Sutcliffe	The Oval	1949
Best Bowling in an innings	for Surrey:	8-33	P.J.Loader	The Oval	1958
	for NZ:	6-47	T.B.Burtt	The Oval	1949
Best Bowling in a match	for Surrey:	9-42	P.J.Loader	The Oval	1958
	for NZ:	8-209	W.E.Merritt	The Oval	1927

Best Wicket Partnership for Surrey:-

1st	180	J.B.Hobbs & A.Sandham	The Oval	1927

Best Wicket Partnership for New Zealanders:-

1st	229	B.Sutcliffe & V.J.Scott	The Oval	1949

SURREY v PAKISTANIS

Home		P	W	L	D
The Oval	1954-1987	7	-	3	4
HOME TOTAL		7	-	3	4

Highest Innings Total	for Surrey:	348-9d		The Oval	1962
	for Pak:	388-6d		The Oval	1962
Lowest Innings Total	for Surrey:	166		The Oval	1971
	for Pak:	195		The Oval	1987
Highest Individual innings	for Surrey:	119	P.B.H.May	The Oval	1962
	for Pak:	123	Waqar Hassan	The Oval	1954
Best Bowling in an innings	for Surrey:	5-66	M.A.Feltham	The Oval	1987
	for Pak:	7-57	Intikhab Alam	The Oval	1971
Best Bowling in a match	for Surrey:	5-94	M.A.Feltham	The Oval	1987
	for Pak:	9-124	Intikhab Alam	The Oval	1971

Best Wicket Partnership for Surrey:-

3rd	147	M.A.Lynch & G.R.J.Roope	The Oval	1978

Best Wicket Partnership for Pakistanis:-

5th	192	Waqar Hassan & Wazir Mohammad	The Oval	1954

SURREY v SOUTH AFRICANS

Home		P	W	L	D
The Oval	1901-1965	16	3	5	8
HOME TOTAL		16	3	5	8

Highest Innings Total	for Surrey:	363-7d		The Oval	1904
	for SA:	572		The Oval	1935
Lowest Innings Total	for Surrey:	112		The Oval	1947
	for SA:	83		The Oval	1947
Highest Individual innings	for Surrey:	127	T.F.Shepherd	The Oval	1924
	for SA:	195	B.Mitchell	The Oval	1935
Best Bowling in an innings	for Surrey:	6-50	T.Richardson	The Oval	1901
	for SA:	8-76	H.J.Tayfield	The Oval	1955
Best Bowling in a match	for Surrey:	11-125	T.Richardson	The Oval	1901
	for SA:	13-98	H.J.Tayfield	The Oval	1955

Best Wicket Partnership for Surrey:-

6th	159	A.Sandham & P.G.H.Fender	The Oval	1929

Best Wicket Partnership for South Africans:-

1st	330	B.Mitchell & E.A.B.Rowan	The Oval	1935

SURREY v SRI LANKANS

Home		P	W	L	D
The Oval	1984-1988	2	1	0	1
HOME TOTAL		2	1	0	1

Highest Innings Total	for Surrey:	250-9d		The Oval	1984
	for SL:	300-6d		The Oval	1988
Lowest Innings Total	for Surrey:	208-8d		The Oval	1984
	for SL:	105		The Oval	1984
Highest Individual innings	for Surrey:	77	G.P.Howarth	The Oval	1984
	for SL:	124	L.R.D.Mendis	The Oval	1988
Best Bowling in an innings	for Surrey:	3-52	M.A.Feltham	The Oval	1988
	for SL:	5-89	V.B.John	The Oval	1984
Best Bowling in a match	for Surrey:	5-68	G.Monkhouse	The Oval	1984
	for SL:	7-163	V.B.John	The Oval	1984

Best Wicket Partnership for Surrey:-

1st	113	A.Needham & G.P.Howarth	The Oval	1984

Best Wicket Partnership for Sri Lankans:-

4th	116	M.A.R.Samarasekera & R.S.Madugalle	The Oval	1988

SURREY v WEST INDIANS

Home		P	W	L	D	A
The Oval	1906-1976	14	2	4	8	1
HOME TOTAL		14	2	4	8	1

Highest Innings Total	for Surrey:	470		The Oval	1933
	for WI:	537-5d		The Oval	1950
Lowest Innings Total	for Surrey:	87		The Oval	1923
	for WI:	121		The Oval	1906
Highest Individual innings	for Surrey:	221	J.B.Hobbs	The Oval	1933
	for WI:	232	E.de C.Weekes	The Oval	1950
Best Bowling in an innings	for Surrey:	8-94	F.R.Brown	The Oval	1939
	for WI:	7-76	O.H.Layne	The Oval	1906
Best Bowling in a match	for Surrey:	9-160	F.R.Brown	The Oval	1939
	for WI:	10-76	G.N.Francis	The Oval	1923

Best Wicket Partnership for Surrey:-

1st	253*	J.B.Hobbs & A.Sandham	The Oval	1928

Best Wicket Partnership for West Indians:-

4th	279	R.E.Marshall & C.L.Walcott	The Oval	1950

SURREY v ZIMBABWEANS

Home		P	W	L	D
The Oval	1985-1993	2	-	-	2
HOME TOTAL		2	-	-	2

Highest Innings Total	for Surrey:	343-5d		The Oval	1985
	for Zim:	226		The Oval	1985
Lowest Innings Total	for Surrey:	189-9d		The Oval	1993
	for Zim:	196-6		The Oval	1993
Highest Individual innings	for Surrey:	138	A.D.Brown	The Oval	1993
	for Zim:	82	A.Flower	The Oval	1993
Best Bowling in an innings	for Surrey:	5-58	A.J.Murphy	The Oval	1993
	for Zim:	3-58	I.P.Butchart	The Oval	1985
Best Bowling in a match	for Surrey:	7-127	A.J.Murphy	The Oval	1993
	for Zim:	6-132	S.G.Peall	The Oval	1993

Best Wicket Partnership for Surrey:-

4rd	165	A.W.Smith & A.D.Brown	The Oval	1993

Best Wicket Partnership for Zimbabweans:-

2nd	92	A.Flower & A.D.R.Campbell	The Oval	1993

OTHER MATCHES

SURREY v AUSTRALIAN IMPERIAL FORCES

Home		P	W	L	D
The Oval	1919	2	-	-	2
HOME TOTAL		2	-	-	2

SURREY v CAMBRIDGESHIRE

Home		P	W	L	D	Away		P	W	L	D
The Oval	1857-1871	5	3	1	1	Cambridge (Fenner's)	1857-1862	3	1	1	1
HOME TOTAL		5	3	1	1	AWAY TOTAL		3	1	1	1
GRAND TOTAL		8	4	2	2						

Highest Innings Total	Surrey:	277		The Oval	1862
	Cambs:	329		The Oval	1861
Lowest Innings Total	Surrey:	68		Cambridge	1857
	Cambs:	65		Cambridge	1857
Highest Individual innings	Surrey:	111	J.Caesar	The Oval	1861
	Cambs:	112	T.Hayward	Cambridge	1861
Best Bowling in an innings	Surrey:	7-19	W.Caffyn	Cambridge	1857
	Cambs:	8-45	G.F.Tarrant	Cambridge	1862
Best Bowling in a match	Surrey:	10-92	W.Caffyn	The Oval	1858
	Cambs:	10-71	F.W.Bell	Cambridge	1857

Best Wicket Partnership - Surrey:-

1st	71	H.Jupp & R.Humphrey	The Oval	1871

Best Wicket Partnership - Cambridgeshire:-

3rd	212	R.Carpenter & T.Hayward	The Oval	1861

SURREY v COMBINED SERVICES

Home		P	W	L	D
The Oval	1946-1960	4	1	-	3
Kingston	1946	1	-	-	1
HOME TOTAL		5	1	-	4

SURREY v ENGLAND

Home		P	W	L	D	Away		P	W	L	D
The Oval	1848-1895	16	6	4	6	Lord's	1849-1852	2	1	1	-
HOME TOTAL		16	6	4	6	Scarborough	1892	1	-	-	1
						AWAY TOTAL		3	1	1	1
GRAND TOTAL		19	7	5	7						

SURREY v GENTLEMAN OF ENGLAND

Home		P	W	L	D
The Oval	1905-1908	4	3	-	1
HOME TOTAL		4	3	-	1

SURREY v KENT & SUSSEX

Home		P	W	L	D	Away		P	W	L	D
The Oval	1858-1859	2	1	-	1	Brighton	1858-1859	2	2	-	-
HOME TOTAL		2	1	-	1	AWAY TOTAL		2	2	-	-
GRAND TOTAL		4	3	-	1						

SURREY v LONDON COUNTY

Home		P	W	L	D
The Oval	1900-1904	5	3	1	1
HOME TOTAL		5	3	1	1
GRAND TOTAL		10	3	3	4

Away		P	W	L	D
Crystal Palace	1900-1904	5	-	2	3
AWAY TOTAL		5	-	2	3

SURREY v MANCHESTER

Away		P	W	L	D
Eccles	1857	1	-	1	-
AWAY TOTAL		1	-	1	-

SURREY v M.C.C.

Home		P	W	L	D	T
The Oval	1847-1969	8	1	6	-	1
HOME TOTAL		8	1	6	-	1
GRAND TOTAL		53	13	23	16	1

Away		P	W	L	D	T
Lord's	1847-1972	45	12	17	16	-
AWAY TOTAL		45	12	17	16	-

SURREY v NORTH OF ENGLAND

Home		P	W	L	D
The Oval	1857-1863	7	5	2	-
HOME TOTAL		7	5	2	-
GRAND TOTAL		13	7	2	4

Away		P	W	L	D
Manchester	1859-1863	5	1	2	2
Sheffield	1857	1	1	-	-
AWAY TOTAL		6	2	2	2

SURREY v PHILADELPHIANS

Home		P	W	L	D
The Oval	1897-1908	3	2	1	-
HOME TOTAL		3	2	1	-

SURREY v REST OF ENGLAND

Home		P	W	L	D
The Oval	1955-1956	2	-	2	-
HOME TOTAL		2	-	2	-
GRAND TOTAL		3	1	2	-

Away		P	W	L	D
Scarborough	1957	1	1	-	-
AWAY TOTAL		1	1	-	-

SURREY v RHODESIA

Away		P	W	L	D
Bulawayo	1959	1	-	-	1
Salisbury	1959	1	-	1	-
AWAY TOTAL		2	-	1	1

SURREY v SCOTLAND

Home		P	W	L	D
The Oval	1913-1923	3	2	-	1
HOME TOTAL		3	2	-	1
GRAND TOTAL		4	2	-	2

Away		P	W	L	D
Glasgow	1923	1	-	-	1
AWAY TOTAL		1	-	-	1

SURREY v SOUTH OF ENGLAND

Home		P	W	L	D
The Oval	1864-1865	2	-	-	2
HOME TOTAL		2	-	-	2

SECTION 10 - PLAYERS' RECORDS

SURREY CAPTAINS 1846-1994

1846-1850	C.H.Hoare	1911-1913	M.C.Bird
1851-1857	F.P.Miller	1914-1920	C.T.A.Wilkinson
1858-1865	F.Burbidge	1921-1931	P.G.H.Fender
1866	E.Dowson	1932-1933	D.R.Jardine
1867	W.J.Collyer	1934-1938	E.R.T.Holmes
1868	C.Calvert	1939	H.M.Garland-Wells
1869-1870	S.H.Akroyd	1946	N.H.Bennett
1871	J.C.Gregory	1947-1948	E.R.T.Holmes
1872-1875	G.Strachan	1949-1951	M.R.Barton
1876	A.Chandler	1952-1956	W.S.Surridge
1877-1878	G.Strachan	1957-1962	P.B.H.May
1879	A.P.Lucas	1963-1972	M.J.Stewart
1880-1893	J.Shuter	1973-1977	J.H.Edrich
1894-1899	K.J.Key	1978-1983	R.D.V.Knight
1900-1902	D.L.A.Jephson	1984-1985	G.P.Howarth
1903	L.Walker	1986	P.I.Pocock
1904	*No appointment*	1987-1991	I.A.Greig
1905-1907	Lord Dalmeny	1992-1994	A.J.Stewart
1908-1910	H.D.G.Leveson-Gower		

SURREY CAPS 1884-1994

R.Abel	1884	W.S.Lees	1898
E.Barratt	1884	E.G.Hayes	1899
M.P.Bowden	1884	E.H.L.Nice	1899
E.J.Diver	1884	H.B.Richardson	1899
C.E.Horner	1884	F.Stedman	1899
G.G.Jones	1884	H.D.G.Leveson-Gower	1900
K.J.Key	1884	E.M.Dowson	1902
J.M.Read	1884	W.C.Smith	1902
W.W.Read	1884	H.P.Clode	1903
W.E.Roller	1884	H.Strudwick	1903
J.Shuter	1884	L.Walker	1903
H.Wood	1884	A.Baker	1904
J.Beaumont	1887	H.B.Chinnery	1904
T.Bowley	1887	Lord Dalmeny	1904
G.A.Lohmann	1887	L.V.Harper	1904
R.Henderson	1888	H.C.McDonell	1904
W.H.Lockwood	1889	J.E.Raphael	1904
J.W.Sharpe	1889	R.A.Sheppard	1904
W.Brockwell	1891	W.E.Davis	1905
E.C.Streatfeild	1891	J.B.Hobbs	1905
G.W.Ayres	1894	N.A.Knox	1905
T.W.Hayward	1894	H.S.Bush	1906
T.Richardson	1894	J.N.Crawford	1906
F.E.Smith	1894	P.R.May	1906
E.A.Street	1894	T.Rushby	1906
C.Baldwin	1895	A.Ducat	1908
N.F.Druce	1896	J.W.Hitch	1908
V.F.S.Crawford	1898	E.C.Kirk	1908
F.C.Holland	1898	A.Marshal	1908
D.L.A.Jephson	1898	M.C.Bird	1909

G.J.W.Platt	1909
W.J.Abel	1910
I.P.F.Campbell	1910
E.G.Goatly	1911
H.S.Harrison	1911
W.A.Spring	1911
H.S.Altham	1912
D.J.Knight	1912
E.B.Myers	1912
F.S.Gillespie	1913
A.Sandham	1913
P.G.H.Fender	1914
C.T.A.Wilkinson	1914
M.Howell	1920
J.H.Lockton	1920
H.A.Peach	1920
G.M.Reay	1920
T.F.Shepherd	1920
A.Jeacocke	1921
F.C.G.Naumann	1922
D.R.Jardine	1923
W.T.Cook	1924
S.Fenley	1924
W.C.H.Sadler	1924
E.R.T.Holmes	1926
A.C.T.Geary	1927
H.T.Barling	1928
E.W.J.Brooks	1928
R.J.Gregory	1928
M.J.C.Allom	1929
E.F.Wilson	1929
H.M.Garland-Wells	1930
A.R.Gover	1930
R.S.Machin	1931
E.J.Sheffield	1931
H.S.Squires	1931
F.R.Brown	1932
E.A.Watts	1934
L.B.Fishlock	1935
J.F.Parker	1937
R.de W.K.Winlaw	1937
G.S.Mobey	1939
E.W.Whitfield	1939
A.V.Bedser	1946
N.H.Bennett	1946
A.J.W.McIntyre	1946
E.A.Bedser	1947
D.G.W.Fletcher	1947
J.C.Laker	1947
M.R.Barton	1948
J.W.McMahon	1948
W.S.Surridge	1948
G.J.Whittaker	1949
B.Constable	1950
G.A.R.Lock	1950
P.B.H.May	1950
T.H.Clark	1952
P.J.Loader	1953
R.Subba Row	1953
K.F.Barrington	1955
M.J.Stewart	1955
R.Swetman	1958
J.H.Edrich	1959
D.Gibson	1960
A.B.D.Parsons	1961
A.Long	1962
D.A.D.Sydenham	1962
R.A.E.Tindall	1962
M.D.Willett	1962
R.Harman	1964
R.I.Jefferson	1964
S.J.Storey	1964
M.J.Edwards	1966
G.G.Arnold	1967
P.I.Pocock	1967
W.A.Smith	1968
Intikhab Alam	1969
G.R.J.Roope	1969
D.J.S.Taylor	1969
Younis Ahmed	1969
R.D.Jackman	1970
C.E.Waller	1972
G.P.Howarth	1974
A.R.Butcher	1975
L.E.Skinner	1975
R.D.V.Knight	1978
C.J.Richards	1978
S.T.Clarke	1980
G.S.Clinton	1980
D.M.Smith	1980
M.A.Lynch	1982
D.J.Thomas	1982
G.Monkhouse	1984
A.H.Gray	1985
T.E.Jesty	1985
A.Needham	1985
A.J.Stewart	1985
I.A.Greig	1987
K.T.Medlycott	1988
M.P.Bicknell	1989
D.J.Bicknell	1990
C.K.Bullen	1990
M.A.Feltham	1990
Waqar Younis	1990
D.M.Ward	1990
G.P.Thorpe	1991
J.E.Benjamin	1993
A.D.Brown	1994

MOST APPEARANCES FOR SURREY

598	J.B.Hobbs	1905-1934	315	S.J.Storey	1960-1974
593	T.W.Hayward	1893-1914	314	W.Brockwell	1886-1903
554	H.Strudwick	1902-1927	309	J.C.Laker	1946-1959
525	A.Sandham	1911-1937	305	T.Richardson	1892-1904
514	R.Abel	1881-1904	305	W.H.Lockwood	1889-1904
500	E.G.Hayes	1896-1919	304	J.W.Hitch	1907-1925
498	M.J.Stewart	1954-1972	304	M.A.Lynch	1977-1994
485	P.I.Pocock	1964-1986	300	D.G.W.Fletcher	1946-1961
443	E.A.Bedser	1939-1961	298	P.J.Loader	1951-1963
434	B.Constable	1939-1964	288	K.J.Key	1882-1904
422	A.Ducat	1906-1931	286	H.Wood	1884-1900
414	P.G.H.Fender	1914-1935	283	A.R.Butcher	1972-1986
413	R.J.Gregory	1925-1947	282	F.C.Holland	1894-1908
410	J.H.Edrich	1958-1978	278	J.M.Read	1880-1895
402	H.S.Squires	1928-1949	274	J.Shuter	1877-1909
389	H.T.Barling	1927-1948	262	Younis Ahmed	1965-1978
385	G.A.R.Lock	1946-1963	260	T.H.Clark	1947-1959
376	A.J.W.McIntyre	1938-1963	256	E.Pooley	1861-1883
371	A.V.Bedser	1939-1960	256	C.J.Richards	1976-1988
366	W.W.Read	1873-1897	254	W.S.Surridge	1947-1959
362	K.F.Barrington	1953-1968	252	H.Jupp	1862-1881
354	T.F.Shepherd	1919-1932	240	E.A.Watts	1933-1949
352	A.Long	1960-1975	236	M.J.Edwards	1961-1974
354	E.W.J.Brooks	1925-1939	234	G.S.Clinton	1979-1990
347	L.B.Fishlock	1931-1952	232	Intikhab Alam	1969-1981
343	W.S.Lees	1896-1911	229	W.C.Smith	1900-1914
342	G.R.J.Roope	1964-1982	228	T.Rushby	1903-1921
338	R.D.Jackman	1966-1982	218	G.G.Arnold	1963-1977
336	A.R.Gover	1928-1947	208	P.B.H.May	1950-1963
334	J.F.Parker	1932-1952	207	A.J.Stewart	1981-1994
324	H.A.Peach	1919-1931	205	D.J.Thomas	1977-1987

YOUNGEST PLAYERS ON DEBUT FOR SURREY

G.A.R.Lock	17y 8d	v Kent	The Oval	1946
V.F.S.Crawford	17y 72d	v Oxford University	The Oval	1896
D.J.Knight	17y 115d	v Somerset	The Oval	1911
D.M.Smith	17y 123d	v Cambridge University	Cambridge	1973
M.P.Bicknell	17y 144d	v Derbyshire	The Oval	1986
A.P.Lucas	17y 146d	v Middlesex	The Oval	1874
C.J.M.Fox	17y 186d	v Gloucestershire	The Oval	1876
J.N.Crawford	17y 247d	v Kent	Canterbury	1904
Younis Ahmed	17y 260d	v South Africans	The Oval	1965
W.W.Read	17y 261d	v Yorkshire	The Oval	1873
M.P.Bowden	17y 274d	v Somerset	The Oval	1883
R.F.Lowe	17y 278d	v Glamorgan	Cardiff (AP)	1923
P.I.Pocock	17y 281d	v Cambridge University	The Oval	1964
F.Buckle	17y 289d	v Kent	Gravesend	1867
K.J.Key	17y 293d	v Kent	The Oval	1882
C.J.Richards	17y 311d	v Cambridge University	Cambridge	1976
W.H.Game	17y 323d	v Yorkshire	The Oval	1871

OLDEST PLAYERS ON DEBUT FOR SURREY

W.Clarke	53y 162d	v England	The Oval	1852
F.J.Titmus	45y 202d	v Kent	Tunbridge Wells	1978
N.Wanostrocht (Felix)	41y 263d	v Kent	The Oval	1846
T.Box	41y 131d	v England	Lord's	1849
W.D.Baker	40y †	v MCC	Lord's	1847
A.Christy	39y 121d	v Cambridgeshire	Cambridge	1857
D.Day	39y 11d	v Kent	The Oval	1846
T.A.Beard	39y †	v Cambridgeshire	Cambridge	1857
J.Heath	38y 225d	v Kent	The Oval	1846
J.H.Vincett	38y 39d	v Hampshire	Bournemouth	1921

† *W.D. Baker was born c. 1806 and T.A. Beard was born c. 1817.*

OLDEST PLAYERS FOR SURREY

(Age given as on the last day of last match)

J.Shuter	54y 134d	v Oxford University	Reigate	1909
W.Clarke	53y 164d	v England	The Oval	1852
J.Southerton	51y 287d	v Gloucestershire	Cirencester	1879
J.B.Hobbs	51y 258d	v Glamorgan	Cardiff (AP)	1934
E.R.T.Holmes	49y 307d	v Oxford University	Guildford	1955

LONGEST CAREER FOR SURREY

J.Shuter	31y 315d	1877-1909
E.R.T.Holmes	30y 313d	1924-1955
J.B.Hobbs	29y 130d	1905-1934
A.Sandham	26y 81d	1911-1937
D.J.Knight	25y 316d	1911-1937
H.Strudwick	25y 129d	1902-1927
B.Constable	25y 41d	1939-1964
A.J.W.McIntyre	25y 22d	1938-1963
H.Thompson	25y 22d	1894-1919

LONGEST LIVED SURREY PLAYERS

	Age	*Career*	*Born*	*Died*
J.Kenrick	96y 77d	1876	13.11.1852	29. 1.1949
D.Adams	95y 214d	1902	8. 6.1880	8. 1.1976
W.W.C.Lane	93y 242d	1868-1870	1. 8.1845	31. 3 1939
C.Tillard	92y 324d	1874-1875	18. 4.1851	7. 3.1944
P.G.H.Fender	92y 297d	1914-1935	22. 8.1892	15. 6.1985
N.Miller	92y 188d	1899-1903	27. 8.1874	3. 3.1967
C.M.Wells	92y 154d	1892-1893	21. 3.1871	22. 8.1963
Lord Dalmeny	92y 142d	1903-1908	8. 1.1882	30. 5.1974
A.Sandham	91y 288d	1911-1937	6. 7.1890	20. 4.1982
S.C.B.Ponsonby	91y 262d	1846-1853	14. 3.1824	1.12.1915
W.Caffyn	91y 207d	1849-1873	2. 2.1828	28. 8.1919
W.E.Roller	91y 207d	1881-1890	1. 2.1858	27. 8.1949
W.J.Rudd	90y 271d	1904	29. 6.1880	27. 3.1971
H.Strudwick	90y 17d	1902-1927	28. 1.1880	14. 2.1970

FAMILY RELATIONSHIPS OF SURREY PLAYERS

Grandfather		Grandson	
Hayward, D., sen.	(1846-1847)	Hayward, T.W.	(1893-1914)

Father		Son	
Abel, R.	(1881-1904)	Abel, T.E.	(1919-1920)
		Abel, W.J.	(1909-1926)
Allom, M.J.C.	(1927-1937)	Allom, A.T.C.	(1960)
Butcher, A.R.	(1972-1986)	Butcher, M.A.	(1992-1994)
Chester, J.	(1846-1858)	Chester, A.	(1872-1883)
Dowson, E.	(1860-1870)	Dowson, E.M.	(1900-1903)
Earnshaw, A.	(1847)	Earnshaw, G.R.B.	(1880)
Hayward, D., sen.	(1846-1847)	Hayward, D., jun.	(1854)
Hayward, D., jun.	(1854)	Hayward, T.W.	(1893-1914)
Howell, R.	(1878-1879)	Howell, M.	(1919-1925)
Sewell, T., sen.	(1846-1849)	Sewell, T., jun.	(1859-1868)
Smith, W.A.	(1961-1970)	Smith, A.W.	(1993-1994)
Stewart, M.J.	(1954-1972)	Stewart, A.J.	(1981-1994)
Street, J.	(1863-1878)	Street, A.E.	(1892-1898)
Surridge, W.S.	(1947-1959)	Surridge, S.S.	(1978-1980)

Father-in-law		Son-in-law	
Clarke, C.F.C.	(1873-1882)	Tufnell, N.C.	(1922)

Brothers			
Abel, T.E.	(1919-1920)	Abel, W.J.	(1909-1926)
Akroyd, B.N.	(1872-1873)	Akroyd, S.H.	(1869-1878)
Bedser, A.V.	(1939-1960)	Bedser, E.A.	(1939-1961)
Bicknell, D.J.	(1987-1994)	Bicknell, M.P.	(1986-1994)
Burbidge, A.	(1857)	Burbidge, F.	(1854-1866)
Bush, F.W.	(1879-1885)	Bush, H.S.	(1901-1912)
Butcher, A.R.	(1972-1986)	Butcher, M.S.	(1982)
Caesar, F.B.	(1859-1862)	Caesar, J.	(1849-1867)
Cattley, A.C.	(1882)	Cattley, S.W.	(1879-1883)
Clarke, C.F.C.	(1873-1882)	Clarke, M.C.	(1875-1880)
Crawford, J.N.	(1904-1921)	Crawford, V.F.S.	(1896-1902)
Douglas, A.P.	(1887)	Douglas, R.N.	(1890-1891)
Humphrey, R.	(1870-1881)	Humphrey, T.	(1862-1874)
Humphrey, J.	(1862 Surrey Club)	Humphrey, W.	(1864)
Knox, F.P.	(1899-1902)	Knox, N.A.	(1904-1910)
Lane, C.G.	(1856-1861)	Lane, W.W.C.	(1868-1870)
Marshall, A.	(1849-1857)	Marshall, H.	(1853-1854)
Noble, C.	(1868)	Noble, J.W.	(1866-1869)
Pickering, E.H.	(1844)	Pickering, W.P.	(1846-1848)
Pooley, E.	(1861-1883)	Pooley, F.W.	(1876-1877)
Pratt, D.E.	(1954-1957)	Pratt, R.E.C.	(1952-1959)
Read, F.H.	(1881)	Read, J.M.	(1880-1895)
Roller, C.T.	(1886)	Roller, W.E.	(1881-1890)
Shuter, J.	(1877-1909)	Shuter, L.A.	(1876-1883)
Trodd, W.	(1869)	Trodd, J.	(1855 Surrey Club)

Half-brothers

Chinnery, E.F.	(1906)	Chinnery, H.B.	(1897-1904)
Lee, F.	(1861)	Lee, J.M.	(1847-1850)

Brothers-in-law

Pratt, J.	(1868)	Southerton, J.	(1854-1879)
Gover, A.R.	(1928-1947)	Watts, E.A.	(1933-1949)

Uncle		**Nephew**	
Bayley, J.	(1846-1847)	Bayley, M.	(1866)
Brockwell, G.	(1846-1857)	Brockwell, W.	(1886-1903)
Butcher, M.S.	(1982)	Butcher, M.A.	(1992-1994)
Caffyn, W.W.	(1844)	Caffyn, W.	(1849-1873)
Stephenson, H.H.	(1853-1871)	Read, J.M.	(1880-1895)
		Read, F.H.	(1881)

Cousins

Jupp, H.	(1862-1881)	Jupp, W.T.	(1876)

UNIVERSITY BLUES

CAMBRIDGE

M.J.C.Allom	Wellington	1927-1928
C.J.Aworth	Tiffins	1973-1975
R.E.H.Baily	Harrow	1908
H.W.Bainbridge	Eton	1884-1886
H.T.Bartlett	Dulwich	1934-1936
R.A.Bayford	Kensington G.S.	1857-1859
C.T.Bennett	Harrow	1923-1925
S.A.Block	Marlborough	1929
E.Bray	Westminster	1871-1872
F.R.Brown	The Leys	1930-1931
N.J.Cosh	Dulwich	1966-1968
P.J.Dickinson	K.C.S. Wimbledon	1939
R.N.Douglas	Dulwich	1890-1892
E.M.Dowson	Harrow	1900-1903
N.F.Druce	Marlborough	1894-1897
A.E.R.Gilligan	Dulwich	1919-1920
S.C.Griffith	Dulwich	1935
A.W.G.Hadingham	St. Paul's	1932
W.J.Hammersley	Private	1847
L.V.Harper	Rossall	1901-1903
A.M.Hoare	Private	1844
R.I.Jefferson	Winchester	1961
D.L.A.Jephson	Manor House Clapham	1890-1892
R.D.V.Knight	Dulwich	1967-1970
R.B.Lagden	Marlborough	1912-1914
F.Lee	Rugby	1860
J.M.Lee	Oundle	1846-1848
H.K.Longman	Eton	1901
A.P.Lucas	Uppingham	1875-1878

H.C.McDonell	Winchester	1903-1905
R.S.Machin	Lancing	1927
E.MacNiven	Eton	1846
P.B.H.May	Charterhouse	1950-1952
P.R.May	Private	1905-1906
W.B.Money	Harrow	1868-1871
P.H.Morton	Rossall	1878-1880
D.R.Owen-Thomas	K.C.S. Wimbledon	1969-1972
A.B.D.Parsons	Brighton	1954-1955
W.P.Pickering	Eton	1840-1842
A.Ratcliffe	Rydal	1930-1932
S.G.Russell	Tiffins	1965-1967
M.W.W.Selvey	Battersea G.S.	1971
E.C.Streatfeild	Charterhouse	1890-1893
R.Subba Row	Whitgift	1951-1953
A.S.Tabor	Eton	1872-1874
C.Tillard	Repton	1873-1874
N.C.Tufnell	Eton	1909-1910
O.J.Wait	Dulwich	1949-1951
C.M.Wells	Dulwich	1891-1893
R.de W.K.Winlaw	Winchester	1932-1934

OXFORD

H.S.Altham	Repton	1911-1912
M.R.Barton	Winchester	1936-1937
I.P.F.Campbell	Repton	1911-1913
W.J.H.Curwen	Charterhouse	1906
I.J.Curtis	Whitgift	1980-1982
J.L.Cuthbertson	Rugby	1962-1963
H.W.F.Franklin	Christ's Hospital	1924
W.H.Game	Sherborne	1873-1876
H.M.Garland-Wells	St. Paul's	1928-1930
J.H.Gordon	Winchester	1906-1907
R.Hankey	Harrow	1853-1855
E.R.T.Holmes	Malvern	1925-1927
M.Howell	Repton	1914-1919
D.R.Jardine	Winchester	1920-1923
K.J.Key	Clifton	1884-1887
D.J.Knight	Malvern	1914-1919
F.P.Knox	Dulwich	1899-1901
C.G.Lane	Westminster	1856-1860
H.D.G.Leveson-Gower	Winchester	1893-1896
M.A.McCanlis	Cranleigh	1926-1928
N.L.Majendie	Winchester	1962-1963
F.C.G.Naumann	Malvern	1914-1919
F.W.Oliver	Westminster	1856-1857
V.R.Price	Bishop's Stortford	1919-1922
J.E.Raphael	Merchant Taylors	1903-1905
G.W.Ricketts	Westminster	1887
G.O.Smith	Charterhouse	1895-1896
H.Teesdale	Winchester	1908
A.C.Von Ernsthausen	Uppingham	1902-1904
E.M.Wellings	Cheltenham	1929-1931
G.A.Wheatley	Uppingham	1946

SURREY PLAYERS' TEST CAREER RECORDS

		Batting								Bowling							
		M	*I*	*NO*	*Runs*	*HS*	*Avge*	*100*	*50*	*Runs*	*Wkts*	*Avge*	*Best*	*5 WI*	*10 WM*	*Ct*	*St*
Abel, R.	1888- 1896	13	22	2	744	132*	37.20	2	2							13	
Allom, M.J.C.	1929/30-1930/31	5	3	2	14	8*	14.00	-	-	265	14	18.92	5-38	1	-	-	
Arnold, G.G.	1967- 1975	34	46	11	421	59	12.02	-	1	3254	115	28.29	6-45	6	-	9	
Barrington, K.F.	1955- 1968	82	131	15	6806	256	58.67	20	35	1300	29	44.82	3-4	-	-	58	
Bedser, A.V.	1946- 1955	51	71	15	714	79	12.75	-	1	5876	236	24.89	7-34	15	5	26	
Benjamin, J.E.	1994	1	1	0	0	0	0.00	-	-	80	4	20.00	4-42	-	-	-	
Bird, M.C.	1909/10-1913/14	10	16	1	280	61	18.66	-	2	120	8	15.00	3-11	-	-	5	
Bowden, M.P.	1888- 1889	2	2	0	25	25	12.50	-	-							-	
Braund, L.C.	1901/02-1907/08	23	41	3	987	104	25.97	3	2	1810	47	38.51	8-81	3	-	39	
Brockwell, W.	1893- 1899	7	12	0	202	49	16.83	-	-	309	5	61.80	3-33	-		6	
Brown, F.R.	1931- 1953	22	30	1	734	79	25.31	-	5	1398	45	31.06	5-49	1	-	22	
Butcher, A.R.	1979	1	2	0	34	20	17.00	-	-	9	0	-	-	-	-	-	
Clarke, S.T.	1977/78-1981/82	11	16	5	172	35*	15.63	-	-	1170	42	27.85	5-126	1	-	2	
Crawford, J.N.	1905/06-1907/08	12	23	2	469	74	22.33	-	2	1150	39	29.48	5-48	3	-	13	
Druce, N.F.	1897/98	5	9	0	252	64	28.00	-	1							5	
Ducat, A.	1921	1	2	0	5	3	2.50	-	-							1	
Edrich, J.H.	1963- 1976	77	127	9	5138	310*	43.54	12	24	23	0	-	-	-	-	43	
Fender, P.G.H.	1920/21-1929	13	21	1	380	60	19.00	-	2	1185	29	40.86	5-90	2	-	14	
Fishlock, L.B.	1936- 1946/47	4	5	1	47	19*	11.75	-	-							1	
Gilligan, A.E.R.	1922/23-1924/25	11	16	3	209	39*	16.07	-	-	1046	36	29.05	6-7	2	1	3	
Gover, A.R.	1936- 1946	4	1	1	2	2*	-	-	-	359	8	44.87	3-85	-	-	1	
Gray, A.H.	1986/87	5	8	2	48	12*	8.00	-	-	377	22	17.13	4-39	-	-	6	
Greig, I.A.	1982	2	4	0	26	14	6.50	-	-	114	4	28.50	4-53	-	-	-	
Griffith, S.C.	1947/48-1948/49	3	5	0	157	140	31.40	1	-							5	
Hayes, E.G.	1905/06-1912	5	9	1	86	35	10.75	-	-	52	1	52.00	1-28	-	-	2	
Hayward, T.W.	1895/96-1909	35	60	2	1999	137	34.46	3	12	514	14	36.71	4-22	-	-	19	
Hitch, J.W.	1911/12-1921	7	10	3	103	51*	14.71	-	1	325	7	46.42	2-31	-	-	4	
Hobbs, J.B.	1907/08-1930	61	102	7	5410	211	56.94	15	28	165	1	165.00	1-19	-	-	17	
Holmes, E.R.T.	1934/35-1935	5	9	2	114	85*	16.28	-	1	76	2	38.00	1-10	-	-	4	
Howarth, G.P.	1974/75-1984/85	47	83	5	2531	147	32.44	6	11	271	3	90.33	1-13	-	-	29	
Intikhab Alam	1959/60-1976/77	47	77	10	1493	138	22.28	1	8	4492	125	35.93	7-52	5	2	20	
Jackman, R.D.	1980/81-1982	4	6	0	42	17	7.00	-	-	445	14	31.78	4-110	-	-	-	
Jardine, D.R.	1928- 1933/34	22	33	6	1296	127	48.00	1	10	10	0	-	-	-	-	26	
Jupp, H.	1876/77	2	4	0	68	63	17.00	-	1							2	
Knight, D.J.	1921	2	4	0	54	38	13.50	-	-							1	
Knox, N.A.	1907	2	4	1	24	8*	8.00	-	-	105	3	35.00	2-39	-	-	-	
Laker, J.C.	1947/48-1958/59	46	63	15	676	63	14.08	-	2	4101	193	21.24	10-53	9	3	12	
Lees, W.S.	1905/06	5	9	3	66	25*	11.00	-	-	467	26	17.96	6-78	2	-	2	
Leveson-Gower, H.D.G.	1909/10	3	6	2	95	31	23.75	-	-							1	
Loader, P.J.	1954- 1958/59	13	19	6	76	17	5.84	-	-	878	39	22.51	6-36	1	-	2	
Lock, G.A.R.	1952- 1967/68	49	63	9	742	89	13.74	-	3	4451	174	25.58	7-35	9	3	59	
Lockwood, W.H.	1893- 1902	12	16	3	231	52*	17.76	-	1	883	43	20.53	7-71	5	1	4	
Lohmann, G.A.	1886- 1896	18	26	2	213	62*	8.87	-	1	1205	112	10.75	9-28	9	5	28	
Lucas, A.P.	1878/79-1884	5	9	1	157	55	19.62	-	1	54	0	-	-	-	-	1	
McIntyre, A.J.W.	1950- 1955	3	6	0	19	7	3.16	-	-							-	
May, P.B.H.	1951- 1961	66	106	9	4537	285*	46.77	13	22							42	
Mills, C.H.	1891/92	1	2	0	25	21	12.50	-	-	83	2	41.50	2-83	-	-	2	
Pocock, P.I.	1967/68-1984/85	25	37	4	206	33	6.24	-	-	2976	67	44.41	6-79	3	-	15	
Read, J.M.	1882- 1893	17	29	2	463	57	17.14	-	2							8	
Read, W.W.	1882/83-1893	18	27	1	720	117	27.69	1	5	63	0	-	-	-	-	16	
Richards, C.J.	1986/87-1988	8	13	0	285	133	21.92	1	-							22	1
Richardson, T.	1893- 1897/98	14	24	8	177	25*	11.06	-	-	2220	88	25.22	8-94	11	4	5	
Roope, G.R.J.	1972/73-1978	21	32	4	860	77	30.71	-	7	76	0	-	-	-	-	35	
Sandham, A.	1921- 1929/30	14	23	0	879	325	38.21	2	3							4	
Selvey, M.W.W.	1976- 1976/77	3	5	3	15	5*	7.50	-	-	343	6	57.16	4-41	-	-	1	
Sharpe, J.W.	1890- 1891/92	3	6	4	44	26	22.00	-	-	305	11	27.72	6-84	1	-	2	
Shuter, J.	1888	1	1	0	28	28	28.00	-	-							-	
Smith, D.M.	1985/86	2	4	0	80	47	20.00	-	-							-	
Southerton, J.	1876/77	2	3	1	7	6	3.50	-	-	107	7	15.28	4-46	-	-	2	
Stewart, A.J.	1989/90-1994	43	78	5	2982	190	40.84	7	15	13	0	-	-	-	-	53	4
Stewart, M.J.	1962- 1963/64	8	12	1	385	87	35.00	-	2							6	
Strudwick, H.	1909/10-1926	28	42	13	230	24	7.93	-	-							60	12
Subba Row, R.	1958- 1961	13	22	1	984	137	46.85	3	4	2	0	-	-	-	-	5	
Swetman, R.	1958/59-1959/60	11	17	2	254	65	16.93	-	1							24	2
Thorpe, G.P.	1993- 1994	10	19	2	708	114*	41.64	1	6	15	0	-	-	-	-	14	
Titmus, F.J.	1955- 1974/75	53	76	11	1449	84*	22.29	-	10	4931	153	32.22	7-79	7	-	35	
Tufnell, N.C.	1909/10	1	1	0	14	14	14.00	-	-							-	1
Waqar Younis	1989/90-1994	31	37	6	276	29	8.90	-	-	3383	180	18.79	7-76	19	4	4	
Willis, R.G.D.	1970/71-1984	90	128	55	840	28*	11.50	-	-	8190	325	25.20	8-43	16	-	39	
Wood, H.	1888- 1891/92	4	4	1	204	134*	68.00	1	1							2	1
Younis Ahmed	1969/70-1986/87	4	7	1	177	62	29.50	-	1	6	0	-	-	-	-	-	

SURREY CAREER RECORDS

		Batting							Bowling								
		M	I	NO	Runs	HS	Avge	100	Runs	Wkts	OW	Avge	Best	5 WI	10 WM	Ct	St
Abbott, W.	1877	3	5	0	9	5	1.80	-								7	2
Abel, R.	1881-1904	514	813	59	27605	357*	36.61	64	5966	256	-	23.30	6-15	3	-	492	
Abel, T.E.	1919-1920	12	13	1	224	50*	18.66	-	718	23	-	31.21	3-30	-	-	3	
Abel, W.J.	1909-1926	170	245	29	4984	117	23.07	1	5685	184	-	30.89	5-28	3	-	146	
Adams, D.	1902	1	2	0	26	14	13.00	-	83	1	-	83.00	1-28	-	-	2	
Adams, H.J.	1887-1889	4	7	4	25	9	8.33	-								4	2
Akroyd, B.N.	1872-1873	6	12	0	108	30	9.00	-	14	0	-	-	-	-	-	6	
Akroyd, S.H.	1869-1878	23	40	0	622	87	15.55	-								2	
Alexander, G.C.	1869	1	1	0	0	0	0.00	-								-	
Alikhan, R.I.	1989-1993	45	78	6	2346	138	32.58	2	165	5	-	35.00	2-43	-	-	23	
Allom, A.T.C.	1960	1	1	1	0	0*	-	-	53	0	-	-				-	
Allom, M.J.C.	1927-1937	100	107	17	952	64	10.57	-	7546	333	-	22.66	7-71	18	1	50	
Altham, H.S.	1908-1912	10	14	2	237	51	19.75	-								2	
Anstead, W.H.	1870-1872	7	12	2	61	17	6.10	-	542	48	-	11.29	6-27	5	1	2	
Arnold, G.G.	1963-1977	218	217	52	2302	63	13.95	-	14857	745	-	19.94	8-41	32	2	78	
Ashby, D.	1874	1	2	0	0	0	0.00	-	8	0	-	-	-	-	-	-	
Atkins, P.D.	1988-1993	24	44	3	1081	114*	26.36	1								9	
Avory, H.K.	1876	2	4	0	82	42	20.50	-								-	
Aworth, C.J.	1974-1976	26	47	4	965	115	22.44	1	353	5	-	70.60	2-23	-	-	9	
Ayres, G.W.	1892-1896	25	33	1	407	44	12.71	-	27	0	-	-	-	-	-	10	
Baggallay, T.W.	1865-1874	8	13	0	178	82	13.69	-								4	
Baily, R.E.H.	1904-1906	5	10	0	155	61	15.50	-								2	
Bainbridge, H.W.	1883-1885	11	17	1	175	32	10.93	-	89	2	-	44.50	1-18	-	-	4	
Baker, A.	1900-1907	104	162	18	3729	155*	25.89	5	34	1	-	34.00	1-3	-	-	38	
Baker, R.P.	1973-1978	54	56	30	563	91	21.65	-	2942	104	-	28.28	6-29	1	-	24	
Baker, W.D.	1847-1851	4	6	0	48	16	8.00	-								1	
Baldwin, C.	1892-1898	80	126	12	2757	234	24.18	3	87	0	-	-	-	-	-	55	
Baldwin, H.G.	1922-1930	32	46	8	509	63*	13.39	-	321	3	-	107.00	2-83	-	-	10	
Bale, E.W.	1904	1	1	0	6	6	6.00	-								2	
Barker, K.E.M.	1899-1903	6	8	0	141	52	17.62	-	25	0	-	-	-	-	-	2	
Barker, W.	1882	1	2	0	1	1	0.50	-	40	0	-	-	-	-	-	-	
Barling, H.T.	1927-1948	389	605	54	18995	269	34.47	34	530	7	-	75.71	3-46	-	-	170	
Barnato, J.W.	1928-1930	6	8	1	23	7	3.28	-								19	1
Barratt, E.	1876-1885	130	210	48	1403	67	8.66	-	12227	706	-	17.31	8-28	62	16	63	
Barrington, K.F.	1953-1968	362	564	99	19197	207	41.28	43	4729	133	-	35.55	5-46	4	-	381	
Bartlett, H.T.	1933-1935	3	5	1	86	61	21.50	-								1	
Barton, M.R.	1948-1954	110	183	13	3975	132	23.38	5								79	
Batchelar, A.	1862	2	3	1	11	8*	5.50	-	16	1	-	16.00	1-16	-	-	-	
Bayford, R.A.	1860-1861	4	6	0	24	10	4.00	-								1	
Bayley, J.	1846-1847	3	5	4	36	17*	36.00	-	-	-	2	-	1-?	-	-	4	
Bayley, M.	1866	1	1	1	8	8*	-	-	19	0	-	-	-	-	-	1	
Beard, T.A.	1857-1858	3	6	1	29	10	5.80	-								2	
Beauchamp, J.	1854-1855	5	10	1	56	30	6.22	-								1	
Beaumont, J.	1885-1890	91	120	38	741	60	9.03	-	6222	404	-	15.40	8-40	28	7	29	
Bedser, A.V.	1939-1960	371	429	148	4108	126	14.61	1	27918	1459	-	19.13	8-18	72	11	228	
Bedser, E.A.	1939-1961	443	669	78	14148	163	23.93	9	19831	797	-	24.88	7-33	24	4	226	
Bell, R.	1876	1	2	0	4	3	2.00	-								-	
Benjamin, J.E.	1992-1994	50	60	16	392	42*	8.90	-	5141	185	-	27.78	6-19	9	1	13	
Bennett, C.T.	1922	4	6	0	82	26	13.66	-								2	
Bennett, N.H.	1946	31	45	2	688	79	16.00	-	25	1	-	25.00	1-1	-	-	6	
Berrington, E.H.	1872	1	2	0	16	8	8.00	-	4	0	-	-	-	-	-	-	
Berry, F.	1934-1939	46	64	11	1004	104*	18.94	1	2192	75	-	29.22	5-61	1	-	27	
Bickley, J.	1852	1	1	0	0	0	0.00	-	63	8	-	7.87	5-33	1	-	1	
Bicknell, D.J.	1987-1994	143	252	26	9400	235*	41.59	23	287	3	-	95.66	2-62	-	-	55	
Bicknell, M.P.	1986-1994	131	150	42	1996	88	18.48	-	11598	454	-	25.54	9-45	20	2	49	
Bigwood, A.	1878	1	2	1	5	4	5.00	-								2	
Bird, M.C.	1909-1921	127	203	8	4880	151	25.02	4	2858	114	-	25.07	5-48	2	1	70	
Birley, F.H.	1879	1	2	0	7	6	3.50	-								-	
Blacklidge, H.G.	1908-1913	7	9	2	100	45	14.28	-	334	10	-	33.40	4-26	-	-	8	
Blackman, A.	1878	1	2	0	5	3	2.50	-								2	
Blamires, E.	1878-1881	32	55	12	406	31	9.44	-	2576	127	-	20.28	8-77	9	2	27	
Block, S.A.	1928-1933	30	46	3	1135	117	26.39	1	21	2	-	10.50	1-0	-	-	16	
Bloomfield, H.O.	1921-1922	4	7	2	180	107*	36.00	1								2	
Boardman, A.J.	1878-1880	9	17	2	157	33	10.47	-	37	0	-	-	-	-	-	1	
Boiling, J.	1988-1994	43	53	22	425	34*	13.70	-	3192	79	-	40.40	6-84	2	1	38	
Boult, F.H.	1872-1873	22	41	0	536	65	13.07	-	1117	52	-	21.48	5-32	1	-	10	
Boultbee, St.J.	1867	2	4	1	20	10	6.66	-	76	3	-	25.33	2-54	-	-	5	
Bowden, M.P.	1883-1888	72	109	11	1880	189*	19.18	2	14	0	-	-	-	-	-	66	6
Bowley, T.	1885-1891	76	100	26	695	46	9.39	-	4182	256	-	16.33	7-64	9	1	38	
Box, T.	1849	2	4	0	48	19	12.00	-								2	1
Braund, L.C.	1896-1898	21	28	2	409	85	15.73	-	193	2	-	96.50	1-12	-	-	23	1
Bray, E.	1870-1878	14	26	4	184	36	8.36	-	742	48	-	15.45	7-32	4	2	5	

		Batting							Bowling								
		M	I	NO	Runs	HS	Avge	100	Runs	Wkts	OW	Avge	Best	5 WI	10 WM	Ct	St
Brazier, A.F.	1948-1954	36	56	11	979	92	21.75	-	7	0	-	-	-	-	-	10	
Bridges, J.H.	1876	2	2	0	9	8	4.50	-								-	
Bristow, J.	1867-1873	32	58	8	514	79	10.28	-	1503	73	-	20.58	7-45	5	-	17	1
Brockwell, G.	1846-1857	33	56	6	571	57	11.42	-	136	5	30	27.20	4-?	-	-	14	
Brockwell, W.	1886-1903	314	472	45	11830	225	27.70	20	12273	500	-	24.54	8-22	21	-	219	1
Brooks, E.W.J.	1925-1939	354	437	96	4437	70	13.01	-	6	0	-	-	-	-	-	712	96
Brooks, R.	1889	1	1	0	4	4	4.00	-								-	1
Brown, A.D.	1992-1994	47	74	6	3171	175	46.63	8	131	0	-	-	-	-	-	40	
Brown, G.E.	1986-1989	10	11	8	59	13*	19.66	-								19	2
Brown, F.R.	1931-1948	106	159	16	3982	212	27.84	9	10548	429	-	24.58	8-34	30	5	68	
Brown, T.	1868-1874	9	15	2	58	10	4.46	-	123	7	-	17.57	4-16	-	-	6	
Bryant, J.M.	1852	2	3	2	8	5	8.00	-	65	2	-	32.50	2-54	-	-	-	
Bryson, R.E.	1992	11	13	2	257	76	23.36	-	1256	23	-	54.60	5-48	2	-	-	
Buckle, F.	1867-1872	15	25	4	156	31	7.42	-	165	6	-	27.50	2-40	-	-	4	
Budgen, H.	1904-1909	3	4	0	58	30	14.50	-	213	3	-	71.00	3-112	-	-	1	
Bullen, C.K.	1982-1991	30	35	7	663	65	23.68	-	1078	38	-	28.37	6-119	1	-	30	
Bullock, B.	1922-1924	5	8	1	121	40	17.29	-								-	
Burbidge, A.	1857	2	4	0	24	8	6.00	-								-	
Burbidge, F.	1854-1866	41	68	9	799	101	13.54	1								37	
Burls, C.W.	1873-1880	10	17	0	99	16	5.82	-								3	
Burnett, J.D.	1862	1	2	0	9	5	4.50	-								-	
Burrows, M.B.	1921	1	2	1	26	24*	26.00	-	117	3	-	39.00	2-58	-	-	-	
Burton, H.H.	1904	3	6	1	126	48*	25.20	-								-	
Bush, F.W.	1879-1885	7	12	0	70	22	5.83	-	216	6	-	36.00	1-13	-	-	1	
Bush, H.S.	1901-1912	70	109	7	2532	135	24.82	4	161	2	-	80.50	1-12	-	-	38	
Bush, R.T.	1864-1868	2	4	1	21	8*	7.00	-								-	
Bushell, R.H.	1857-1858	2	4	0	23	17	5.75	-								1	
Busher, S.E.	1908	1	1	0	52	52	52.00	-	92	7	-	13.14	4-41	-	-	1	
Buss, C.H.H.	1934	1	2	0	47	42	23.50	-	143	2	-	71.50	2-90	-	-	-	
Butcher, A.R.	1972-1986	283	479	43	14571	216*	33.42	29	4689	125	-	37.51	6-48	1	-	130	
Butcher, D.H.	1900-1913	7	11	1	187	71	18.70	-								1	
Butcher, M.A.	1992-1994	20	32	6	883	134	33.96	1	1221	32	-	38.15	4-31	-	-	25	
Butcher, M.S.	1982	1	0	0	0	-	-	-	2	0	-	-	-	-	-	1	
Caesar, F.B.	1859-1862	7	13	1	95	23	7.91	-	6	0	-	-	-	-	-	3	
Caesar, J.	1849-1867	121	202	17	3314	132*	17.91	2	123	5	-	24.60	2-1	-	-	123	
Caesar, W.C.	1922	1	-	did not bat		-	-	-	38	0	-	-	-	-	-	-	
Caffaray, J.	1881-1882	3	5	0	18	6	3.60	-	44	0	-	-	-	-	-	2	
Caffyn, W.	1849-1873	89	154	15	3226	103	23.20	2	4299	321	10	13.39	8-25	29	6	72	
Calvert, C.	1868	13	23	2	266	67*	12.66	-	27	1	-	27.00	1-9	-	-	8	
Campbell, G.V.	1912	1	1	0	1	1	1.00	-	26	0	-	-	-	-	-	-	
Campbell, I.P.F.	1910-1927	25	39	0	829	88	21.25	-								9	
Carmichael, J.	1876-1881	14	24	1	243	47	10.56	-	9	0	-	-	-	-	-	11	3
Carter, W.J.	1871-1874	7	12	3	77	21*	8.55	-	41	4	-	10.25	2-15	-	-	2	
Carver, G.J.	1907	1	2	0	36	36	18.00	-	42	1	-	42.00	1-42	-	-	-	
Cattley, A.C.	1882	1	2	0	45	45	22.50	-								1	
Cattley, S.W.	1879-1883	23	41	1	562	89	14.05	-	13	0	-	-	-	-	-	9	
Chandler, A.	1873-1877	27	47	0	633	74	13.46	-								16	
Charman, W.	1875	1	2	0	11	7	5.50	-	24	0	-	-	-	-	-	-	
Cheatle, R.G.L.	1980-1983	20	13	9	62	27*	15.50	-	894	27	-	33.11	5-28	2	-	11	
Chenery, C.J.	1872-1873	12	22	2	298	40*	14.90	-	48	1	-	48.00	1-11	-	-	4	
Chester, A.	1872-1883	17	27	2	272	54*	10.88	-								5	
Chester, J	1846-1858	26	45	2	625	64	14.53	-	4	0	15	-	3-?	-	-	4	
Chinnery, E.F.	1906	1	1	0	47	47	47.00	-								-	
Chinnery, H.B.	1897-1904	30	47	2	957	149	21.26	1	212	6	-	35.33	4-51	-	-	9	
Christy, A.	1857	1	2	0	0	0	0.00	-								-	
Clark, T.H.	1947-1959	260	421	35	11458	191	29.68	12	2233	73	-	30.58	5-23	1	-	104	
Clarke, A.F.	1890-1892	8	8	2	61	30	10.16	-								8	6
Clarke, C.F.C.	1873-1882	10	16	1	103	19	6.86	-	84	2	-	42.00	1-12	-	-	7	
Clarke, M.C.	1875-1880	9	17	1	115	26	7.18	-								6	
Clarke, S.T.	1979-1989	152	155	18	2130	100*	15.55	1	11226	591	-	18.99	8-62	39	6	97	
Clarke, W.	1852	1	2	1	12	11	12.00	-								-	
Clifford, G.	1871-1878	15	28	1	255	45	9.44	-	355	13	-	27.30	3-15	-	-	7	
Clinton, G.S.	1979-1990	234	392	50	11838	192	34.61	20	192	2	-	96.00	2-77	-	-	84	
Clode, H.P.	1899-1903	40	56	6	596	50*	11.92	-	2884	111	-	25.98	6-31	6	1	20	
Collett, W.E.	1869-1874	4	8	0	44	19	5.50	-								1	
Collyer, W.J.	1866-1869	18	34	3	386	69	12.45	-								6	
Colman, S.	1882	6	10	0	81	63	8.10	-								2	
Coltson, C.	1847-1851	9	16	1	122	24*	8.13	-								5	
Comber, G.	1880-1885	6	11	2	44	19	4.88	-								2	1
Comber, R.H.	1851	1	2	0	20	17	10.00	-								-	
Constable, B.	1939-1964	434	681	81	18224	205*	30.37	26	2585	49	-	52.75	3-68	-	-	173	
Cook, W.T.	1921-1933	32	52	3	1032	84	21.06	-	48	1	-	48.00	1-1	-	-	9	
Cooper, S.H.	1936	2	2	1	11	11*	11.00	-								2	3
Cosh, N.J.	1969	6	9	1	165	55	20.62	-								6	
Cowderoy, J.	1876	1	2	0	4	2	2.00	-	11	0	-	-	-	-	-	-	

					Batting							Bowling					
		M	I	NO	Runs	HS	Avge	100	Runs	Wkts	OW	Avge	Best	5 WI	10 WM	Ct	St
Cox, D.F.	1949-1957	42	52	17	660	57	18.85	-	2316	68	-	34.05	7-22	2	1	39	
Crawford, J.N.	1904-1921	120	182	22	5217	232	32.60	8	8765	450	-	19.47	8-24	27	6	74	
Crawford, V.F.S.	1896-1902	110	164	15	4280	159	28.72	8	246	3	-	82.00	2-18	-	-	64	
Crouch, H.R.	1946	1	1	0	4	4	4.00	-								-	
Cuffy, C.E.	1994	12	15	8	42	10	6.00	-	1082	36	-	30.05	4-70	-	-	1	
Cumberlege, C.F.	1872	2	4	0	30	26	7.50	-								1	
Cumbes, J.	1968-1969	29	22	13	76	25*	8.44	-	1989	93	-	21.38	6-35	5	-	11	
Curtis, I.J.	1983-1984	14	11	5	23	7	3.83	-	726	18	-	40.33	6-28	1	-	3	
Curwen, W.J.H.	1909	4	7	0	23	8	3.28	-								-	
Cuthbertson, J.L.	1963	7	9	3	118	34	19.66	-	204	3	-	68.00	1-13	-	-	1	
Daily, C.E.	1923-1929	45	60	4	998	91	17.82	-	11	1	-	11.00	1-11	-	-	15	
Daley, J.V.	1936-1938	28	34	24	75	26*	7.50	-	1942	67	-	28.98	6-47	3	1	13	
Dalmeny, Lord	1903-1908	94	151	5	3386	138	23.19	2	73	3	-	24.33	2-16	-	-	42	
Davies, A.G.	1985	1	1	1	26	26*	-	-								3	
Davis, J.	1850	2	2	0	0	0	0.00	-								1	
Davis, W.E.	1903-1911	111	176	12	3419	112	20.84	3	823	13	-	63.30	2-34	-	-	75	
Day, D.	1846-1852	23	36	10	127	19	4.88	-	657	47	86	13.97	8-?	14	4	24	
Deane, M.W.	1880	1	2	0	1	1	0.50	-								-	1
Dible, W.G.	1882	1	2	0	8	4	4.00	-	5	0	-	-	-	-	-	-	
Dickinson, P.J.	1939	10	12	1	132	49*	12.00	-	70	0	-	-	-	-	-	7	
Diver, E.J.	1883-1886	75	122	4	2643	143	22.39	1	103	0	-	-	-	-	-	46	
Dolbey, H.O.	1899-1902	3	6	2	21	18*	5.25	-	235	7	-	33.57	4-96	-	-	1	
Doughty, R.J.	1985-1987	27	33	4	631	65	21.76	-	2047	66	-	31.02	6-33	1	-	22	
Douglas, A.P.	1887	1	2	1	63	51*	63.00	-								2	
Douglas, R.N.	1890-1891	4	4	0	92	72	23.00	-								2	
Dowson, E.	1860-1870	54	90	5	1394	87	16.40	-								30	
Dowson, E.M.	1900-1903	44	71	6	1669	123	25.67	3	2185	56	-	39.01	7-72	4	-	24	
Driver, B.N.	1847-1852	3	4	0	11	10	2.75	-								-	
Druce, N.F.	1895-1897	12	16	1	286	51*	19.06	-								6	
Ducat, A.	1906-1931	422	657	59	23108	306*	38.64	52	903	21	-	43.00	3-12	-	-	202	
Dunn, J.	1881	4	8	1	85	33*	12.14	-								-	
Earle, G.F.	1911-1921	4	6	0	124	48	20.66	-	389	13	-	29.92	5-137	1	-	1	
Earnshaw, A.	1847	4	8	0	50	15	6.25	-								-	
Earnshaw, G.R.B.	1880	2	4	1	31	13*	10.33	-	4	0	-	-	-	-	-	1	
Edrich, J.H.	1958-1978	410	716	80	29305	226*	46.07	81	16	0	-	-	-	-	-	243	
Edwards, F.	1909	1	2	0	8	6	4.00	-	54	3	-	18.00	3-31	-	-	-	
Edwards, M.J.	1961-1974	236	415	24	10581	137	27.06	12	34	0	-	-	-	-	-	262	
Eglington, R.	1938	2	3	0	59	34	19.66	-								1	
Elliott, G.F.	1875-1880	44	80	5	1037	53	13.82	-	472	8	-	59.00	1-2	-	-	7	
Estridge, G.T.	1859-1860	5	8	1	89	34	12.71	-								1	
Falkner, N.J.	1984-1987	16	24	3	734	102	34.95	2	9	1	-	9.00	1-3	-	-	10	
Feltham, M.A.	1983-1992	114	142	38	2526	101	24.28	1	9266	292	-	31.73	6-53	6	-	48	
Fender, P.G.H.	1914-1935	414	556	52	14117	185	28.00	17	38200	1586	-	24.08	8-24	86	14	470	
Fenley, S.	1924-1929	116	111	45	396	26	6.00	-	9904	345	-	28.70	8-69	19	4	51	
Fielding, F.	1889	2	2	0	76	75	38.00	-								3	2
Finlay, I.W.	1965-1967	23	35	3	654	103	20.43	1	56	1	-	56.00	1-19	-	-	10	
Fishlock, L.B.	1931-1952	347	588	41	22138	253	40.47	50	433	9	-	48.11	4-62	-	-	187	
Fletcher, D.G.W.	1946-1961	300	494	40	13646	194	30.05	21								174	
Fox, C.J.M.	1876	1	2	0	4	4	2.00	-								-	
Franklin, H.W.F.	1921	1	2	1	22	12	22.00	-								-	
Freeman, A.	1871-1875	29	54	5	399	32	8.14	-	458	8	-	57.25	2-47	-	-	18	
Freeman, A.J.	1919	1	1	1	0	0*	-	-	67	0	-	-	-	-	-	-	
Frost, M.A.	1988-1989	13	13	1	22	7	1.83	-	1005	25	-	40.20	5-40	1	-	2	
Gamble, F.C.	1933-1935	19	25	10	132	29	8.80	-	1555	40	-	38.87	4-82	-	-	10	
Gamble, G.F.	1906	8	8	4	28	7	7.00	-	470	18	-	26.11	5-78	1	-	4	
Game, W.H.	1871-1883	39	71	4	1084	84*	16.17	-	226	2	-	113.00	1-31	-	-	22	
Garland, E.	1846	1	1	0	0	0	0.00	-								-	
Garland-Wells, H.M.	1928-1939	130	185	11	3617	103	20.78	1	4137	97	-	42.64	5-25	2	-	94	
Geary, A.C.T.	1922-1931	90	90	27	670	40	10.63	-	6068	198	-	30.64	6-50	6	1	33	
Gentry, J.S.B.	1922-1923	10	11	4	65	13	9.28	-	761	36	-	21.13	4-36	-	-	3	
Gibson, D.	1957-1969	183	211	45	3143	98	18.93	-	12213	550	-	22.20	7-26	26	1	76	
Gilbert, C.A.W	1877-1878	2	4	1	25	17*	8.33	-								-	
Gillespie, F.S.	1913	6	11	0	249	72	22.63	-								2	
Gilligan, A.E.R.	1919	3	5	0	33	15	6.60	-	247	3	-	82.33	2-59	-	-	1	
Goatly, E.G.	1901-1914	126	198	21	4419	147*	24.96	3	733	19	-	38.57	4-48	-	-	22	
Gooder, L.M.H.	1901-1905	19	29	2	312	35	11.55	-	1862	54	-	34.48	5-66	3	1	7	
Gordon, J.H.	1906-1907	3	5	1	118	69*	29.50	-								1	
Gore, S.W.	1874-1875	2	3	0	52	36	17.33	-	51	0	-	-	-	-	-	2	
Gover, A.R.	1928-1947	336	386	154	2170	41*	9.35	-	34101	1437	-	23.73	8-34	87	15	164	
Graburn, W.T.	1894	1	1	0	39	39	39.00	-								-	
Gray, A.H.	1985-1990	48	34	6	245	35	9.42	-	4234	199	-	21.27	8-40	11	2	18	
Green, W.	1883	1	2	0	2	2	1.00	-								1	

		M	I	NO	Batting Runs	HS	Avge	100	Bowling Runs	Wkts	OW	Avge	Best	5 WI	10 WM	Ct	St
Greenfield, G.P.	1867-1869	3	5	1	115	102	28.75	1	67	4	-	16.75	3-38	-	-	-	
Greenwood, J.F.	1874	3	5	0	17	8	3.40	-								3	
Gregory, J.C.	1870-1871	19	35	5	630	70	21.00	-	12	0	-	-	-	-	-	8	
Gregory, R.J.	1925-1947	413	622	76	18978	243	34.75	38	13877	434	-	31.97	6-21	11	1	283	
Greig, I.A.	1987-1991	115	157	27	4298	291	33.06	4	4280	118	-	36.27	6-34	2	-	64	
Griffin, N.F.	1963	1	2	1	90	83*	90.00	-	45	0	-	-	-	-	-	-	
Griffith, G.	1856-1871	165	288	15	4604	142	16.86	2	9122	549	-	16.61	9-130	45	7	138	2
Griffith, S.C.	1934	1	1	0	19	19	19.00	-								1	
Groom, R.	1846	2	4	1	11	4	3.66	-								1	
Gunn, T.W.	1863-1869	6	11	3	52	13	6.50	-								1	
Haden, J.V.	1882	7	10	0	42	22	4.20	-								2	
Hadfield, G.H.	1903-1904	4	4	1	21	10	7.00	-	419	14	-	29.93	5-52	1	-	3	
Hadingham, A.W.G.	1932	1	-	-	-	-	-	-								-	
Hall, C.J.	1868-1873	8	13	1	71	15	5.91	-	13	1	-	13.00	1-4	-	-	1	
Hall, J.K.	1958-1962	13	11	3	19	5	2.37	-	787	36	-	21.86	5-30	1	-	7	
Hammersley, W.J.	1848-1850	4	7	0	68	27	9.71	-	11	0	-	-	-	-	-	-	
Hanbury, E.C.	1871	3	6	2	44	17	11.00	-								-	
Hankey, R.	1855	1	2	0	5	5	2.50	-	26	0	-	-	-	-	-	-	
Hansell, T.M.G.	1975-1977	14	26	5	319	54	15.19	-								2	
Harman, R.	1961-1968	141	144	50	924	34	9.82	-	8708	369	-	23.59	8-12	18	3	84	
Harper, L.V.	1904	6	9	0	145	67	16.11	-								-	
Harris, S.S.	1904	1	2	0	9	8	4.50	-								1	
Harrison, H.S.	1909-1923	164	254	33	5226	155*	23.64	2	726	20	-	36.30	2-14	-	-	117	
Hartley-Smith, H.	1880	1	2	0	17	11	8.50	-								-	
Hartnell, E.G.	1853	1	2	0	5	3	2.50	-								1	
Harwood, F.	1851-1865	4	5	1	8	5	2.00	-	158	7	-	22.57	3-39	-	-	3	
Hayes, E.G.	1896-1919	500	802	45	25062	276	33.10	45	12761	473	-	26.97	8-22	12	2	561	
Hayward, D., jun.	1854	1	1	0	1	1	1.00	-								1	
Hayward, D., sen.	1846-1847	2	4	1	33	24	11.00	-								2	
Hayward, T.W.	1893-1914	593	932	79	36175	315*	42.40	88	9342	436	-	21.42	8-89	17	2	420	
Hearsum, J.	1871	2	4	0	43	25	10.75	-	59	0	-	-	-	-	-	-	
Heartfield, J.	1860-1867	9	13	2	24	10*	2.18	-	338	21	-	16.09	6-28	2	-	2	
Heath, J.	1846-1854	19	35	4	218	35	7.03	-								19	
Heath, W.G.H.	1919	3	5	1	82	58*	20.50	-								5	
Henderson, R.	1883-1896	141	219	28	3466	106	18.14	1	1248	59	-	21.15	6-17	1	-	86	
Hillyer, W.R.	1849	2	4	1	71	30	23.66	-	-	-	18	-	7-?	2	1	1	
Hinkly, E.	1848-1853	2	3	2	11	7*	11.00	-	91	8	-	11.37	4-24	-	-	-	
Hitch, J.W.	1907-1925	304	423	41	6765	107	17.70	3	26550	1232	-	21.55	8-38	90	21	204	
Hoare, A.M.	1846-1847	2	3	0	77	59	25.66	-								-	
Hoare, C.H.	1846-1853	17	27	3	308	58	12.83	-								7	
Hoare, C.T.	1871-1874	4	7	0	98	35	14.00	-								1	
Hobbs, J.B.	1905-1934	598	956	80	43554	316*	49.71	144	1948	86	-	22.65	7-56	3	-	239	
Holland, F.C.	1894-1908	282	425	29	10323	171	26.06	12	570	13	-	43.84	2-20	-	-	232	
Hollioake, A.J.	1993-1994	22	32	3	1074	138	37.03	4	1263	31	-	40.74	4-48	-	-	16	
Holmes, E.R.T.	1924-1955	198	298	40	8837	206	34.25	15	6135	173	-	35.46	6-16	3	-	145	
Homer, C.E.	1882-1886	53	80	26	468	37*	8.66	-	3630	217	-	16.72	8-35	14	2	18	
Hooper, J.M.M.	1967-1971	21	36	10	406	41*	15.61	-	10	1	-	10.00	1-10	-	-	14	
Hore, F.S.	1861	1	1	1	8	8*	-	-								-	
Howarth, G.P.	1971-1985	188	323	25	9284	183	31.15	18	848	16	-	53.00	3-20	-	-	109	
Howell, L.S.	1869-1880	13	24	5	330	96	17.36	-								8	
Howell, M.	1919-1925	36	55	8	1117	99	23.76	-	6	0	-	-	-	-	-	10	
Howell, R.	1878-1879	3	5	1	31	10	7.75	-								-	
Humphrey, R.	1870-1881	145	268	16	4433	116*	17.59	1								61	
Humphrey, R.G.	1964-1970	2	2	1	63	58	63.00	-								4	1
Humphrey, T.	1862-1874	159	289	10	5215	144	18.69	4	2285	107	-	21.35	6-29	5	-	80	
Humphrey, W.	1864	4	6	0	49	18	8.16	-	148	2	-	74.00	1-19	-	-	1	
Hyndson, J.G.W.	1927	2	2	0	19	18	9.50	-	125	4	-	31.25	2-30	-	-	1	
Intikhab Alam	1969-1981	232	338	45	5707	139	19.47	4	18871	629	-	30.00	8-74	25	2	73	
Jackman, R.D.	1966-1982	338	386	132	4823	92*	18.98	-	26969	1206	-	22.36	8-58	61	7	152	
Jackson, M.T.	1903-1907	11	17	8	21	9	2.33	-	660	33	-	20.00	7-96	3	-	6	
Jardine, D.R.	1921-1933	141	194	36	7037	167	44.53	14	916	25	-	36.64	2-13	-	-	102	
Jeacocke, A.	1920-1934	132	205	15	5608	201*	29.51	8	576	14	-	41.14	2-24	-	-	100	
Jefferson, R.I.	1961-1966	76	106	23	1663	136	20.03	2	5582	206	-	27.09	6-25	7	1	27	
Jennings, T.S.	1921-1924	18	17	3	194	37*	13.85	-	1094	37	-	29.56	6-51	3	1	4	
Jephson, D.L.A.	1894-1904	165	237	32	6566	213	32.02	9	5747	249	-	23.08	7-51	10	1	82	
Jesty, T.E.	1985-1987	68	102	14	3281	221	37.36	7	884	29	-	30.48	6-81	1	-	37	
Johnson, F.	1878-1883	20	32	8	158	21*	6.58	-	1302	51	-	25.52	6-42	4	1	14	
Jones, G.G.	1875-1888	98	156	23	1152	63	8.66	-	5409	321	-	16.85	7-20	15	2	60	
Judd, P.E.	1960	1	-	did not bat		-	-	-	14	0	-	-	-	-	-	1	
Jupp, H.	1862-1881	252	467	40	11452	165	26.81	12	316	7	-	45.14	3-75	-	-	148	6
Jupp, W.T.	1876	2	3	1	25	11	12.50	-	57	0	-	-	-	-	-	2	
Keene, J.W.	1897	2	2	1	3	3	3.00	-	174	4	-	43.50	3-61	-	-	2	

		Batting							Bowling								
		M	*I*	*NO*	*Runs*	*HS*	*Avge*	*100*	*Runs*	*Wkts*	*OW*	*Avge*	*Best*	*5 WI*	*10 WM*	*Ct*	*St*
Kelleher, H.R.A.	1955	3	-	-	-	-	-	-	179	12	-	14.91	5-23	2	1	-	
Kember, O.D.	1962-1963	4	7	2	56	19*	11.20	-								6	2
Kendrick, N.M.	1988-1994	55	72	19	862	55	16.26	-	4825	133	-	36.27	7-115	6	1	47	
Kenlock, S.G.	1994	2	-	-	-	-	-	-	186	3	-	62.00	3-104	-	-	1	
Kennis, G.J.	1994	1	2	0	41	23	20.50	-								2	
Kenrick, J.	1876	1	1	0	11	11	11.00	-	44	1	-	44.00	1-26	-	-	-	
Kersey, G.J.	1993-1994	19	31	4	399	39	14.77	-								50	5
Kersley, T.	1899	3	4	1	23	15*	7.66	-	145	7	-	20.71	3-36	-	-	1	
Key, K.J.	1882-1904	288	423	55	9654	179	26.23	8	195	5	-	39.00	2-36	-	-	80	
Killick, W.	1876	1	2	0	3	3	1.50	-								-	
King, K.C.W.	1936-1938	31	39	8	334	64	10.77	-	1148	33	-	34.78	4-38	-	-	18	
King, P.	1871	1	2	0	16	13	8.00	-	18	0	-	-	-	-	-	1	
Kingsford, R.K.	1872-1874	3	5	0	80	30	16.00	-								2	
Kirby, G.N.G.	1948-1953	19	17	8	141	32	15.66	-								37	8
Kirk, E.C.	1906-1921	36	50	7	406	43	9.44	-	3079	128	-	24.05	7-130	6	1	11	
Knight, D.J.	1911-1937	106	159	11	4390	146	29.66	9	2	3	-	0.66	2-0	-	-	52	
Knight, R.D.V.	1968-1984	174	290	32	8712	142	33.76	15	5549	163	-	34.04	5-44	2	-	137	
Knox, F.P.	1899-1902	7	12	2	196	42	19.60	-	223	8	-	27.87	3-28	-	-	3	
Knox, N.A.	1904-1910	73	106	30	670	27*	8.81	-	7269	347	-	20.94	8-48	31	8	27	
Lagden, R.B.	1912	1	1	0	3	3	3.00	-								-	
Laker, J.C.	1946-1959	309	387	70	5531	113	17.44	2	24236	1395	-	17.37	10-88	93	24	223	
Lane, C.G.	1856-1861	18	30	3	487	72	18.03	-	63	3	-	21.00	3-31	-	-	3	
Lane, W.W.C.	1868-1870	2	4	0	56	36	14.00	-	7	0	-	-	-	-	-	-	
Lawrence, C.	1854-1857	2	3	0	42	22	14.00	-	35	2	-	17.50	1-8	-	-	1	
Leaf, H.	1877	1	2	0	8	7	4.00	-								-	
Lee, F.	1861	1	2	0	42	30	21.00	-								1	
Lee, J.M.	1847-1850	7	11	2	140	40	15.55	-	-	-	2	-	2-?	-	-	3	
Lees, W.S.	1896-1911	343	488	68	7237	137	17.23	2	28542	1331	-	21.44	9-81	92	20	118	
Leveson-Gower, H.D.G.	1895-1920	122	174	27	3308	155	22.50	2	211	2	-	105.50	1-12	-	-	38	
Lewis, R.M.	1968-1973	38	68	9	1746	87	29.59	-	7	0	-	-	-	-	-	26	
Ligertwood, D.G.C.	1992	4	7	0	63	28	9.00	-								7	1
Lindsay, W.	1876-1882	33	62	5	987	74	17.31	-								17	
Loader, P.J.	1951-1963	298	291	87	1827	81	8.95	-	20685	1108	-	18.66	9-17	65	13	100	
Lock, G.A.R.	1946-1963	385	451	100	5391	70	15.35	-	29835	1713	-	17.41	10-54	123	31	532	
Lock, H.C.	1926-1932	32	29	8	89	20*	4.23	-	2381	75	-	31.74	4-34	-	-	10	
Lock, N.W.	1934	1	2	1	1	1	1.00	-								-	
Lockton, J.H.	1919-1926	32	34	9	409	77*	16.36	-	2071	78	-	26.55	5-80	1	-	26	
Lockwood, W.H.	1889-1904	305	446	33	9299	165	22.51	14	21266	1182	-	17.99	9-59	105	27	117	
Lockyer, T.	1849-1866	124	197	31	2588	108*	15.59	1	1742	93	-	18.73	6-33	9	1	168	62
Lohmann, G.A.	1884-1896	186	269	25	5070	115	20.77	2	16108	1221	-	13.19	9-67	128	41	203	
Long, A.	1960-1975	352	409	90	4999	92	15.67	-								702	103
Long, R.	1870	2	4	0	0	0	0.00	-	20	0	-	-	-	-	-	-	
Longman, H.K.	1901-1908	5	8	0	98	33	12.25	-								4	
Lowe, R.F.	1923	10	11	3	15	7	1.87	-	557	26	-	21.42	5-15	1	-	3	
Lowles, G.W.	1887	1	2	1	1	1*	1.00	-								-	
Lucas, A.C.	1874	1	2	0	50	29	25.00	-								1	
Lucas, A.P.	1874-1882	41	76	6	1721	115	24.58	2	1011	62	-	16.30	5-23	2	-	31	
Luff, A.	1867	3	6	1	25	8	5.00	-	111	2	-	55.50	1-25	-	-	-	
Lutterlock, E.	1874	3	6	0	23	8	3.83	-								-	
Lynch, M.A.	1977-1994	304	491	59	15674	172*	36.28	33	1251	24	-	52.12	3-6	-	-	314	
Lyons, G.L.	1880	1	2	0	8	8	4.00	-								-	
Lywood, L.W.	1927-1928	2	2	0	7	7	3.50	-	177	1	-	177.00	1-22	-	-	-	
McCanlis, M.A.	1926-1927	2	3	2	44	19*	44.00	-	209	3	-	69.66	1-41	-	-	1	
McDonell, H.C.	1901-1904	13	22	3	269	46	14.15	-	892	41	-	21.75	7-44	2	1	8	
McEntyre, K.B.	1965-1966	3	3	0	33	15	11.00	-								-	
Machin, R.S.	1927-1930	8	9	2	33	17	4.71	-								19	1
McIntyre, A.J.W.	1938-1963	376	544	75	10893	143*	23.22	7	180	4	-	45.00	1-10	-	-	617	145
Mack, A.J.	1976-1977	10	9	0	42	16	4.66	-	760	7	-	108.57	2-50	-	-	-	
McKelvey, P.J.	1959-1960	2	-	-	-	-	-	-	19	1	-	19.00	1-7	-	-	1	
Mackintosh, K.S.	1981-1983	14	12	9	117	31	39.00	-	1135	36	-	31.52	6-61	1	-	5	
McMahon, J.W.	1947-1953	84	106	52	344	23*	6.37	-	6903	234	-	29.50	8-46	9	1	55	
McMurray, T.	1933-1939	33	54	6	892	62	18.58	-	23	1	-	23.00	1-3	-	-	14	
McNiven, E.	1851	1	1	0	8	8	8.00	-								1	
Majendie, N.L.	1963	8	6	1	11	6	2.20	-								26	3
Marriott, D.A.	1965-1967	19	13	6	88	24*	12.57	-	1244	43	-	28.93	4-45	-	-	3	
Marshal, A.	1907-1910	98	158	11	4195	176	28.53	-	2121	101	-	21.00	7-41	6	1	90	
Marshall, A.	1849-1857	14	23	5	146	23*	8.11	-								8	
Marshall, C.	1893-1899	43	60	13	341	42	7.25	-								82	15
Marshall, H.	1853-1854	2	4	0	20	8	5.00	-								1	
Marten, W.G.	1871-1872	24	42	13	163	18	5.62	-	1672	79	-	21.16	6-11	3	1	21	
Martingell, W.	1846-1859	49	78	12	620	49	9.39	-	1523	130	39	11.71	8-37	13	2	36	
Mathews, F.J.	1883	2	3	0	14	9	4.67	-								-	
May, P.B.H.	1950-1963	208	327	46	14168	211*	50.41	39								182	

					Batting							Bowling					
		M	I	NO	Runs	HS	Avge	100	Runs	Wkts	OW	Avge	Best	5 WI	10 WM	(	
May, P.R.	1902-1909	12	19	4	188	32	12.53	-	988	22	-	44.90	6-88	1	-	[illegible]	
Mayo, H.E.	1868-1870	14	27	1	246	53	9.46	-	112	4	-	28.00	2-13	-	-	8	
Mays, C.S.	1987-1989	4	3	2	20	13*	20.00	-	303	3	-	101.00	1-36	-	-	3	
Meads. J.W.	1905	3	4	0	9	4	2.25	-	135	7	-	19.28	4-36	-	-	-	
Medlycott, K.T.	1984-1991	134	173	37	3586	153	26.36	3	10726	331	-	32.40	8-52	17	5	88	
Merrall, J.E.	1932-1933	2	2	0	10	5	5.00	-	153	6	-	25.50	3-24	-	-	1	
Meymott, C.	1847	1	2	0	0	0	0.00	-								-	
Miller, F.P.	1851-1867	80	132	14	1540	105	13.05	1	2713	130	1	20.86	6-36	2	-	57	
Miller, N.	1899-1903	9	12	1	346	124	31.45	1	114	1	-	114.00	1-28	-	-	1	
Mills, C.H.	1888	2	3	0	6	4	2.00	-	17	0	-	-	-	-	-	2	
Mills, E.	1885-1887	7	12	2	54	11*	5.40	-	344	15	-	22.93	5-33	1	-	5	
Mobey, G.S.	1930-1948	77	105	19	1526	75	17.74	-								127	10
Molony, T.J.	1921	3	4	0	2	2	0.50	-	89	4	-	22.25	3-11	-	-	-	
Money, W.B.	1869	2	4	0	50	19	12.50	-	203	4	-	50.75	4-136	-	-	1	
Monkhouse, G.	1981-1986	74	85	33	1158	100*	22.26	1	4589	170	-	26.99	7-51	2	-	35	
Montgomery, W.	1901-1904	14	19	2	60	12	3.52	-	580	22	-	26.36	4-17	-	-	11	
Morgan, C.	1871	4	7	0	31	15	4.42	-	170	2	-	85.00	1-36	-	-	1	
Morris, N.	1873	5	10	0	177	64	17.70	-								-	3
Mortlock, W.	1851-1870	138	236	22	4125	106	19.27	3	2339	128	-	18.27	7-42	7	2	67	
Morton, P.H.	1884	2	3	1	20	19*	10.00	-	79	4	-	19.75	2-26	-	-	-	
Moulder, J.H.	1902-1906	24	34	4	451	48	15.03	-	203	8	-	25.37	3-41	-	-	8	
Mudie, W.	1856-1865	37	56	9	547	79	11.63	-	748	47	-	15.91	7-61	3	-	23	
Murphy, A.J.	1989-1994	67	67	32	298	38	8.51	-	6666	175	-	38.09	6-97	6	-	11	
Myers, E.B.	1910-1914	11	17	1	217	40	13.56	-	211	3	-	70.33	1-10	-	-	3	
Naumann, F.C.G.	1919-1921	11	17	1	216	52	13.50	-	610	15	-	40.66	5-51	1	-	4	
Needham, A.	1977-1986	91	132	17	2620	138	22.78	4	5079	104	-	48.83	6-30	5	-	42	
Nevell, W.T.	1939	1	1	0	6	5	5.00	-	35	0	-	-	-	-	-	-	
Newman, F.C.W.	1919-1921	5	7	0	123	54	17.57	-								1	
Newnham, S.W.	1932	1	1	0	4	4	4.00	-	13	2	-	6.50	2-13	-	-	1	
Nice, E.H.L.	1895-1905	69	96	10	1247	66	14.50	-	4394	174	-	25.25	8-83	5	1	34	
Nightingale, J.	1868	1	1	1	2	2*	-	-	8	0	-	-	-	-	-	1	
Noble, C.	1868	4	7	0	53	17	7.57	-								2	
Noble, J.W.	1866-1869	26	45	2	521	71	12.11	-	268	12	-	22.33	4-36	-	-	5	
O'Gorman, J.G.	1927	3	4	3	106	42*	106.00	-	167	4	-	41.75	2-49	-	-	1	
Oliver, F.W.	1855-1856	2	4	0	71	30	17.75	-								2	
Owen, J.G.	1930-1933	15	13	3	196	54	19.60	-	710	16	-	44.37	3-15	-	-	8	
Owen-Thomas, D.R.	1970-1975	73	118	14	2604	112	25.03	3	6	0	-	-	-	-	-	31	
Palmer, W.T.	1872-1876	19	36	0	289	54	8.02	-	15	0	-	-	-	-	-	4	
Parfitt, J.J.A.	1881-1882	8	16	2	111	23	7.92	-	477	25	-	19.08	7-33	1	1	1	
Parker, J.F.	1932-1952	334	512	70	14068	255	31.82	20	15387	538	-	28.60	6-34	8	-	316	
Parr, G.	1852	1	2	1	4	4	4.00	-								-	
Parsons, A.B.D.	1958-1963	119	203	18	5307	125	28.68	3	4	0	-	-	-	-	-	48	
Pauline, D.B.	1979-1985	49	76	6	1803	115	25.75	1	595	16	-	37.18	5-52	1	-	18	
Payne, I.R.	1977-1984	29	37	5	338	43	10.56	-	1127	26	-	43.34	5-13	1	-	30	
Peach, H.A.	1919-1931	324	411	50	8497	200*	23.53	4	20261	778	-	26.04	8-60	30	1	177	
Penfold, A.G.	1929	3	4	1	12	6	4.00	-	201	13	-	15.46	4-36	-	-	1	
Peters, N.H.	1988-1991	16	18	8	101	25*	10.10	-	1246	40	-	31.15	6-31	1	-	7	
Peto, J.	1847	1	2	1	12	7	12.00	-								-	1
Pickering, W.P.	1846-1848	2	3	0	23	21	7.66	-								2	
Pierpoint, F.G.	1936-1946	8	11	7	15	4	3.75	-	592	13	-	45.53	3-60	-	-	3	
Piggott, J.I.	1910-1913	3	5	1	153	84	38.25	-								5	
Pigott, A.C.S.	1994	8	11	0	160	40	14.54	-	737	29	-	25.41	6-46	1	-	1	
Pilkington, A.F.	1926	1	1	0	4	4	4.00	-	29	1	-	29.00	1-29	-	-	-	
Platt, G.J.W.	1906-1914	33	49	8	396	49	9.65	-	2042	102	-	20.01	6-61	6	1	28	
Pocock, P.I.	1964-1986	485	503	144	4400	75*	12.25	-	35577	1399	-	25.43	9-57	53	7	153	
Ponsonby, S.C.B.	1846-1853	2	4	1	12	12	4.00	-								1	
Pontifex, D.D.	1881	9	17	1	303	89	18.93	-	13	0	-	-	-	-	-	1	
Pooley, E.	1861-1883	256	453	37	6642	97	15.96	-	371	6	-	61.83	2-39	-	-	357	250
Pooley, F.W.	1876-1877	3	4	0	13	11	3.25	-								4	
Potter, C.W.	1869-1871	17	31	3	385	31	13.75	-	17	1	-	17.00	1-17	-	-	3	
Potter, J.	1875-1881	35	62	12	325	27*	6.50	-	1961	98	-	20.01	7-31	7	3	29	
Powell, E.O.	1882	4	7	0	95	53	13.57	-								-	
Pratt, D.E.	1954-1957	9	12	4	171	33	21.37	-	392	13	-	30.15	6-119	1	-	4	
Pratt, J.	1868	1	2	0	10	9	5.00	-	12	0	-	-	-	-	-	2	
Pratt, R.E.C.	1952-1959	69	102	14	1900	120	21.59	1	138	3	-	46.00	1-8	-	-	53	
Pretty, H.C.	1899	8	11	0	233	124	21.18	1	15	0	-	-	-	-	-	5	
Price, V.R.	1919	1	1	0	25	25	25.00	-	179	1	-	179.00	1-156	-	-	-	
Ransom, V.J.	1951-1955	2	2	0	3	2	1.50	-	82	1	-	82.00	1-21	-	-	-	
Raphael, J.E.	1903-1909	39	64	7	1614	111	28.31	1	49	0	-	-	-	-	-	15	
Ratcliff, J.	1876	4	8	0	69	27	8.62	-								1	
Ratcliffe, A.	1932-1933	7	10	2	142	34	17.75	-	8	0	-	-	-	-	-	3	
Read, F.H.	1881	1	1	0	4	4	4.00	-								-	

					Batting							Bowling					
		M	I	NO	Runs	HS	Avge	100	Runs	Wkts	OW	Avge	Best	5 WI	10 WM	Ct	St
Read, H.D.	1933	2	2	1	0	0*	0.00	-	152	6	-	25.33	4-26	-	-	2	
Read, J.M.	1880-1895	278	450	35	10840	186*	26.12	8	1610	64	-	25.15	6-41	1	-	165	
Read, W.W.	1873-1897	366	580	41	17683	338	32.80	31	2830	84	-	33.69	4-27	-	-	300	18
Reay, G.M.	1913-1923	27	34	2	410	54	12.81	-	1859	89	-	20.88	5-22	3	-	12	
Redgewell, L.J.	1922-1923	3	4	2	5	4	2.50	-								4/1	
Reeves, E.	1948-1952	9	14	2	125	25	10.41	-								1	
Reiner, C.F.	1906	1	2	0	50	26	25.00	-								-	
Richards, C.J.	1976-1988	256	328	79	7142	172*	28.68	7	219	5	-	43.80	2-42	-	-	534	66
Richards, J.H.	1881	2	4	0	9	8	2.25	-	89	2	-	44.50	2-40	-	-	-	
Richardson, H.B.	1899	22	31	5	585	72	22.50	-	1	0	-	-	-	-	-	8	
Richardson, T.	1892-1904	305	396	106	2853	69	9.83	-	31732	1775	-	17.87	10-45	169	60	106	
Ricketts, G.W.	1887	3	5	0	48	26	9.60	-	12	0	-	-	-	-	-	-	
Roberts, D.	1921	1	2	0	15	14	7.50	-	31	1	-	31.00	1-31	-	-	1	
Roberts, F.	1867-1868	4	7	2	20	7	4.00	-	159	9	-	17.66	7-72	1	-	1	
Robertson, F.M.	1877	1	2	1	7	4	7.00	-	49	2	-	24.50	2-32	-	-	-	
Robinson, J.D.	1988-1992	31	49	10	898	79	23.02	-	1152	28	-	41.14	3-22	-	-	12	
Robson, A.G.	1991	2	3	0	3	3	1.00	-	103	1	-	103.00	1-72	-	-	-	
Rogers, G.R.	1870	5	10	1	34	18	3.77	-								-	
Roller, C.T.	1886	1	2	0	15	14	7.50	-								-	
Roller, W.E.	1881-1890	102	162	10	3343	204	21.99	7	3190	164	-	19.45	6-44	4	-	63	
Roope, G.R.J.	1964-1982	342	554	118	16226	171	37.21	22	7725	211	-	36.61	5-14	3	-	513	2
Rose, J.	1878	1	2	0	0	0	0.00	-	2	1	-	2.00	1-2	-	-	-	
Rudd, W.J.	1904	1	2	0	4	4	2.00	-								-	
Rushby, T.	1903-1921	228	289	129	1192	58*	7.45	-	19544	954	-	20.48	10-43	58	9	64	
Rushworth, W.R.	1946	1	1	0	0	0	0.00	-	86	2	-	43.00	1-15	-	-	3	
Russell, S.G.	1967	1	-	-	-	-	-	-	77	2	-	38.50	2-63	-	-	2	
Rutty, A.W.F.	1910	1	2	2	18	12*	-	-								1	
Sadiq, Z.A.	1988-1989	6	10	0	177	64	17.70	-								4	
Sadler, W.C.H.	1923-1925	51	65	22	646	68	15.02	-	3907	167	-	23.39	6-50	7	2	20	
Sandham, A.	1911-1937	525	830	71	33312	292*	43.88	83	386	16	-	24.12	3-27	-	-	129	
Sarel, W.G.M.	1904-1909	4	8	0	120	57	15.00	-	46	1	-	46.00	1-20	-	-	1	
Sargeant, N.F.	1989-1994	50	65	11	778	49	14.40	-	88	1	-	88.00	1-88	-	-	109	16
Selvey, M.W.W.	1968-1971	6	8	4	19	14*	4.75	-	445	21	-	21.19	6-58	1	-	-	
Sewell, T., jun.	1859-1868	109	179	39	1756	62	12.54	-	4834	248	-	19.49	8-54	11	-	42	
Sewell, T., sen.	1846-1849	7	13	0	86	25	6.61	-								1	1
Shadwell, F.B.	1880	1	2	0	16	15	8.00	-	18	0	-	-	-	-	-	-	
Sharpe, J.W.	1889-1893	59	79	27	503	36	9.67	-	4183	275	-	15.21	9-47	19	6	35	
Sheffield, E.J.	1930-1932	23	17	3	176	64*	12.57	-	1492	68	-	21.94	7-123	2	-	15	
Shepherd, T.F.	1919-1932	354	520	60	18254	277*	39.68	41	13478	439	-	30.70	6-78	12	-	267	
Shepherd, W.	1864-1865	13	17	6	56	18	5.09	-	709	38	-	18.65	8-49	2	-	8	
Sheppard, R.A.	1904-1905	12	16	1	356	82	23.73	-	526	20	-	26.30	4-33	-	-	5	
Sherman, T.	1847-1870	51	81	19	422	32	6.80	-	1781	125	107	14.24	8-?	20	7	32	
Shuter, J.	1877-1909	274	447	19	9369	135	21.89	8	37	0	-	-	-	-	-	141	
Shuter, L.A.	1876-1883	37	65	2	1039	88	16.49	-	75	1	-	75.00	1-10	-	-	16	
Simmonds, A.	1872-1873	6	12	0	149	50	12.41	-								1	
Skinner, E.A.	1871-1881	3	6	1	37	10	7.40	-	112	3	-	37.33	2-33	-	-	1	
Skinner, L.E.	1971-1977	71	115	14	2255	93	22.32	-								108	13
Slater, P.H.	1911	1	1	0	1	1	1.00	-								-	
Smith, A.W.	1993-1994	28	44	7	1084	202*	29.29	1	1727	33	-	52.33	5-103	1	-	10	
Smith, D.M.	1973-1988	169	260	57	6723	160	33.12	11	1463	27	-	54.19	3-40	-	-	109	
Smith, E.	1858	1	2	1	18	9*	18.00	-								1	
Smith, F.E.	1893-1908	56	69	18	492	45	9.64	-	3121	169	-	18.46	6-12	9	3	26	
Smith, G.O.	1896	3	5	0	17	9	3.40	-								1	
Smith, T.	1876	1	2	0	16	13	8.00	-	20	0	-	-	-	-	-	1	
Smith, W.A.	1961-1970	144	242	18	5024	103	22.42	2	1	0	-	-	-	-	-	52	
Smith, W.C.	1900-1914	229	318	62	3193	69*	12.47	-	17616	1036	-	17.00	9-31	92	27	144	
Soden, F.B.	1870-1871	3	6	1	35	18*	7.00	-	17	2	-	8.50	1-2	-	-	1	
Southerton, J.	1854-1879	152	261	77	1665	82	9.04	-	13793	994	-	13.87	8-34	115	29	109	
Spicer, W.B.	1870	1	2	0	16	14	8.00	-	17	1	-	17.00	1-17	-	-	-	
Spring, W.A.	1906-1913	68	106	13	1968	135	21.16	2	2093	71	-	29.47	6-38	3	1	54	
Squires, H.S.	1928-1949	402	643	44	18636	236	31.11	36	10496	297	-	35.34	8-52	7	-	137	
Stacey, C.F.	1901	1	1	1	0	0*	-	-	148	1	-	148.00	1-78	-	-	-	
Stafford, J.P.	1864	1	2	0	0	0	0.00	-	31	0	-	-	-	-	-	-	
Staveley, M.	1870	1	2	0	3	3	1.50	-	51	1	-	51.00	1-24	-	-	-	
Stedman, F.	1899-1908	134	184	67	1484	62	12.68	-	53	0	-	-	-	-	-	253	46
Stephenson, H.H.	1853-1871	179	312	24	5338	119	18.53	2	3342	191	-	17.49	7-58	12	3	91	11
Stevens, J.	1874-1875	3	4	0	36	16	9.00	-								1	
Stewart, A.J.	1981-1994	207	334	42	11506	206*	39.40	21	353	3	-	117.66	1-7	-	-	271	7
Stewart, M.J.	1954-1972	498	844	91	25007	227*	33.20	48	48	1	-	48.00	1-4	-	-	604	
Stockley, A.J.	1968	3	2	0	5	5	2.50	-	194	10	-	19.40	4-74	-	-	3	
Stoner, A.	1899-1900	6	9	0	98	61	10.88	-	344	14	-	24.57	4-16	-	-	2	
Storey, S.J.	1960-1974	315	468	58	10402	164	25.37	12	12903	490	-	26.33	8-22	11	2	318	
Strachan, G.	1872-1880	54	93	5	1186	84	13.47	-	2085	118	-	17.66	6-33	5	-	38	
Strahan, W.	1846-1849	2	4	0	6	3	1.50	-								-	
Streatfeild, E.C.	1890-1892	9	13	1	185	39	15.41	-	231	19	-	12.15	5-26	1	-	5	

		Batting							Bowling								
		M	I	NO	Runs	HS	Avge	100	Runs	Wkts	OW	Avge	Best	5 WI	10 WM	Ct	St
Street, A.E.	1892-1898	50	66	6	1356	161*	22.60	1	393	15	-	26.20	3-44	-	-	16	
Street, J.	1863-1878	139	239	70	1280	50	7.57	-	11435	534	-	21.41	7-141	36	6	71	
Stroud, E.G.	1930	7	7	3	63	22*	15.75	-	526	23	-	22.86	4-17	-	-	2	
Strudwick, H.	1902-1927	554	695	197	5485	93	11.01	-	60	0	-	-	-	-	-	1040	183
Subba Row, R.	1953-1954	41	58	11	1663	128	35.38	3	131	1	-	131.00	1-10	-	-	35	
Sullivan, D.	1914-1921	8	10	4	34	12*	5.66	-								10	2
Surridge, S.S.	1978-1980	1	1	1	2	2*	-	-								1	
Surridge, W.S.	1947-1959	254	316	32	3697	87	13.01	-	13753	464	-	29.64	7-49	19	1	360	
Swan, J.J.	1870-1876	32	59	5	637	62	11.79	-	83	2	-	41.50	1-15	-	-	16	
Swetman, R.	1954-1961	129	178	29	3073	93	20.62	-								230	37
Sydenham, D.A.D.	1957-1972	142	131	64	483	24*	7.20	-	9548	481	-	19.85	9-70	26	3	52	
Tabor, A.S.	1878	1	2	0	0	0	0.00	-								-	
Tanner, W.	1866-1868	2	4	2	2	1*	1.00	-	26	0	-	-	-	-	-	1	
Taylor, A.	1865	1	1	0	1	1	1.00	-	13	1	-	13.00	1-13	-	-	-	
Taylor, D.J.S.	1966-1969	10	8	1	137	56	19.57	-								16	5
Taylor, E.F.	1865-1867	2	4	0	48	27	12.00	-	135	7	-	19.28	4-59	-	-	2	
Taylor, N.S.	1984-1985	10	9	3	63	21*	10.50	-	833	28	-	29.75	7-44	1	-	3	
Taylor, W.	1852-1855	3	6	1	15	10	3.00	-	43	1	1	43.00	1-23	-	-	-	
Tazelaar, D.	1989	4	4	1	65	29	21.66	-	417	10	-	41.70	3-88	-	-	1	
Teesdale, H.	1906-1908	2	3	0	65	26	21.66	-								2	
Thain, C.	1923	2	2	1	4	4*	4.00	-	88	3	-	29.33	3-38	-	-	-	
Thomas, D.J.	1977-1987	205	172	35	2850	119	20.80	2	10155	303	-	33.51	6-36	6	-	47	
Thompson, D.J.	1994	1	2	0	39	22	19.50	-	123	3	-	41.00	2-37	-	-	-	
Thompson, H.	1894-1919	12	20	4	138	44*	8.62	-	663	31	-	21.38	5-59	2	1	4	
Thorpe, G.P.	1988-1994	110	183	29	6588	216	42.77	14	923	18	-	51.27	4-40	-	-	71	
Tillard, C.	1874-1875	3	4	0	51	22	12.75	-	149	7	-	21.28	3-10	-	-	2	
Tindall, R.A.E.	1956-1966	172	256	38	5383	109*	24.69	2	4846	150	-	32.30	5-41	2	-	129	
Titmus, F.J.	1978	1	2	1	4	4*	-	-	35	1	-	35.00	1-35	-	-	1	
Topley, T.D.	1985	1	1	1	6	6*	-	-	64	2	-	32.00	2-42	-	-	1	
Trodd, J.T.	1879-1880	4	8	5	10	5	3.33	-	70	4	-	17.50	2-13	-	-	1	
Trodd, W.	1869	6	11	0	65	16	5.90	-	146	3	-	48.66	2-38	-	-	1	
Trollope, W.S.	1877-1882	7	14	0	154	35	11.00	-	99	4	-	24.75	2-2	-	-	3	
Trouncer, C.A.	1888	3	5	1	51	26	12.75	-	25	0	-	-	-	-	-	1	
Tufnell, N.C.	1922	1	2	0	9	7	4.50	-	5	0	-	-	-	-	-	1	
Verrinder, A.O.C.	1974-1976	3	2	0	0	0	0.00	-	105	4	-	26.25	2-42	-	-	2	
Vigar, H.E.	1906-1911	15	21	2	226	33*	11.89	-								21	2
Vince, J.	1870	11	22	1	60	10*	2.85	-	454	15	-	30.26	4-58	-	-	11	
Vincett, J.H.	1921	2	4	1	31	23*	10.33	-	50	2	-	25.00	2-46	-	-	2	
Von Emsthausen, A.C.	1900-1901	2	3	0	24	13	8.00	-	95	1	-	95.00	1-37	-	-	2	
Voss, R.	1883-1886	3	5	2	10	7	3.33	-	53	2	-	26.50	2-31	-	-	-	
Vyse, E.W.	1857	2	4	0	34	24	8.50	-								-	
Wait, O.J.	1950-1951	7	9	3	11	4	1.83	-	400	14	-	28.57	3-27	-	-	3	
Walker, L.	1900-1903	56	93	8	1609	84	18.92	-	354	8	-	44.25	3-54	-	-	22	
Waller, C.E.	1967-1973	40	31	13	173	47	9.61	-	2195	96	-	22.86	7-64	4	-	13	
Walter, C.R.	1859	1	1	0	0	0	0.00	-								-	
Wanostrocht, N.(Felix)	1846-1852	23	38	1	659	82	17.81	-	-	-	1	-	1-?	-	-	10	
Waqar Younis	1990-1994	45	47	16	447	31	14.41	-	4420	232	-	19.05	7-33	20	4	11	
Ward, I.J.	1992	1	1	0	0	0	0.00	-	35	0	-	-	-	-	-	1	
Ward, D.M.	1985-1994	150	236	33	7931	294*	39.06	16	113	2	-	56.50	2-66	-	-	116	3
Waterman, P.A.	1983-1985	11	6	3	7	6*	2.33	-	727	18	-	40.38	3-22	-	-	4	
Watney, J.	1851	1	2	0	9	8	4.50	-								-	
Watts, E.A.	1933-1949	240	350	68	6005	123	21.29	2	18757	722	-	25.97	10-67	24	2	152	
Watts, G.H.	1890-1892	8	16	2	79	20	5.64	-	21	0	-	-	-	-	-	13	4
Watts, T.	1922-1926	6	8	5	42	21*	14.00	-	327	8	-	40.87	2-32	-	-	3	
Weeks, D.	1933	2	2	0	2	1	1.00	-	165	2	-	82.50	1-25	-	-	-	
Wellings, E.M.	1931	4	4	1	33	10	11.00	-	195	2	-	97.50	1-30	-	-	-	
Wells, C.M.	1892-1893	4	7	1	49	20	8.16	-	216	15	-	14.40	7-31	1	-	5	
Westerman, P.	1949-1951	9	12	5	25	10*	3.57	-	596	21	-	28.38	5-49	2	-	1	
Whale, G.	1861-1867	4	6	0	40	26	6.66	-	288	5	-	57.60	3-94	-	-	1	
Wheatley, G.A.	1947	5	7	1	119	37*	19.83	-								5	2
Wheeler, A.	1872-1873	2	3	0	15	9	5.00	-								-	
Wheeler, W.C.	1875	5	10	1	33	13	3.66	-	88	5	-	17.60	2-10	-	-	1	
White, A.C.	1881	1	2	1	15	9*	15.00	-								-	
White, C.	1850	1	1	0	0	0	0.00	-								1	
White, Capt.	1850	1	2	0	3	3	1.50	-								1	
White, J.	1926	1	-	-	-	-	-	-	103	1	-	103.00	1-56	-	-	1	
Whitfield, E.W.	1930-1939	106	157	21	3498	198	25.72	6	1354	31	-	43.67	4-63	-	-	32	
Whitley, R.T.	1873	1	2	0	8	5	4.00	-								2	
Whittaker, G.J.	1937-1953	124	183	18	4584	185*	27.78	6	47	1	-	47.00	1-31	-	-	45	
Wilkinson, C.T.A.	1909-1920	53	76	8	1734	135	25.50	3	706	23	-	30.69	6-43	1	-	25	
Willett, M.D.	1955-1967	172	273	45	6535	126	28.66	8	1105	23	-	48.04	3-36	-	-	95	
Willis, H.	1868	1	2	0	7	7	3.50	-								-	
Willis, R.G.D.	1969-1971	34	34	20	228	33	16.28	-	2428	96	-	25.29	5-78	1	-	13	

					Batting							Bowling					
		M	*I*	*NO*	*Runs*	*HS*	*Avge*	*100*	*Runs*	*Wkts*	*OW*	*Avge*	*Best*	*5 WI*	*10 WM*	*Ct*	*St*
Wilson, C.W.	1881	1	2	0	10	9	5.00	-								2	
Wilson, E.F.	1928-1936	81	120	12	2516	110	23.29	1	43	0	-	-	-	-	-	16	
Wilson, P.H.L.	1978-1982	37	23	15	80	15	10.00	-	1814	55	-	32.98	4-39	-	-	6	
Wiltshire, E.	1902-1903	13	22	2	219	33	10.95	-								3	
Wingfield, W.	1881	3	6	0	13	5	2.16	-								2	
Winlaw, R.de W.K.	1932-1934	17	26	5	650	91	30.95	-	13	0	-	-	-	-	-	8	
Winterborne, G.	1986	1	-	-	-	-	-	-	47	0	-	-	-	-	-	-	
Wood, H.	1884-1900	286	378	89	4948	83	17.12	-	29	0	-	-	-	-	-	523	96
Wood, W.	1883	2	4	0	9	8	2.25	-	44	1	-	44.00	1-22	-	-	1	
Woodgate, T.W.	1877	1	2	0	11	11	5.50	-								-	
Wyatt, G.N.	1877-1879	10	18	0	251	58	13.94	-	17	0	-	-	-	-	-	7	
Wyld, W.G.	1879-1887	10	16	1	169	34*	11.26	-	113	3	-	37.66	1-12	-	-	4	
Yates, G.	1851-1854	2	3	0	9	6	3.00	-								2	
Yeatman, R.H.	1946-1947	5	8	1	53	21	7.57	-	18	0	-	-	-	-	-	1	
Younis Ahmed	1965-1978	262	448	63	14112	183*	36.65	19	602	17	-	35.41	4-10	-	-	144	

OW indicates wickets in matches for which no bowling analyses survive.